# gardens
## their hidden life

Unnoticed plants and unseen animals

# gardens
## their hidden life

Unnoticed plants and unseen animals

**Colin Spedding**

B L O O M S B U R Y

LONDON · BERLIN · NEW YORK · SYDNEY

Published 2012 by Bloomsbury Publishing Plc
50 Bedford Square, London WC1B 3DP

ISBN (print) 978-1-4081-5868-5

A CIP catalogue record for this book is available from the
British Library

This book is produced using paper that is made from
wood grown in managed sustainable forests. It is natural,
renewable and recyclable. The logging and manufacturing
processes conform to the environmental regulations of the
country of origin.

Commissioning editor: Lisa Thomas
Copy editor: Marianne Taylor
Design: Marc Dando, Fluke Art

Printed in China by C & C Offset Printing Co Ltd

10 9 8 7 6 5 4 3 2 1

Visit www.acblack.com/naturalhistory to find out more
about our authors and their books. You will find extracts,
author interviews and our blog, and you can sign up for
newsletters to be the first to hear about our latest releases
and special offers.

A Great Tit drinking from a pond.

# Contents

A swallow.

# List of tables

# List of boxes

Hummingbird Hawk Moth.

# Acknowledgements

Most importantly, I wish to thank my Secretary, Mrs Mary Jones, for her tireless help, over many years, in preparing this book for publication.

I am indebted to my son-in-law, Neal Weston, for the photograph of the German Shepherd dog in Chapter 17.

I am also pleased to thank Lisa Thomas, Commissioning Editor at Bloomsbury Publishing, for her enthusiastic help in seeing the book through the press and Marc Dando of Fluke Art for his attractive design and excellent drawings.

Some of the drawings were used in my two children's books, *What's in your Garden?* (2010) and *Biology in my Garden* (in press), published by Brambleby Books.

A Chiffchaff, amidst spring blossom. They are most easily distinguished by their song which gives the birds their name.

# Foreword

This book is not a gardening book nor is it a traditional wildlife field guide or textbook. It is intended for gardeners who enjoy wildlife and wildlife watchers who love their gardens. Much of the material is based on a personal account of many years of observing wildlife in a large garden in the south-east of England.

The primary purpose of the book is to alert readers to the vast array of wild plants and the many animals, from tiny invertebrates to foxes, badgers and even deer, that they may encounter in a garden. It may be argued that by no means all of the wildlife covered is actually 'hidden': after all most of us see birds outside the window on a daily basis, pull out weeds and enjoy butterflies and bumblebees. And a deer eating the rosebush on the front lawn is not difficult to spot.

But even those creatures that we do see in the garden are actually somewhat mysterious to most of us. Do you know where a bumblebee nests? A Grass Snake? Or even the ubiquitous Grey Squirrel or easily seen bird such as a Blackbird or Song Thrush? We know that there are millions of Field Voles but how do you get to see a live one – even in a country garden? Many animals that visit gardens on a regular basis are nocturnal and only seen if actively sought, including many insects, owls and bats. But if you know how and where to look, you may be rewarded with some entrancing experiences.

Beginning with a summary of the purpose of gardens, the book explores the garden environment, discussing how plants and animals communicate and giving ideas for ways of starting to watch wildlife in the garden including my tried and tested method of laying down dustbin lids that can act as nest, shelter and food store for a wide range of animals.

The text then looks at the various types of plants and the way that they live, reproduce and interact with other plants and with animals and reflects on the range of animals that can be seen in a garden of even modest size. Later chapters cover specific environments such as ponds and bog gardens and show how much can be found in and around the walls and roofs of buildings. The end of the book takes a seasonal look at what can be seen in the garden, including in the apparently silent winter depths. The last chapter suggests lots of questions that could be asked to unlock the garden's hidden world – and shows a number of projects for studying wild plants and small animals more closely.

Even 'weeds' such as this Bindweed are fascinating to study if you want to understand how they work.

# Introduction

I have lived in my cottage in Hurst, Berkshire, since 1973 – so long that one of the Balsam Poplar trees that I planted grew to such a height that it was blown over on to one end of my roof! I am now more careful where I plant trees.

The cottage lies in 3½ acres (1½ ha) of largely wooded, rather boggy land, where the water table rises at times to form a lake (up to 1½m deep) and a number of smaller ponds. A wide range of bird species are therefore attracted, especially water birds and tree-dwellers. I have a lawn and some flowerbeds but the major part of the land is 'wild'.

At one end, it abuts on to the local Primary School (St Nicholas) and in 1993 a pupil wrote to ask if they could come and have a look round what they called 'the plantation'. From then on, and continuing today, I have been showing parties of children round my garden, and particularly the wildlife it supports.

Of course, a party of 30 primary school children would normally see very little so I was led to devise ways (such as dustbin lids – see Chapter 4) in which I could be sure to find small creatures to show them. This led to my widening my interest in natural history and continual observation so that I always had new and interesting plants and animals to show the children – several times a year.

In 2003, I wrote my first book about the garden, *The Natural History of a Garden* and, when I found that parents and grandparents were using it to answer children's questions, I decided to write books directly for them. So *What's in your Garden* (for 7-11 year olds) appeared in 2010 and *Biology in My Garden* (for 11+) scheduled for publication a year later.

However, my observations – and what I had learned about how to make them – became so extensive that I decided to write the present book, covering all aspects of life in gardens, what you might expect to find (when and where) and how to observe more of the exciting life to be found in all gardens, whatever their size.

*An adult Meadow Brown butterfly feeding on a bramble in the garden.*

*A damp Nuthatch at the edge of a birdbath.*

# 1 Gardens

There are an estimated 15 million gardens in Britain. Together they cover an area of about 16 million acres (c.7.3 million hectares) – a larger area than all our nature reserves combined. About 8 per cent of England is in National Parks and a similar area (8.6 per cent) is built on. About half the adult population participate in gardening, the proportion increasing with age and income. On this basis, it has been claimed that gardening represents the most popular form of 'active' leisure.

In addition, the audience for television gardening programmes is in the millions and vast numbers of gardening books are available (some 80,000 titles currently listed on amazon.co.uk) with about 1,000 new ones being published annually. In addition, there are numerous gardening periodicals. There is thus a large 'reflective' or 'armchair' interest in gardening, as well as the 'sleeves-up' active participation. Gardens vary enormously, of course, in size, location, shape and purpose. A number of specific types or categories can be identified by purpose.

*A Hoverfly feeding on a scabious flower – note that it has only two wings and the widely-spaced eyes show that it is a female.*

## Organic

Sometimes called 'chemical-free' (quite erroneously, since all living and non-living things contain chemicals) organic gardens avoid as far as possible the use of manufactured chemicals, in the form of fertilisers, herbicides and pesticides. That does not mean that no attempt is made to control weeds and pests, but organic gardens are often claimed to be 'wildlife-friendly'. In fact, organic Standards allow the use of 'organic pesticides', some of them synthetic, and 'natural' pesticides such as the insecticide Pyrethrum (made from chrysanthemum flowers hand-picked in Kenya), which is a blend of nerve toxins.

However, many other practices are available to avoid major pest and disease problems, such as mixing different species of vegetables together, using barriers round carrots and grease bands on fruit tree trunks (to stop climbing Winter Moths), and encouraging predators, such as ladybirds, hoverflies and birds. Timing of sowing can also be helpful and removal of weeds before they set seed is very important.

# Wildlife gardens

Most people are in favour of wildlife but our attitudes to wildlife are highly selective – we tend to prefer furry or feathery creatures over those that are slimy, slithery or equipped with lots of legs. Relatively few people seem to like slugs or snails and even those 'creepy-crawlies' recognised as good and useful to the gardener (which, oddly enough, do not usually include spiders!) such as earthworms, while welcome, are not really liked.

Therefore, gardens designed to attract wildlife tend to aim at butterflies (rather than moths), ladybirds (though they need aphids to feed on) and birds. Fewer gardeners make efforts to attract animals that are difficult to observe, such as small mammals. Methods used to make a garden attractive to wildlife are reviewed in Chapter 13 and features that actually deter it are considered in Chapter 17. Attracting wildlife is often the purpose of quite large gardens, such as those open to the public. Much less attention is paid to encouraging wild flowers, but wild flower meadows are becoming popular.

# Wild flower meadows

Over the last 60 years, it is estimated that 95 per cent of our wild flower-rich meadows have disappeared, due to changes in farming practices (such as feeding livestock on silage rather than hay). However, a 'meadow' can be created in your garden with only a few square metres. The key to success may be remembering that many wild flowers respond best to hardship and trauma and do best on impoverished soil.

Of course, different species flourish on different soil types and in different areas. There is now a 'Postcode Plants Database' (at www.nhm.ac.uk/ science/projects/fff) which generates lists of native plants suitable for any postal district in the UK.

It is recommended that a wild flower meadow be cut once, at the end of the summer, and the debris removed (and composted). One popular seed mixture contains poppies, Larkspur, Love-in-a-mist and Cornflowers, which flower all summer long.

*Providing a variety of feeders in a garden can attract a wide range of birds including, if you are lucky, the Great Spotted Woodpecker.*

*Sometimes considered weeds, wildflowers in a meadow garden can make a vivid display.*

## Public gardens

Many public gardens are simply large recreational spaces, dominated by mown grass, trees and lakes – parks rather than gardens. Those that specialise in wildlife do so predominantly for birds, and many large parks and some nature reserves contain areas designated as 'wildlife gardens' and managed accordingly.

The local park may be the nearest thing to a garden available to people, especially those on lower incomes, in towns and cities. For example, London has a population of about 7.43 million, with 1.6 million children under 18, many in one-parent families, and 44 per cent of these children live in homes where income is below the national average. London has some 3,000 parks, covering 15 per cent of its total area, so its public green spaces form an important resource.

A great many public gardens focus on spectacular flower displays, and visitors are encouraged to visit at particular times of year. Even wildlife gardens may be stated to be 'at their best in June and July'. There are few public gardens that consider the whole panoply of wildlife, though some wildlife centres do cover a fairly wide range and illustrate the characteristic features of each month.

As every gardener knows, each month (perhaps each day) is different and part of the fun of a garden depends on this variety: if a garden looked exactly the same every day it would become uninteresting very quickly. One of the benefits of looking for all forms of wildlife is that it greatly increases the number of interesting things to see, even in winter (see Chapter 20).

## Conservation gardens

There are some gardens (and other areas) devoted to the conservation of endangered species, but these are rarely open to the public – for obvious reasons. Conservation more widely interpreted, such as the encouragement of diversity (of species), is sometimes fairly specialised. Themes could include 'gardening by the sea' or 'gardens on islands'. However, the most important message is that all gardens can contribute to conservation and biodiversity and most could contribute much more than they currently do.

It has been estimated that the average garden (though this is very hard to visualise in any meaningful way) may contain as many as 2,000 animal species and larger gardens two or three times as many. Most of these are never seen, so there is little immediate incentive to encourage them or increase their numbers. Apart from the encouragement of wild flower meadows, including their use in urban green spaces, and setting aside areas of rough grass to encourage such flowers, there is little interest in growing what are called 'weeds', even though they support much more biodiversity than non-native garden flowers. Indeed, almost by definition, a weed is something we do not want and, unless it has a pretty flower, to many gardeners it has no redeeming features. However, many of our wild flowers have declined and are in need of conservation. Chapter 15 explores this topic further.

Most conservation gardens have limited or no access, although some private gardens do have 'open' days, usually to display cultivated plants or design features.

## Gardens for schools

The main aims of school gardens are to provide a wide range of wildlife habitats for use in cross-curricula teaching, to involve the children in the management, development and monitoring of the garden, and often to encourage involvement of the local community (initially parents).

The site has to be properly organised with regard to safety, visual attractiveness and access for study with minimum disturbance. Such gardens introduce the biology of a plant and animal community, but also the skills of growing plants and keeping animals, thus leading to some understanding of farming. Indeed, this whole activity may be linked to farm visits. Children are encouraged to take more interest in their own family gardens and, of course, they tell their parents about their activities in the school gardens.

## Gardens for pets

There are designs for pet-friendly gardens, mainly for dogs and cats, and some of these also have the objective of minimising the effects that pets may have on wildlife. This is explored further in Chapter 17.

*sampling pond life.*

# Gardens for the disabled

For those people with a sensory disability in one way or another, it is quite possible to design gardens that minimise the disadvantage. In some ways, physical disabilities are easier to provide for. Gardens for those with limited mobility must be designed to make access to all parts as easy as possible.

For people who are blind or partially sighted, three things are required: a means of finding one's way about; a means of knowing what is there when you arrive; and guidance in the use of the other senses; taste, hearing, smell and, particularly, touch. For scent, favourite plants include lavenders, jasmines, roses, Sage, Thyme, mints and Rosemary.

Gardens and gardening also offer opportunities to those with learning difficulties or other mental health problems to learn how to perform useful tasks, perhaps leading to employment at some point. Organisations such as 'Thrive' specialise in the provision of gardens for those suffering from dementia, helping to stimulate their memories: this can be done by planting older varieties, especially honeysuckles, roses and lavenders, and a traditional kitchen garden. Potting tables and benches for sowing seeds can help to provide self-confidence and self-esteem, as well as a place for conversation with others.

# Kitchen gardens

Kitchen gardens can be wildlife-friendly and offer educational opportunities, but they are primarily for the production of edible vegetables and fruits, and flowers and other decorative vegetation. Fruits may come from orchards, which are not normally considered to be part of the kitchen garden, or fruit bushes and isolated trees (against walls or supported by fences) which are. Orchards are dealt with in Chapter 8.

However, not many people nowadays are obliged economically to grow their own food, whether in gardens or allotments. So, although production is the aim, many people find pleasure in growing their own food and do so because the food is fresher and tastier.

Kitchen gardens often include glasshouses, cold frames and even heated beds, all extending the range of plants that can be cultivated and the length of the growing seasons. They offer considerable insights into the way food is produced and, for children, particularly, help to demonstrate the origins of familiar packaged foodstuffs like fruit juice and chips. What kitchen gardens cannot do is convey a picture of the complexity of current food chains and the extent of global trade in food.

In general, wildlife is less welcome in kitchen gardens, with the exception of the well-known predators (such as ladybirds) on familiar pests (such as aphids). The balance between organisms is vastly more complex, even in kitchen gardens, than is generally supposed and food production benefits from an improved understanding of the way in which animals and plants interact and the balance of nature that can be achieved (see Chapter 10).

Planting fragrant plants, such as lavender, can make a garden a sensory experience for those with limited sight.

One issue to understand is that all the species grown for food have been specially bred (selected) for production. Plants in the wild have evolved adaptations to avoid being eaten. Indeed, many produce discouraging thorns and other forms of protection, including poisons and unpleasant tastes, to avoid being eaten – just as animals do not with to be eaten and avoid it in any way they can. So the idea that plants are there for us to eat is not one that plants would share and most are only suitable for us to eat because we have brought about genetic changes to avoid their protective mechanisms. Even so, we have to cook many of them (such as potatoes) in order to render their contents usable and, in some cases, safe to eat.

Cultivated plant variants that have had their natural defences 'bred out' to make life easier for us may as a result be more vulnerable to pests and disease than their wild ancestors. However, selective breeding can also be used to develop enhanced resistance to certain pests.

*A substantial vegetable garden such as this one gives the opportunity to grow a variety of produce.*

## Cottage gardens

No longer a major part of the garden scene, cottage gardens, as their name implies, were small patches associated with small cottages. They were almost uniquely English and characteristically are packed with plants, great mixtures of flowers, sweet-smelling herbs, trees and shrubs. They often included many small plants and plants were chosen to provide flowers in all seasons. Solomon's Seal, bleeding-hearts (or lyre plants), euphorbias, pulmonarias (the old smaller varieties), primroses and astrantias were typical, as were fumitories, sunflowers, lilies, golden-rods, phloxes, veronicas and a whole range of daisies.

Many other species often arrived by themselves, including candytufts, evening primroses, marigolds, nasturtiums, forget-me-nots and Honesty – as they still do in modern gardens. Cottage walls were also used as props for winter- and summer-flowering jasmines, honeysuckles, hops, vines, Virginia Creeper, japonicas, roses, clematis and ivy were all used extensively. Even window boxes and potted plants often meant a great deal to their owners.

You might think that the small size of cottage gardens precluded trees and limited the use of shrubs. However, some are hard to exclude (such as Elder) but fuschias and snowberries were encouraged and, apart from the odd apple or pear tree, the most common trees were probably laburnums and hawthorns (for blossom and scent). Other species deliberately planted for their scent were Rosemary, various kinds of mint, chamomiles, lavenders and Sweet-briar.

A classic cottage garden, stocked with a wide range of flowers, shrubs and trees for colour and scent.

# English country gardens

These are traditional in the same way as cottage gardens, but tend to be somewhat larger (though not necessarily with acres of parkland). They tend to contain a mixture of formal and informal areas, often containing statues, a sundial or an elegant bird-bath. Roses can be either laid in formal beds or grown as climbers that cover trees, buildings and pergolas. Other climbers include honeysuckles, clematis, Virginia Creeper, ivy and grape vines.

Herbaceous borders contain such plants as delphiniums, oriental poppies, lady's mantle, asters, aquilegia, foxgloves, hollyhocks and forget-me-nots. Trees, especially fruit trees, and hedges, especially evergreens such as yew, box and holly, add attractive features during the winter.

Gardens attached to large country houses – such as this one at Brodsworth Hall in South Yorkshire – often have elaborate formal areas close to the house with more casual 'wild' areas in the surrounding park.

# Roof gardens

These are virtually confined to suitably strengthened flat roofs and the range of plants tends to be limited. Wild flower meadows can be sown, but the most common species used are mosses, lichens and slow-growing plants like stonecrops (*Sedum* spp) and houseleeks, all of which require minimal management and can survive the periodic drying-out to which roofs are exposed. In the UK, it is estimated that about 100,000m² of 'sedum blanket' are now laid annually.

The advantages claimed are temperature control and efficient use of rainwater. Green roofs can lower the surrounding air temperature by up to 11°C and thus cool buildings in hot weather, as well as insulating them in cold weather. They absorb up to 60 per cent of rainwater and thus reduce run-off in heavy rain. They are commonly combined with water-storage systems.

In Michigan, it has been found that roof gardens can absorb up to 375g of carbon per square metre over two years. However, in this study it took seven years for the roof to offset the carbon used for its building materials.

# Life in gardens

The theme of this book is simply that all gardens, of whatever kind, are full of life, both plants and animals, most of them not put there deliberately by the gardeners. Many of the plants that find their way into gardens are thought of as weeds but quite a number (especially mosses, liverworts and ferns) are simply not noticed at all, and the same applies to lichens and fungi.

Most of the animals are small and never seen, even though they may be essential to pest control, pollination and soil fertility. All these organisms are full of interest and enrich the experience of a garden but most gardeners only see the plants they have planted themselves and then only the above-ground parts. However, understanding how these plants grow, survive and reproduce requires some knowledge of the unseen (or unnoticed life going on around them).

Most people think of a walk round the garden as a visit to old friends (plants they put there) to see how they are getting on and see the changes in growth, development, colour and so on. I think of a walk in the garden as a voyage of discovery, seeing the living things you didn't know were there, how they got there and what they are doing, but for this you need to know how and where to look to have any chance of seeing them or traces of their activities. If you wish you can then encourage more living things of all kinds, or you can just observe them to help you understand how your garden lives and grows.

A range of sedum plants typically used to make a 'living roof garden.

# 2 Environment

You will notice that this chapter is not entitled 'The Environment', since there is no such thing. Imagine if you really meant the whole environment, including the world and all the myriads of organisms within it. No library or computer could accommodate its description, even if you were aware of all the known components, never mind the species and processes that we are yet to discover. So referring to the environment as a whole is so vague as to be meaningless: it would be more helpful if, when we referred to an effect on the environment, we simply specified which bit.

Albert Einstein claimed that "the environment is everything that isn't me!", but since each of us could take that view, it is clear that there would be as many different environments as there are people. He could have said that this was *his* environment; even so, it would have included many things that did not affect him at all and, indeed, many organisms not yet discovered. Clearly, every one of us and every plant and animal has an environment and each may be part of another's environment.

My definition of my environment (which can be applied to every other individual) is "everything that affects me and that I affect". However, some generalisations are possible. For example, every individual has a macroclimate and a microclimate within which it lives.

## Macroclimate

This is usually described in terms of temperature, rainfall and solar radiation. In the UK, there is marked seasonal variation and even the seasons appear to be changing somewhat in response to 'global warming' (see Chapter 21). Because of this, average measures are not very helpful, since they not only vary between years and seasons but even from day to day and between day and night.

The British climate used to be described in terms of a moderate range of temperatures and well distributed rainfall. It is still true that different regions of the country have different average annual rainfall, but distribution of rainfall and temperatures at given times of year are becoming harder to predict. Only solar radiation is relatively constant, in terms of daily totals and day-length, but cloud cover is very variable, so the sunlight received at ground level may therefore be very variable, too. Both plants and animals are greatly affected by all these factors but species show a range of adaptations to light, temperature and water supply. These adaptations are both physiological and behavioural.

*A House Sparrow – now becoming scarce in many parts of the country.*

A Rabbit at the entrance to its burrow where it can seek shelter when the weather is poor.

In general, plants and larger animals are exposed to the elements of the macroclimate, but animals can move about and seek shelter. Plants are fixed once established but their seeds and spores may only develop in certain habitats – so they have an initial 'choice' of where they grow, modified by survival. Smaller animals, however, are able to select protected habitats characterised by more favourable microclimates.

## Microclimate

This describes the combination of light, temperature and humidity in the organism's immediate surroundings. It applies to both plants and animals but, in both cases, especially the smaller ones. For example, a herb in the bottom of a hedgerow is exposed to more sheltered conditions than apply to the hedge itself. Very small animals can live in soil, tree bark crevices or other sheltered places. Mature trees, on the other hand, have little choice and are exposed to the weather at all times. By contrast, aquatic plants may benefit from relatively constant temperature and guaranteed water supply, though they will still be exposed to variations in day-length and solar radiation.

Because they can seek out a favourable microclimate, small creatures, such as earwigs, woodlice, centipedes and insects can generally control their exposure to light, humidity and, to a limited extent, temperature. This also applies to reptiles and even more to amphibians.

No British wild mammals are so large that they cannot find some shelter, and a few hibernate to avoid the most severe effects of winter. Similarly, British birds can find some shelter, and some species use tree holes or thick vegetation for winter roosts (though nests are built only for reproduction). Squirrels, on the other hand, build nests (called 'dreys') for use at all times of the year and Foxes, Badgers, Moles, rats and mice use underground refuges.

In relation to the impact of their immediate environments, all endothermic or 'warm-blooded' animals (mammals and birds) have the ability to control their body temperature, virtually independent of their surroundings. Even plants may create their own microclimate by the density of the canopy they grow, within which temperature, humidity and light levels may be quite different close to the ground compared to a few centimetres higher.

Although plants cannot move to a different microclimate, the wind does actually move several environmental features past them. For example, a large tree with a radius of 10m, when exposed to a wind speed of, say, 10m per second, has its 'air' changed by the passage of about ¼ of a cubic km per 24-hour day!*

Solar radiation cannot be evaluated as simply as may first appear. For example, visible light is only about 45 per cent of the total. Of the visible light received by leaves, about a quarter may be reflected (or the leaves would be invisible to us!) and the rest absorbed. Not all the energy absorbed is used in photosynthesis (in fact, only about 2 per cent of the whole solar radiation may be so used) and much energy is used in transpiration (the evaporation of

*This is a complex calculation, based on 10m radius tree having a cross-section of c.300m² and a wind speed of 10m/s for 24 hours.

water from the leaves). Furthermore, the amount of solar radiation received by an individual leaf varies with its size, shape, position (how shaded it is) and angle relative to the sun.

*Although they themselves are static, the plants in this garden feel the effects of a number of 'moving' environmental factors.*

## Soil

Soil is made up of organic matter, minerals (including clay, silt and sand), air and water. The texture or 'feel' of the soil varies with the proportions of the constituents. Sandy soils are 'light', clay soils are 'heavy', and the proportion of organic matter (derived from dead vegetation and animal droppings) determines how much water soils can hold. All these attributes affect the 'workability' of the soil and the kind of plants that can be grown.

Soil also varies in its depth and its pH, acid soils having a low pH and alkaline or limey soils have a higher pH (the neutral value is about 7). Plants vary in their tolerance to pH – rhododendrons and azaleas, for example, are so-called 'acid-lovers', preferring a pH of 4–5. In fact, colour changes may occur when plants take up aluminium from the soil (and this is controlled by the pH – some hydrangeas produce blue flowers on acid soils). Adding organic matter may lower the pH and adding lime will raise it.

All this, however, represents the physical structure within which millions of organisms operate. Most are detrivores – organisms that break down the organic matter, physically and chemically. Their activity is mostly unseen, simply because it is below ground, but the majority of the organisms (bacteria and fungi) are extremely small and will not be visible without a microscope.

*springtails are minute arthropods that may occur in tremendous numbers in soils.*

Then there are vast populations of nematodes and protozoans that live by consuming the bacteria and fungi. The protozoans are simple, single-celled creatures, such as amoebae, while nematodes are small, often parasitic, worms, often called roundworms or eelworms (because of their appearance – they are not segmented like earthworms). The larger soil invertebrates include the micro- and macro-arthropods (e.g. about eight species of woodlice in gardens, the springtails (*Collembola* spp) which are only c.5mm long (top left), and the earthworms.

The protozoans probably consume most of the bacteria and the nematodes and micro-arthropods are the main fungus-eaters, but all these microorganisms need organic matter in a finely divided form. This is provided mainly by earthworms.

## Earthworms

There are two major earth-movers in gardens. One, the Mole, is not normally welcomed by gardeners. The other is the earthworm – a major asset, although not always appreciated on the lawn. In 1881, Charles Darwin estimated that the annual weight of worm casts in English pastures was 18.7 to 40.3 tonnes per ha (or about a 5mm layer) and this contains a higher concentration of plant nutrients than surrounding soil. The Common Earthworm is very good at breaking down tree leaves as well as other senescing vegetation. Its burrows also aid drainage. It may go down over 4 metres, but half that would be more usual. It proceeds through the soil either by pushing it aside or by eating through it!

There are several earthworm species found in gardens, of which the following are most likely to be seen. Besides the Common Earthworm, other cast-formers are *Allolobophora longa* and *A. nocturna*. The activities of these three species result in several centimetres of stone-free soil under an established lawn. The Brandling Worm needs copious amounts of decaying organic matter, which is why it is found in compost heaps where it is of great value. It is easily identified by its transverse rings of alternate yellow and maroon. The Common or Garden Field Worm operates mainly below the surface but does not burrow as deeply as the Common Earthworm. It is usually more numerous and thus probably turns over more soil than others, and is often encountered during digging.

Earthworms, like most small creatures, do not usually live for very long, from a few months to a year, but this is due to the fact that they are preyed upon by many species rather than their innate longevity, which may be several years. They are hermaphrodite organisms but need to mate in order to reproduce, lying alongside each other to exchange sperm. Eggs and sperm are then shed in a cocoon that the worm slips over its head! Incidentally, a worm chopped in half does not become two worms, but if the tail end is chopped off, a new tail may be regenerated.

*Earthworms on the soil surface.*

## Roots

It may seem odd to deal with roots here, since they are important parts of plants, but they do also form a major constituent of the soil. The living roots, in most terrestrial plants, derive their water and mineral nutrients from the soil and the latter have to be soluble in order to be taken in with the water. Dead roots, on the other hand, form an important soil constituent, providing a major part of its organic matter.

In a grass lawn, for example, there would normally be two or three times as many dead roots as living ones, which themselves represent about half of the weight of the short (cut) grass above. Each time grass is cut, a substantial number of the roots die. Of course, in other plants, the situation is quite different.

The largest of the tree roots function as supports to anchor the tree and prevent it falling (or being blown) over. Plants with tap roots generally use them as storage organs, to give them a good start in the spring, as well as to penetrate deeply into the soil for water.

Other plants have underground storage organs, such as the rhizomes of irises: these are not strictly roots but modified stems. Tubers (such as potatoes) are also storage organs but may arise as swollen roots or stems. The Lesser Celandine has underground 'bulbils' at the base of the leaf-stalks: these, and the root tubers, are the overwintering parts of the plant and give rise to new shoots in the spring.

Soil nutrients tend to be concentrated near the surface, in the top 15cm or so, which is why droughts can be so severe. Legumes such as clovers often do better in a drought because, although they have less roots than grass, they have nodules full of bacteria that fix nitrogen from the atmosphere, the only real source of nutrition that is independent of water flow into the roots. Grass may continue to transpire water from depth but derives little mineral nutrition that way.

*Legumes such as White Clover are better adapted to drought than grasses (right).*

## Composting

Composting is a biologically controlled process by which micro-organisms break down organic matter into 'humus', consisting largely of carbon, hydrogen and oxygen.

The process needs water (c.50–60 per cent), oxygen (at least 5 per cent), high temperatures (c.40°C) which are self-generating, and a pH of between 5.5 and 8. Maintaining this temperature is easier in fairly large masses of organic matter (at least 1 cubic metre).

Compost is dug into the soil as a form of fertiliser. Stable manure is also commonly available to gardeners and contains nitrogen, phosphorus and potassium in almost equal amounts (but not as high as poultry droppings; pigeon droppings are even higher!).

## Plant nutrients
(generally obtained in water solution)

### Plants require

Nitrogen (N)

Phosphorous (P)

Potassium (K)

Calcium (Ca)

Magnesium (Mg) and

Sulphur (S)

(the 'macronutrients')

### and the following 'micronutrients'

Iron (Fe)

Manganese (Mn)

Copper (Cu)

Zinc (Zn)

Boron (Bo)

Chlorine (Cl)

Molybdenum (Mo) and

Nickel (Ni)

Some plants also need traces of silicon (Si) and cobalt (Co).

# 3 Colour and communication

Gardeners often choose their plants on the basis of attractive colour combinations. However, flowers have evolved their lovely colours not to appeal to human eyes but to communicate with animals that are much more important to them – the insects that pollinate them. Animals may also use visual signals to communicate with their own and other species, along with an array of other physical and behavioural adaptations.

## Colour

While we think of colour as a property of plants and animals, strictly speaking, they do not actually possess colour – they have shape and texture that reflect wavelengths of light that our brains (and those of other animals) interpret as colour. To do this, we have three types of cone cells in the retinas of our eyes, which detect either blue, green or yellow/red light.

Most mammals have only two types of cone cells, for green and blue. Birds and reptiles see in full colour and most birds and insects have an additional type of cone that perceives ultraviolet light (uv). This last ability means that most birds and insects do not see the garden as we do but can perceive additional 'colours' and patterns. Here are two quite different examples that illustrate the importance of ultraviolet light and need for us to be aware of the ways in which it can explain what we see.

The first is the 'gape' of young Blackbirds (right) and House Sparrows. When the adult approaches the nest with food (or without for that matter) the nestlings open their bills wide to display what we see as a bright yellow 'gape'. Actually, the dominant colour is ultraviolet.

The second example concerns how predatory birds such as owls and Kestrels find the voles they prey on. Voles make tunnels in long grass, which they use to travel about unseen, but, for the benefit of other voles, they mark these tunnels with urine containing pheromones. However, the urine also reflects ultraviolet light that can be detected by owls in the dark and by Kestrels hovering high overhead.

The bright 'gape' of nestlings demanding food.

Large White butterflies collecting nectar from lavender plants.

We tend to think of colours as being due to pigments – after all, this is how we paint – but plants and animals generate colours in other ways, too. Well-known examples are the scales on the wings of butterflies and moths. These often do contain pigments but they also act as multi-layer reflectors and cause iridescence. Butterflies can recognise the sex of others by means of such colours but, importantly, often only when the wings are flapping. The rate of flapping may also be important and the brightness of the resulting flashes may indicate to potential mates how healthy the butterfly is. We, of course, mainly see the colours when the butterfly is at rest provided the wings are opened wide.

Fluorescence also occurs in some birds, due to reflection of ultraviolet light striking atoms in their feathers, releasing a yellow light, and fish scales can generate a metallic lustre that may confuse predators. Bioluminescence is also known (e.g. in glow-worms, and bacteria that live in certain fungi). This light generates no heat, and due to the nature of the chemical reactions that produce it, does not occur in mammals, reptiles or birds.

Finally, there is simple mirror-like reflection giving rise to a silver colour, such as that of the silverfish that you may find in the bath. This reflection comes from the underlying exoskeleton, not the scales.

Most colours have some purpose, since they are the result of evolution and are likely to be advantageous (exceptions include the colours of internal body parts, such as the red colour of mammalian blood). This is because the purpose of colours depends upon vision and most animals have eyes of one sort or another. So predators mostly hunt by vision, and prey species use colour to avoid detection, usually as some form of camouflage. A fairly recent finding is that many animals can see colour even at night and it is now believed that nocturnal colour vision can be found in toads, frogs, bees and wasps, and some aquatic animals.

Since we cannot see ultraviolet radiation, it follows that our view of the garden (by day and night) may be quite different from that perceived by its other animal occupants. For example, Blue Tits may see their caterpillar prey, which humans find hard to detect, as glaringly obvious under ultraviolet light.

The main plant pigments are green chlorophyll, yellow and orange caretenoids, purple betalains and, most interesting in many ways, sugar-containing flavonoids, called anthocyanins. The anthocyanins are responsible for reds, purples and blues depending mainly on the pH of the plant, and this may be affected by the acidity of the soil in which it grows. Pigments also work together – very complex combinations of anthocyanins, flavonoids and metal ions produce the blue flowers of cornflowers and salvias.

*The vivid colours of most butterflies' wings are only visible when the wings are open wide.*

*A hen pheasant amongst dried grasses is almost hidden by the disruptive camouflage that her feather markings provide.*

## Camouflage

Of course, predators digging up prey from underground cannot use vision to detect their quarry. Blackbirds eating earthworms usually wait for them to surface but also stimulate this by the tapping of their feet when moving across the ground. They only dig a little when a worm is detected. However, Green Woodpeckers dig for ants (commonly on the lawn), Rooks dig for insects such as leatherjackets, and Badgers dig for worms (and roots), as do Foxes, to a lesser extent. Badgers and Foxes have an acute sense of smell: in the case of the Badger it is about 800 times a sensitive as ours. Moles, of course, spend most of their time tunnelling underground. So the earthworm is not camouflaged by colour.

Indeed, much camouflage depends upon other factors, in combination with colour. Many animals tend to 'disappear', at least from our sight, if they remain perfectly still, although it is also true that a still animal stands out if its surroundings move (as with vegetation swaying in the wind).

Uniform colour is only useful against a uniform background. This may be the case for small animals (such as caterpillars or shieldbugs on green leaves) or for larger ones against the brown colours often prevalent in undergrowth (Rabbits, Foxes, Wrens). Many other animals have pronounced contrasting patterns. It is remarkable how stripes and spots break up an animal's outline sufficiently to render it very difficult to see against a natural background (above).

It has often been thought that speckled birds' eggs are a form of camouflage but it has recently been found that the spots also function as a means of strengthening the shell where calcium is in short supply. It is also notable that many birds that nest in holes rather than building open nests lay pale or white eggs. Those animals that hide away (such as beetle larvae in decaying wood) have less need for camouflage, and colour is less useful to nocturnal animals.

It is less easy to see whether plants use colour (or any other feature) for camouflage. More usually they use colour to draw attention to their flowers or fruits (a form of communication).

Herbivorous animals are more likely to find their food by smell or taste than by colour. Plants that are green are so because their chlorophyll (essential for photosynthesis) is a green pigment – in other words, it reflects the green wavelengths of light, while absorbing and utilising the wavelengths that correspond to the blue and red parts of the visible spectrum.

One of the most interesting forms of camouflage is the way small animals position themselves to cast little or no shadow. This is achieved either by extreme flattening or by becoming hemispherical.

## Eye-catching

Some animals do use colour to make themselves conspicuous. Most of these are poisonous, venomous, well-armed or otherwise dangerous creatures and they exhibit 'warning colours'. This, therefore, is really a form of general communication.

It seems puzzling that male birds have bright colours to attract their mates, as their increased visibility also runs the risk of alerting predators? One possibility is the recent finding that the coloured areas (often on the head) reflect less ultraviolet light and thus are less visible to raptors, although it is also claimed that male Blue Tits' heads are *more* visible to females because they emit ultraviolet light. The 'handicap' theory of sexual selection says that female birds are attracted to colourful males because they show superior survival skills, having successfully evaded predators despite the handicap of more visible plumage.

Some animals 'play dead' when attacked by a predator. It is a risky strategy but some predators will be unwilling to eat what they think is an already rotting corpse. The Six-spot Burnet moth (opposite) goes further and gives out a yellow, smelly liquid. If it is crushed, its body releases cyanide!

## Warning colours

Some potentially dangerous animals advertise this through striking coloration or patterning. Britain's only venomous snake, the Adder, has no bright colours but has a noticeable zig-zag pattern all the way down its back. However, it is not an aggressive species (towards humans) so the warning pattern is presumably not directed at us but at its most likely predators.

Warning colours are very prominent in ladybirds, most of them (in this country) having coloured spots on a reddish-orange background. The combination of colour and pattern signals 'unpleasant to eat'. The obnoxious feature of the ladybird is the way it exudes caustic blood from its leg joints when attacked.

However, the best known examples of warning colours are those of bees, wasps and hornets, associated with the capacity to sting, injecting unpleasant substances (acidic in the case of the Honey-bee but alkaline in the case of the Common Wasp – hence the old advice of using an alkali as treatment for a bee-sting and acid, such as vinegar, for a wasp sting, though there is no scientific evidence that these treatments are effective).

The following table illustrates other examples of warning colours found in garden insects.

| Insect | Location | Colours |
|---|---|---|
| **Magpie Moth caterpillars** *Abraxus grossulariata* | on Gooseberry and Currant bushes | The moth and its caterpillars are black, white and orange: even the pupa is banded yellow and black |
| **Soldier Beetles** *Rhagonycha fulva* | on umbelliferous flower heads | orange-brown |
| **Sawflies** such as *Croesus septentrionalis* and *Cladius viminalis* | on Poplar in August and September | green with orange markings orange with black markings |
| **Cardinal Beetle** *Pyrochroa coccinea* | on nettles | deep red with jet black legs and antennae |

Many other caterpillars combine colour with irritating hairs that put off most birds (but apparently not the Cuckoo).

The Six-spot Burnet moth's vivid colouration gives a visual warning to potential predators.

# Communication

This may seem to be the opposite of camouflage but is often complementary because most communication is only directed at members of the same species – it is not aimed at drawing everyone's attention to the communicators! Some well-camouflaged animals communicate by short flashes of colour or swift movements of one limb or appendage, so that their camouflage is not compromised. Warning colours are an exception. Many plants are poisonous but only some of them carry warning signs.

Animals, as already discussed, commonly use bright colours to display the message that they are best left alone. It is better if the effect of eating or attacking dangerous animals is less than lethal, so that predators can learn from their experiences. So effective are these warning colours that they are copied by non-dangerous species who benefit from the association – a phenomenon called Batesian mimicry. Of course, to be effective, warning colours have to be visible to the likely predator – which may not have full colour vision.

## Poisonous plants and fungi

| Plant spp. | Poisonous parts |
|---|---|
| **Shrubs** | |
| Broom | Seeds |
| Mistletoe | Berries |
| Rhododendron | Leaves and flowers |
| Privet | Berries and possibly leaves |
| **Trees** | |
| Holly | Berries |
| Yew | Leaves and seeds |
| Laburnum | All, but especially bark and seeds |
| Oak | Leaves and acorns |
| Beech | Nuts |
| **Herbs** | |
| Buttercups | Sap |
| Lily of the valley | All parts |
| Celandine | Sap |
| Bluebell | Bulbs |
| St. John's Wort | Leaves and flowers |
| Rhubarb | Leaves |
| Ragwort | All parts |
| Yellow Vetchling | All, especially seeds |
| Tomato | Stem and leaves |
| Lupins | All, especially seeds, except for sweet lupin |
| Daffodil | Bulbs |
| Yellow Flag | Leaves and rhizomes |
| Hellebores | All parts |
| Marsh marigold | Sap |
| Aquilegia | Possibly all |
| Foxglove | All parts |
| Cuckoo Pint | All, especially berries |
| Tobacco | Leaves |
| **Climbers** | |
| Ivy | Leaves and berries |
| White Bryony | Roots and berries |
| Black Bryony | Roots and berries |
| **Horsetails** | |
| *Equisetum* spp. | Probably all parts |
| **Ferns** | |
| Bracken | Especially the rhizome |
| **Fungi** | |
| *Boletus* | Not certain |
| Agaric | Not certain |
| Ink Cap | Not certain |

In the case of plants, which are mainly stationary, they only have to taste or smell unpleasant and the animal that tastes them is put off before much has been consumed. Toads exude unpleasant-tasting venom from their skin when seized, which may enable them to escape attack. However, shrews are thought to taste unpleasant and are therefore not eaten by most mammalian predators, but this does not seem to prevent them being killed.

Plants are limited in their methods of communication but are able to send internal messages, by soluble hormones, or external ones, by pheromones. Both can be extremely effective. In many plants, the apical cell (or bud) sends hormonal signals downwards that inhibit the development of side-shoots. This has such a dramatic effect that dormant buds lower down the plant may be quite invisible until the apical bud is removed. This is quite spectacular in trees. If the top is removed from a full-grown oak, quite quickly dormant buds all over the remaining trunk will burst into life and produce new branches and leaves. This is why, in grasses, grazing or cutting results in prolific branching (called 'tillering') and a short, dense sward.

## Animal noises

Many animals communicate by sound, with repertoires including clicks, squeaks, barks, whistles, hisses, grunts and songs. Different calls can have distinct meanings. Warning calls can even indicate the nature of the threat, including the species of predator. The loud alarm call of the Blackbird is well known, and alerts all birds in the vicinity to the danger, not just other Blackbirds. Its calls are quite different from its song.

The Moorhen also has a characteristic warning call and, while it has no song, its alarm call is quite distinct from the softer calls it uses to marshal its young chicks when no danger threatens.

It is likely that the calls of Rooks, crows and Jackdaws include a range of meanings that are not obvious to us. It is interesting to speculate whether other species can interpret them better. It is also worth remembering that some animal sounds fall outside our range of hearing. It is well known that bats emit squeaks that are, in the main, too high-pitched for us to hear, though there are now instruments that make this possible.

At the opposite extreme is birdsong, a familiar and welcome feature of life in (virtually) every garden. Not all birds sing, of course, but many species do, though not always in the familiar way. The hooting of the Tawny Owl and drumming of the Great Spotted Woodpecker have the same function as more conventional birdsong.

From a human point of view, the Nightingale (top) and the Blackcap (bottom) are among the most popular songsters. English Nightingales apparently sing 50–200 different phrases with further minor variations. Most species have a much more limited range and, indeed, it is the repetition of characteristic phrases that enables most of us to identify birds from their songs.

Most songs are learnt early in life (they often do have to be learned) but Blackbirds can learn new songs in later years. Indeed, it has recently been found that an adult Canary can learn new songs and, when it does so, it grows new brain cells! This is an extraordinary (and rather encouraging) finding and has now been confirmed in mice, the males of which also sing but ultrasonically so we can't hear it. Adult mice can develop new brain cells, a capacity that is induced by learning and suppressed by stress. These replace those that have died off.

Bird song has two important functions – to acquire and defend territory, and to attract a mate. In most bird species the male sings much more than the female, and in only one species has female song been shown to attract males – it is usually the other way round. Not only can both males and females identify their own species from song but they can differentiate between simple and complex versions.

Males with a wider repertoire of different syllables and phrases are more successful at both territorial acquisition and defence and at attracting females, who clearly prefer more complex songs.

Although, in many species, song is learned early in life, species (and perhaps individuals) vary in their ability to add to their repertoires and, especially in their ability to mimic. The fact that only part of a song is concerned with establishing territory may lead to males singing phrases that females do not and, in Canaries, this apparently leads to males having more developed brains than females.

Most people consider bird song to be beautiful and like to hear it. Many believe that birds may also enjoy singing – they certainly give that impression. However, as the breeding season progresses, birdsong diminishes as the growing chicks place more demands on their parents' time. Birdsong is also less often heard in winter, when feeding and maintaining energy levels takes precedence.

Even insects can emit sounds, a few of which can be heard by us, but it has recently been established that ants can emit sounds: these can now be magnified (greatly) by very sensitive microphones, so that we can get an idea of what is going on – or, at least, that something is going on!

The Nightingale (above) and Blackcap (below) – both renowned for the beauty of their song.

## Other forms of animal communication

Communication by movement is common among animals. Territorial disputes between rival birds and mammals are often settled through a process of physical posturing, accompanied by song. Distinctive stances are also used in courtship displays.

Female moths attract mates by releasing pheromones. Male moths are incredibly sensitive to these chemicals, and can be drawn in from miles around to pinpoint the female – in some cases before she has even emerged from her pupa. Mammals commonly use scent-marking to leave a message of their whereabouts to others of their species. This may serve to attract a mate, or to ward off intruders to the territory.

The 'waggle dance' of Honey-bees (below) is a unique form of communication, whereby bees use coded movements to share information about the whereabouts of food supplies with their hive-mates. This communication comes close to being a language and appears to be unique.

### The 'waggle' dance of the Honey-bee

This dance is a complex 'language' used by a bee returned from foraging to tell other bees where to find a good source of nectar and pollen. It was discovered by von Frisch in the 1940s and 1950s, but John Thorley in 1765 wrote that "bees certainly have a language among themselves which they perfectly understand ...". von Frish described 'round', 'wag-tail' (tracing out a figure of eight) and 'sickle' dances.

Suffice it to say that by means of these dances, the returning bee can communicate to others the direction, distance and quality of the food source. The details are complex but, just to indicate how this can be done:

(a) a vertical run upwards on the comb indicates that the food source lies in the same direction as the sun;

(b) if downwards, the direction is opposite to the sun (bear in mind bees only have to be able to see some blue sky);

(c) distance is indicated by the pattern traced out by the dance and the number of 'waggles';

(d) tasting and smelling the newly delivered nectar tells the bees quite a lot about the flowers to be sought;

(e) the richer the food supply, the more vigorous the dance.

They can even adjust for a head-wind, for example, and the departing bees take with them enough honey to fuel the journey indicated. How do you suppose bees judge the angles from the vertical that tell them how to orientate their flight relative to the sun?

# Communication by plants

We don't usually think of plants as possessing senses, but clearly they are sensitive to light, some leaves and flowers orienting themselves towards sunlight. Plants that are shaded will often increase their stem growth to reach the light. Clearly, too, some are sensitive to touch, such as mimosa and carnivorous plants such as sundews.

This is also true of climbing plants like convolvuluses and honeysuckles, which wrap their stems round others, or peas, beans, vetches and White Bryony, which twine their tendrils round supports. Plants also respond to buffeting by the wind, strengthening the tissues being swayed about.

It is also true that some plants can respond to sound, even at a level of the human voice, by growing faster or by seed germination. However, those carrying out research in this area warn that "you'd have to talk to them for days to have any effect"!

However, plants also have complex and quite sophisticated internal communication systems that govern their shape, how many branches they have and how they respond to defoliation. One example is the effect of removing the apical bud. The communication itself is conveyed by the movement of plant hormones up and down the main stem, auxins going down and cytokinins going up (the amount moving down governs the amount of cytokinin being produced and moving up or into side shoots). Of course, animals have complicated systems of hormone flow, but the fact that it happens in plants is less well known.

A number of climbing plants 'sense' the presence of potential supports and throw out sprung tendrils to grasp onto them like this White Bryony. Note that these early green berries will turn red as they ripen.

# 4 Observing wildlife

To enjoy a garden fully, it is enormously helpful to have a healthy interest in learning more about how and why things work the way they do. Indeed, you may think that this is true of many other interests too. One of the reasons why many people find it so difficult to answer the child's repeated, "*Why?*" question is that it usually arises from something observed that really invites other questions first.

## An enquiring mind

Often we are inspired to start asking questions after observing some animal activity that we don't immediately understand. Activity in plants, though, is usually too slow to be observed, or occasionally, as in some seed dispersal mechanisms, it is actually too fast.

Let us start with animals. A sensible sequence of questions might go as follows: "*What is it?*", "*What is it doing?*" and "*What is the purpose of this behaviour?*" But the enquiring mind should not wait for an animal to pop up. In general, only some animals ever do: many remain completely hidden. So a useful starting point might be: "*What is going on in there/under that/up there?*" This approach can be applied to the water (including under the lily leaves), the soil (including under the fallen leaves in autumn and winter), the treetops (and on the tree trunks), the bushes, the long grass, the flower bed or any other situation.

*This male Blackbird is well aware of the feast that lies beneath the leafy carpet including earwigs, centipedes and millipedes as well as slugs and snails.*

Normally you're only likely to look in the treetops if something (perhaps a squirrel or a bird) catches your attention. Similarly, you only look closely at the water if you see something move, or in the long grass if *it* moves, or within a flower if there's an insect on it. But dead leaves may reveal nothing of what is going on under them. Yet, when the ground is frozen hard in winter, insect-eating birds such as Blackbirds and Redwings continue to forage among these leaves, revealing that they know perfectly well what other creatures may be under there. Squirrels and pigeons do the same looking for acorns. Many of the creatures that live in water are not seen at a casual glance, because they are so small, or transparent, or do not move. In the case of the larvae of the phantom midge they are all three.

To help you to interpret animal behaviour, the most likely activities include: feeding or looking for food; hunting for prey; hiding from enemies; looking for a mate; reproducing (laying eggs or giving birth); looking after (and protecting) their young; creating a home (perhaps by burrowing or nest-building; or sheltering).

*The Bank Vole is a frequent, but elusive, visitor to many country gardens.*

Insects such as honey-bees, bumblebees and butterflies are drawn to the plants they help to pollinate by their colourful blooms.

## The purpose of a plant

To understand how plants live, it can be helpful to look at the various functions of their different parts. The stem could be for: supporting the leaves and flowers; carrying leaves up to the light; spreading the plant horizontally; or twining through bushes or other plants to gain support. The stem is also full of tubes that transport water and nutrients from the roots to the other parts of the plant, and carry sugars made in the leaves back down to the roots.

Plant roots clearly collect water from the soil, along with nutrients from the soil that are dissolved in the water (thanks to the actions of earthworms, fungi and bacteria, that break down organic matter into water-soluble constituents. Obviously the roots also fix the plant to the ground and prevent it being blown over. In fact, in big trees, these structural roots may do little else, or at least this is their most important function.

Leaves are where most of the gaseous exchange takes place. Carbon dioxide and oxygen are both absorbed to fuel the plant's chemical processes, and oxygen is also released as a by-product. Water vapour evaporates from the leaves (if it was not evaporated, how would the water and its nutrients flow up the stem?). This process, called transpiration, may also serve to cool the leaf in hot weather.

Large, colourful flowers attract insects to feed on the nectar they secrete and thus affect pollination. Wind-pollinated flowers tend to be small and inconspicuous. This is most easily seen on trees. The female flowers tend to be separate and quite tiny: try and find them on a hazel bush (they have tiny crimson stigma (about 1mm in length) protruding from a small bud-like growth on small branches). The male catkins are large (about 2.5cm long) and hang down to catch the wind that transports their pollen.

Female flowers, when fertilised, then produce seed and this has to be distributed. Often the seed is embedded in a pulpy fruit that animals enjoy eating: thus the seed gets carried away and deposited either after passing through the animal or when discarded as the fruit is eaten.

The soft flesh of berries such as those of the viburnum attracts birds and berry-loving animals which distribute the seed in their droppings.

# Noticing life in the garden

You could hardly miss a Sunflower in full bloom or a Sycamore tree in leaf, but not all plants or plant activity is so conspicuous. Take the Sycamore. In summer it has big leaves and winged seeds (top right). In the winter it has no leaves, but the seeds can still be found on the ground. Would you notice them? The voles do. If you open the seeds in December or January you will find the tightly rolled-up first leaves (or cotyledons) and in February they may be producing seedlings in large numbers. Voles will collect the seeds and eat the green bits.

Sycamore seeds and leaves.

And what about Hazel bushes? They have characteristic leaves and nuts in the summer. When do you think they produce their catkins? To most people's surprise, these first appear in November but they don't open and start shedding pollen until late January. Even more surprising is to open the (4mm) buds of pussy willow in September and find fully formed silvery catkins inside. Alder (centre right) and Silver Birch also have catkins in January but they are tightly closed up and nowhere near ready to shed pollen. In the case of Silver Birch, the catkins are all erect at this time, which is rather confusing because, eventually, the male catkins hang down and the female ones are erect.

In January, however, only the Hazel bushes may have female flowers – small, scarlet tufts at the tips of small buds (below right). These will only be noticed if you are looking for them, but, like so many of these observations, once you have seen one it becomes easier to spot others.

Alder catkins.

So, you should never suppose that there is nothing to see in the winter. In ponds, and even small pools amongst the dead leaves of a wood, the water is often teeming with tiny invertebrates, just visible to the naked eye. There are *Cyclops*, with females carrying egg sacs, and *Daphnia*, or water fleas (below). Both are pale-coloured and move in a jerky fashion. Using a magnifying glass will reveal more detail about both the way they look and how they move around. Slightly larger creatures such as small fish, dragonfly larvae and, later, newts feed on these little crustaceans.

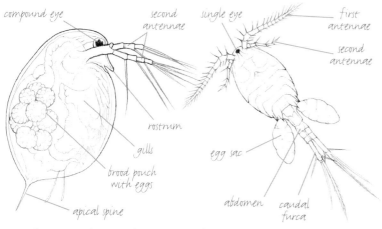

Left the Water Flea (Daphnia) and right Cyclops.

A Hazel twig showing female flowers.

# Tools and record-keeping

The humble magnifying glass is just one of many aids to observation that can help you to see what is in your garden. As well as using tools to make better observations, you can also keep notes and records as a permanent reminder of the more interesting things you observe.

## Magnification

A simple magnifying glass can reveal fascinating detail. For example, if you know that the wings of bees and wasps are hooked together, you may actually want to see this. It's not difficult to find dead bees and wasps as they sometimes enter houses, so there is no problem in obtaining specimens. A magnifying glass is also an excellent present for a child of almost any age.

Insect eyes, flower structure and developing newt eggs are clearer through a magnifying glass, although perfectly visible to the unaided eye (albeit wearing glasses!). But tiny objects such as pollen grains can only be seen using a microscope. Of course, a microscope makes the details on larger objects look clearer and reveals much more, such as the hairs on wasps' wings and the scales on butterfly wings.

For a closer view of distant animals, without running the risk that they will fly or run away when you get too close, use binoculars. Reversing them can also be used to magnify small details, but you have to put the binoculars very close to the object being examined.

## Record-keeping

Keeping records of what you see provides a reference for the future, which can guide you in terms of what you might expect to see and when. The suggestion that you should keep records may not appeal, common reactions being: "How tedious!", "That's not for me." or, "That would spoil my joy in discovery, if I've got to write it down." The answer is that you should only keep records if they *increase* your interest and pleasure. There are three main ways that this can be achieved. Firstly, they help you to remember what you've seen and when you saw it. It can be very irritating not to be able to recall these things. Secondly, they allow you to compare one year with another. We all say things like "this is happening earlier than last year" but actual records surprise me regularly. And finally, they make you take rather more care in the detail of what you observe, which can be rewarding in itself – the closer you look, the more you see.

Written records can be simple handwritten notes or, for example, a diary, which could, of course, be kept on a computer. I make notes about all sorts of interesting statistics (from books, newspapers and the TV) but record most of my own observations in a diary. However, this is not in the form of a separate diary for each year but a cumulative one. This is partly because I would find specific year diaries rather burdensome but mainly because I am interested in what *may* happen *when,* rather that what *did* actually happen in *my* garden on a particular day.

Even the limited enlargement offered by a magnifying glass reveals details of plants and animals hidden to the naked eye. Encourage children to look through a glass on a walk round the garden.

## Visual records

Many of us enjoy taking photographs of wildlife. These may have limited value as records because there are limits to what you can photograph. Some organisms are too small, move too fast, or choose to 'perform' when you don't have your camera with you. The big advantage of photographs is in showing other people unusual events that lose something in written description. Digital cameras now make it possible to take any number of pictures and, via the computer, to enlarge and manipulate them for a variety of purposes.

Drawing pictures or diagrams of what you see actually improves observation greatly, since every important detail has to be put in: you can only do this if you notice it in the first place. Most of us do not observe detail very carefully. It's helpful if you have some ability to draw, but many people discover that they enjoy the activity. I find black ink best because it is permanent, waterproof, easily copied and very sharp (pens are available in different thicknesses, some of them very fine).

For example, when I decided to record the life-cycle of the oak tree, I started, naturally enough, with the acorn. Then I realised that I had no idea when acorns germinated (when I first looked, I was astonished to find it already happening in December). I assumed, correctly as it turned out, that the root emerged first, but which end of the acorn did it come from? I had no idea and found that it was the pointed end. (I subsequently realised that I had even less idea about the Horse Chestnut fruit – the familiar conker.) But where does the shoot emerge? If you draw these things, you have to notice such detail in order to show it.

This is a very simple example but take insects or woodlice. How many legs do they have? How many body segments? Where are the legs attached? How many joints does each leg have? How do the legs end? Are the bodies hairy or smooth? What about eyes and antennae? Drawing does actually force you to observe more closely and this creates a habit that then operates whether you are drawing or not.

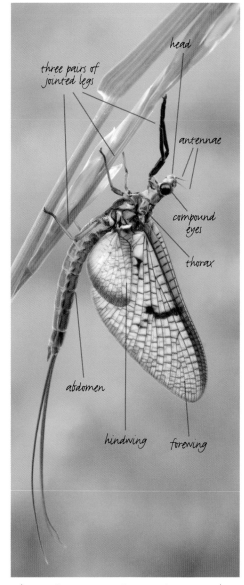

This excellent image of a Mayfly imago shows clearly the structural features that clearly identify it as an insect.

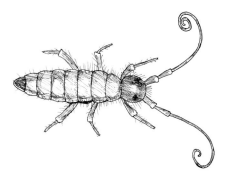

Careful observation of a creature such as this springtail helps to increase understanding of its physical structure.

## Watching and waiting

Direct observation is helped by knowing what to look for, when and where, but your presence may be a major obstacle, since animals may be reluctant to show themselves. Patience is a major virtue here. Standing or sitting still for long enough will often bring its own reward, as animals get used to you and conclude that you are not a threat. Of course, subdued clothing, keeping quiet and avoiding sudden movements all help. For those creatures that are still too shy, the use of a simple hide is often enough.

Some useful observations can be made from inside your house, through the windows, but many animals can see you quite well and move away. However, I have noticed that many species seem unable to see you through double glazing (see page 49).

## Searching and finding

To see most very small creatures, you have to search actively where they are to be found. It helps to know where to look. The obvious places are under logs and stones, for invertebrates of all kinds but also newts and toads will hide under large logs. Rather less obvious are hedge bottoms (for the nests of Wood Mice and bumblebees) and pond edges.

In ponds themselves, the eggs of Pond Snails and the cases of China-mark moths can be found under water lily leaves, whilst emerging dragonflies, damselflies, alder flies and others occur on upright vegetation within the pond, as well as at the edges. In the water, too, small creatures hide under stones and leaves and water fleas and *Cyclops* often concentrate at the edges, especially if there's an overhang. I have often been able to see none of these little animals until I have disturbed the surface water right at the edge.

Go quietly and look in the bushes and you may be rewarded by the sight of a bird, such as this starling, feeding on berries.

Female flowers of shrubs with (male) catkins are often quite inconspicuous. If there are male catkins shedding pollen, there must be female flowers to receive it (although not always on the same tree or bush). Small holes in the ground, even those of mice and bumblebees, are easily overlooked: the much smaller holes of solitary bees and wasps, on lawns or paths, even more so. Even some berries, especially on evergreens like ivy, may not be noticed. Watching birds like thrushes and Blackbirds feeding in autumn or winter will usually draw your attention to them.

## Dustbin lids and corrugated iron sheets

With some small mammals and reptiles, you need some help in increasing your otherwise pretty slim chances of seeing them however hard you look or still you keep. Laying out simple hiding places or 'refugia' can increase your chances of direct observation and of finding indirect evidence of their activity. I regularly find grass snakes under my 14 dustbin lids, and corrugated iron sheets may attract Adders and Slow-worms (which are really legless lizards).

A young Grass Snake that was taking cover beneath one of my dustbin lids.

Dustbin lids give more protection than corrugated sheets, and are often only accessed by tunnels at or below the soil surface. Short-tailed Field Voles, shrews and Wood Mice are regular visitors to my dustbin lids and all have nested, the voles doing so regularly. Their nests are woven mainly of grass and moss but all sorts of other things may get incorporated, such as baler twine, leaves and bits of plastic sheeting. Nests are sometimes open at the top, and young can be readily seen, or tightly closed with access from a tunnel underneath them. At times, the voles store cut grass (up to 10cm in length) under the lids as a food reserve, augmented in winter by nuts, acorns and berries. These signs tell you what's happening even when you see no voles.

Photographed at night, this Field Vole was using the dustbin lid as its food store.

squirrel

Wood Mouse

Bank Vole

Water Vole

Dormouse

Nuts that have been nibbled by a variety of different rodents.

You can tell whether nut remains near your dustbin lid were eaten by a vole or a mouse (or some other animal) by the way the nuts are opened and the associated tooth marks (left). Mice and voles (below) nibble a small, neat hole in the shell. Squirrels, however, rasp off the small end and split the shell in two with their front teeth, while the Nuthatch picks an irregular, ragged hole with its bill. There are other ways of working out who has been active under the lids. Droppings of voles, mice and shrews are quite different from each other, reflecting their differing diets, and shrews leave behind the shells of snails they have been feeding on, as well as earthworms rendered inactive by biting through them. Since no-one removes these shells, a dozen or so may accumulate.

Putting food, such as bread (however stale), old biscuits, nuts or apples, under the lids is an excellent way of keeping track of activities. Be aware though, that these foods may attract rats. Half-eaten remains can easily be observed at any time, whereas sightings of the animals themselves may be infrequent.

Bumblebees mostly nest in holes in the ground, although I have known them use a hole in a wall or a space between hay or straw bales, and seem to prefer old mouse-holes. Carder bees (above right), however, make woven grassy nests above ground: they also seem to be attracted by the smell of voles. In any event, they regularly nest under my dustbin lids. They rarely seem to have a proper entrance to the nest, simply plunging in through the sides. These bees do not establish large colonies, up to 200, but sometimes as few as a dozen individuals, and their 10mm wax cells remain as evidence of their presence.

A Field Vole eating an acorn.

Black Garden Ants are regular occupants and build their nests of soil virtually up to the top of the space available. They behave as though the whole thing is underground, so their eggs and pupal cases are often brought to the surface (depending on the ambient temperature) where they can be easily seen. The adult ants themselves are not worried by observation, unless eggs and pupae are on the surface – in this case they are rapidly carried below. Red Ants seem even less concerned about being revealed and observed and will move their grubs about on dead leaves under a dustbin lid.

Voles seem to get used to being observed and may stay for a short while. Wood Mice exit rapidly by spectacular leaps into the long grass. Other creatures may be found, especially woodlice, but the most frequent and interesting visitors are listed in the Table, right.

### Animals seen under dustbin lids

Grass Snake
*Natrix natrix*

Short-tailed Field Vole
*Microtus agrestis*

Wood Mouse
*Apodemus sylvaticus*

Common Carder Bee
*Bombus pascuorum*

Early Bumblebee
*Bombus pratorum*

Common Shrew
*Sorex araneus*

Black Garden Ant
*Lasius niger*

Common Red Ant
*Myrmica rubra*

Yellow Meadow Ant
*Lasius flavus*

Common Woodlouse
*Oniscus asellus*

Common Pill Woodlouse
*Armadellidium vulgare*

Snails
e.g. *Helix aspersa* the Garden Snail

Slugs
*Linnax* spp

Ground beetles

Black Garden Ants, their eggs and pupal cases – these are frequently found under dustbin lids.

## Pitfall traps

A female Stag Beetle (top) and a Dor Beetle – both 'victims' of a home-made pitfall trap.

To get a closer look at small, terrestrial invertebrates, there are various ways you can trap them without causing them any harm. One of the simplest is the pitfall trap. Simply dig a hole in the ground, and then place a jar or other receptacle in the hole, so its top is level with the surrounding soil. Passing creatures will fall into the jar and be unable to escape. Of course, the trap must be inspected quite frequently so that occupants can be released alive (and not eaten by another occupant!) and precautions have to be taken to avoid the traps becoming full of rainwater. If it is not possible to inspect the trap frequently, it is best to cover it with a well-fitting piece of wood, stiff cardboard, glass or even thick newspaper (weighed down with stones so that it does not blow about).

I constructed a giant pitfall trap from an old aquarium. While refurbishing this large (1m x 25cm x 25cm) aquarium I found that all the glass panes developed cracks which leaked and had dangerous cutting edges. I therefore decided to try out a giant pitfall trap. I buried the tank and placed in the bottom a thick layer of gravel, to absorb rainfall, and a few sizeable rocks so that small mammals (even baby Rabbits) could jump out again.

The results were immediate and rather surprising. Within two weeks, six female Stag Beetles (top left) had fallen in, including two that I had rescued from my large pond (where they regularly appear and where I had assumed that they flew in), along with two Dor Beetles (below left). Suspecting that some of these were repeat offenders, I started marking them with a small blob of paint on the thorax: it has to be a very small amount of waterproof paint, avoiding joints and the head. I avoided the wing cases, on the grounds that it could unbalance flight. I found it wise to wait until the paint had dried before releasing the insects, as they will smear it and rub it off on soil. I also kept in mind that the Stag Beetle is a protected species and must not be harmed. You would have to repeat this many times to get meaningful results on the number of beetles in the area and it would still be affected by whether the same beetles were being counted more than once. I was only able to note that, quite often, the same beetles fell into the trap, and the water, more than once.

The most frequent visitors to the 'tank trap' are usually ground beetles of various sizes and species. These will hide if they can bury themselves in the gravel or under leaves, and may not be noticed. I now find that all these species may arrive at any time of day or night. Only today (in July) two female Stag Beetles and a ground beetle arrived between 2pm and 5pm! These beetles are probably wandering about on foot – it seems unlikely they would fly in. The most surprising visitors are immature pond skaters, which I have never seen other than on the surface of the pond.

# Double glazing

One way in which wildlife can be more readily observed is through double-glazed windows. I have noticed that many birds seemed unaware that I was watching them through double glazing when they would have immediately fled if I had appeared at an ordinary window. So I started recording what I found and discovered it varied between species.

The Table, right shows the results, recorded under three headings – those animals that seemed not to see me through double glazing, those that clearly could, and those that were intermediate or I couldn't be sure about. Of course, lots of variables could influence the results, including relative brightness (inside and outside), brightness of the observer's clothing, the angle at which the animal is to the window (this affects reflection from the glass) and the observer's movement. It seems likely that, if the observer's movements were vigorous enough, most animals would see them and it is possible that loud enough noises could have the same effect.

Some animals, especially Foxes and deer, were not viewed sufficiently often to form a worthwhile judgement. The ones recorded in the table were seen frequently. Many more species appeared unable to see me than could, but of the latter, the most spectacular were Moorhens, which appeared able to see me even from a distance of up to 50m: they scuttled off much as if I had been outside the house.

## Animals that can see through double glazing*

### Those that can't

Blue Tit

Robin

Wren

Blackbird

Pheasant

Rabbit

Squirrels

Vole

Woodpigeon

Stock Dove

Long-tailed Tit

Great Tit

Song Thrush

Chaffinch

### Intermediate

Mallard

### Those that can

Magpie

Moorhen

Jay

Coal Tit

Cats

*Most animals will notice if a light is suddenly switched on.

A Mallard pair, photographed through double glazing.

## A garden pond

It is quite easy to make a basic garden pond, either by digging a hole and lining it with tough plastic or by constructing it above ground (see Chapter 22). The latter makes it much easier to see what is going on, as the surface can be closer to eye-level.

## Seasonal change

When looking for particular plants and animals, it is important to remember that some only live for a limited period or may only be visible at a particular time. We expect this with bulbs such as daffodils, tulips and hyacinths: we even grow them in pots for particular seasons (for example, hyacinths for Christmas). The Lesser Celandine (below) is a quite spectacular example of an ephemerally visible plant, covering the ground with leaves and bright yellow flowers during the early spring and then suddenly dying off completely. Below ground, of course, the roots and their 'bulbils' live on for next year.

*Lesser Celandine at the height of its vigour, with bright flowers and glossy leaves.*

Birds may be summer visitors and only stay a few months, while many insects can only operate at summer temperatures, so they often hibernate (whether as an adult or in an immature stage). Dragonflies only live for a few weeks as adults but for two or three years as nymphs in the water: Mayflies are the most spectacular, living for only one day as winged adults but for a year as their immature stage in the water. One of our largest insects, the Stag Beetle, similarly lives for up to four years as a larva inside decaying wood, usually in an old tree stump, but only for about four weeks as an adult. Thus, if you want to see the splendid adult beetles, which emerge in May or June, you have to search in June or July (in southern England), when the females mainly walk about (and fall into ponds) and the males fly around looking for them (they also fall into water). Incidentally, if you find an apparently drowned beetle in your pond, it may recover (several hours later) if placed somewhere safe to dry out.

Digger wasps emerge in early July, and are very active, stocking their burrows with prey (on which they lay their eggs) but this is all over by the end of August. Solitary bees, such as the Red Mason Bee which nests in cracks in walls, tend to be earlier (when pollen is plentiful) and are numerous in May but their nests are finished and all sealed with cement caps by mid-June. For this species, you can buy or make nestboxes filled with wooden tubes in which it nests (see page 211). In this way, the activities of the bees can be readily observed.

Spiders are numerous for most of the year but breeding is usually confined to a much shorter period. For example, the Nursery Web Spider only constructs its nest tent in June (right). This contains a cocoon of eggs. The newly hatched young stay together for a week or two.

These are all examples of easily observed and interesting activity that can only be seen for a short time and at a particular period of the year. See Chapter 20 for more on what to look for each month.

# Animal and plant groups

As you become more accomplished at finding and studying plants and animals, you are likely to develop more interest in trying to identify what you see. Some plants and animals are very familiar and distinctive, which makes them instantly recognisable without any need to study them closely. Even the most disinterested gardener will be able to name a Magpie, Fox or Daisy. Others, however, are much more difficult. Sometimes it depends on minor features of structure that are very hard to see. In some cases you may never be able to make an exact identification to species level, but you may be able to place the mystery plant or animal in the right family or genus.

Recognising what you know already is particularly relevant to animals (especially birds) where you may only get a fleeting glimpse of them. However, the more familiar you become with any species, the more likely you'll be able to recognise them from even a very short view. For plants, fleeting glimpses only apply if *you* are moving (for example, in a car): otherwise there is plenty of time to look at them in detail.

A Nursery Web spider guarding the nest it has made beneath its web.

## Plant groups

There are, of course, published detailed and comprehensive keys to help you identify all species of plants (as with animals), but here I am suggesting that without going to such lengths, which are often rather off-putting, you can get an initial idea of the 'sort' of plant by means of some simple observation. For instance, what sort of flowers does it have?

## Flowers

Not all plants produce flowers, and those that do often only have them for a short period of the year. In many plants, the flowers are inconspicuous. In trees and shrubs, the male flowers are often prominent catkins but these may only last a few weeks: the female flowers are quite hard to find. However, 'cherchez la femme' can be applied wherever you see catkins: these produce pollen – something must be there, at the same time, to receive it.

Garden plants are frequently grown for their flowers, so they tend to be big, colourful and either long-lasting or appearing in sequence over a long season. This is also true of some 'weeds', for example, the Dandelion and, on a smaller scale, the Daisy. These two belong to the family Compositae, so-called because the flower-heads are composite, containing many flowers with both male and female organs. Other plants have flowers that are two-lipped, some shaped like that of the pea, and produce characteristic pods of seeds. The clovers and vetches are also in this family of plants (Leguminosae). These plants have nodules on their roots, containing bacteria that fix gaseous nitrogen.

Another characteristic flower form is that of the Foxglove, which belongs to the figwort family (Scrophulariaceae). This family includes mainly two-lipped flowers (including snapdragons and toadflaxes) but also the mainly four-petalled speedwells.

Common Figwort (top), Vetch (centre) and Toadflax (below).

Foxglove (left) and Michaelmas daisies (right).

## Stems

These rarely receive much thought but they cannot only be seen but *felt*. What you can see are properties like hairiness, spines and thorns (although, unfortunately, these can also be felt). But what you can discern more easily through touch is the shape. Cross sections, which cannot be seen clearly unless the stem is cut, can nonetheless be felt. Some are round, some square and some triangular.

Round stems are the most common. Square ones are characteristic of the family Labiatae, which includes Self-heal, Ground Ivy, Hemp Nettle, Yellow Archangel and all the mints. Triangular stems are typical of sedges (family Cyperaceae). Stem shape, like flower shape, are just examples of features that may not tell you the exact species but indicate to which family your mystery plant belongs.

## Buds and leaves

Gardeners appreciate leaves and often grow plants just for the colour or shape of their leaves. Trees are readily identifiable from their leaves, except in the winter when you have to depend on their buds. Less often mentioned (except for the sticky buds of the Horse Chestnut), tree buds are all quite different and not difficult to recognise. Buds are, after all, the first stage in leaf development and, long before they burst, contain tightly packed, unexpanded leaves.

Mature leaves vary greatly in colour, shape, texture and hairiness. The main function of a leaf is photosynthesis, the process by which sunlight is used to convert carbon dioxide to carbohydrates, hence the predominantly green colour and flattened shape, but they also have to protect themselves from those that wish to eat them. Hairs may play a part in this (though quite often leaves also contain chemicals that are toxic to animals).

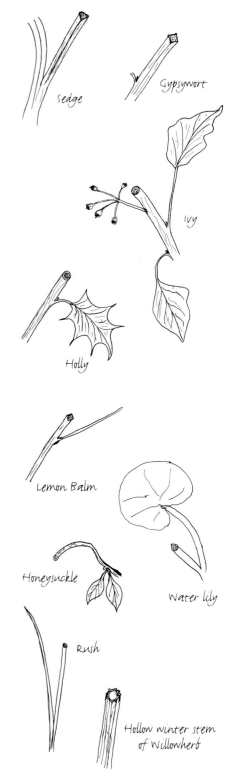

Cross-sections of a variety of plant stems.

Closed (left) and open (right) Horse Chestnut buds. Note the leaf scar in the shape of a horseshoe beneath the closed bud.

## Mammals

Everyone knows when they've seen a Fox, a Rabbit (or was it a hare?), a Hedgehog or a Badger, and it is not all that difficult to tell our various deer species apart. Stoats and Weasels present more problems for most people.

The smaller ground mammals, although there are only a few UK species, move so quickly that you usually only get a brief glimpse. If asked what you saw, you would probably say, "A small, furry, mouse-like creature." The shorter the time you have to see them, the more important it is to note the key features, nose, tail and ears. That is all you actually need to identify them – to a group if not to a particular species. Voles have blunt, rounded noses, small ears and short tails. Mice have sharp pointed noses, big ears and long tails. Shrews have long, narrow, parallel-edged noses, tiny ears and middle-sized tails. A good look at the nose will settle the issue and even a glimpse of the disappearing tail may clinch the matter. Behaviour may also be helpful: mice frequently depart with prodigious leaps, whilst voles and shrews 'scuttle' along, seeking a tunnel to go down.

*Rabbit (above) and Brown Hare (below). Note the larger ears and eyes of the hare.*

### Stoat and Weasel compared

|  | Stoat (*Mustela erminea*) | Weasel (*Mustela nivalis*) |
|---|---|---|
| Size | long (up to 31cm) | small (length about 20cm) |
| Shape | sinuous | cylindrical |
| Tail | long (half the body length) with black tip | shorter – no black tip |
| Colour | Above chestnut brown (sometimes white in winter) Below yellowish-white | chestnut brown white |
| Behaviour | may stand upright | often stands upright |

However, there are differences between the sexes, sometimes between north and south.

*The Stoat and Weasel are superficially similar but the difference in size is striking.*

A Wood Mouse with large ears and very long tail.

A Bank Vole with almost hidden ears and short tail.

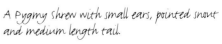

A Pygmy Shrew with small ears, pointed snout and medium length tail.

## Our commonest deer

(Note: colours and antlers vary with the season and sex: males larger than females).

### Red Deer (*Cervus elaphus*)

Largest of UK deer

Shoulder height: male 122cm, female 114cm

Coat short and reddish (esp. in summer)

Creamy rump patch

Large antlers with many points (depending on age)

### Fallow Deer (*Dama dama*)

Smaller than Red Deer

Shoulder height 85–110cm

Antlers palmate in older males, absent in females

Longish tails

Rump patch white but with dark brown outline

Coat chestnut red with rows of white spots

### Roe Deer (*Capreolus capreolus*)

Shoulder height c. 64–67cm

Appears tailless

Females have whitish rump patch with a tuft of white hair projecting backwards between the hind legs

Coat sandy/red brown, black nose with 'moustache'

Antlers short, 3-pointed

### Muntjac (*Muntiacus reevesi*)

Height at shoulder 45–52cm in England

Often stands with 'humped' back

Chestnut above, buff below

Tail ginger, held erect to show white underside when startled

Antlers backward pointing single spikes

Upper canines of males form tusks

## Bats in the garden

All British bats are nocturnal, emerging about 20 minutes after sunset, and all spend much of the winter (November to March) hibernating in a torpid condition that allows them to emerge in warm periods.

Bats can live for 20 years or more but are very dependent on suitable shelter, especially for roosting, in hollow trees, caves or roof spaces.

The species most likely to be encountered in British gardens are:

### Common Pipistrelle (*Pipistrellus pipistrellus*)

The most common and also the smallest. Recently this species has been divided into two very similar but distinct species: the Soprano Pipistrelle (*Pipistrellus pygmaeus*).

Length 3.5–4.5cm, weight 7–12g, wingspan 19–25cm.

### Brown Long-eared Bat (*Plecotus auritus*)

Has huge ears and is said to be able to hear a ladybird walking! The Brown and Grey species are very similar. The Grey Long-eared Bat is distinguished from the Brown by the colour of its fur, the length of the tragus (part of the ear) and its smaller thumbs. It generally occurs further south.

Length 4.5–4.8cm, weight 6–12g, wingspan 23–28cm. The huge ears are 3.3–3.9cm in length.

### Noctule Bat (*Nyctalus noctula*)

Our biggest bat – flies in a straight line.

Length 8cm, weight 18–40g, wingspan 32–40cm.

### Daubenton's Bat (*Myotis daubentonii*)

Known as the 'water bat' because it can fish insects from the water with its feet.

Length 4.5cm, weight 7–12g, wingspan 24–27cm.

Bats require shelter and night-flying insects, which are attracted by light (including security lights on houses), ponds and, above all, by night-flowering, scented flowers. The following plants are particularly attractive to bats:

Honeysuckle

Evening primrose

Night-scented Stock

Mint

Lemon Balm

Borage

Tobacco plant

See also page 195.

Common Pipistrelle

Grey Long-eared Bat

Brown Long-eared Bat

Noctule Bat

Daubenton's Bat

## Birds

In the case of birds, no-one doubts that what they've seen is a bird but which one? The larger garden birds are easily learned and many of the smaller species have distinctive plumage colours or patterns that you'll quickly learn to recognise. Bird song is another important way of identifying birds: indeed animal sounds in general can be used to identify animals that you cannot see (in the dark, for example). Birds can also sometimes be recognised by the way they fly, by their behaviour, by their size, shape and colour, and related species of birds often have some features in common, such as the appearance of their bills, feet and tails.

Bills are extremely varied between species but generally alike within species. As a feeding tool, the bill's shape reflects how its owner eats – whether it tears, crushes or snaps up its food. The illustration below shows the variation between species and indicates the function of each type of bill. It is this function that will often tell us what kind of food the owner of the bill feeds on. Individual birds may show slight variation in bill size and shape over the seasons – for example, tits' bills are thinner in the summer months, better at tackling insect prey, and heavier in winter when their diet becomes dominated by seeds and nuts.

Bills are used for other purposes besides feeding, especially in making nests, including carrying and manipulating mud (for example in House Martins, Song Thrushes, Blackbirds and Nuthatches). Woodpeckers use their bills for 'drumming' – as an aid to establishing territory and attracting a mate. They also use their bills for excavating nesting holes in tree trunks and the Green Woodpecker digs holes in the lawn to find ants.

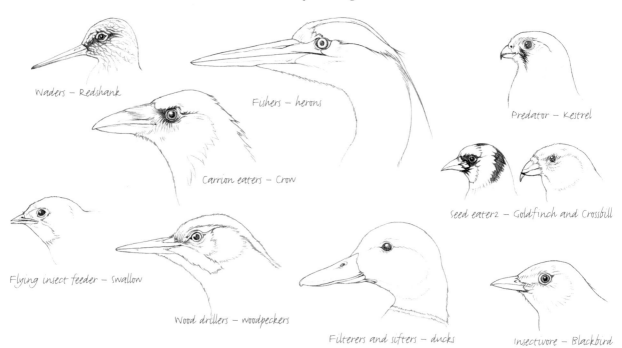

Waders – Redshank

Fishers – herons

Predator – Kestrel

Carrion eaters – Crow

Seed eaters – Goldfinch and Crossbill

Flying insect feeder – swallow

Wood drillers – woodpeckers

Filterers and sifters – ducks

Insectivore – Blackbird

The shapes of birds' bills are strongly related to their diet.

*Woodpeckers are perfectly adapted to life on a vertical tree trunk*

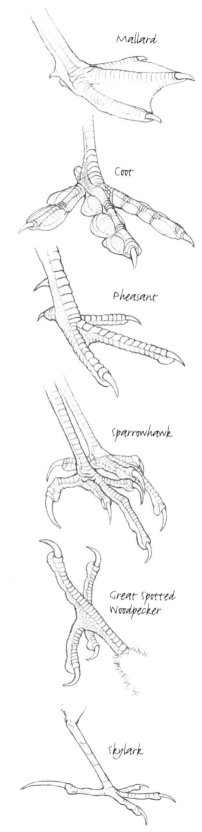

Mallard

Coot

Pheasant

Sparrowhawk

Great Spotted Woodpecker

Skylark

Feet are used for walking (Pheasant), hopping (thrushes, crows), running (Blackbird), swimming (ducks, Moorhens and Coots) and climbing up tree bark (woodpeckers, Treecreepers and Nuthatches). Birds of prey use their feet to strike and seize their prey, while many birds use their feet defensively, to kick at rivals or would-be atttackers.

The illustration right shows the ways in which the foot is modified for these purposes. The subtleties are well illustrated in swimming birds. Most of those that spend a lot of time swimming in the water have fully webbed feet (ducks, geese, swans). There are exceptions though, such as Coots and grebes, which are strong swimmers but have fleshy lobes on their toes rather than webbing between them. Moorhens swim but also climb in trees, and have long toes with no webbing at all. These long toes spread the bird's weight and allow it to walk across floating vegetation.

*A variety of birds' feet showing how they are adapted to their purpose.*

Male and female Bullfinch.

Birds use their tails in flight for balance but the stiff tail feathers of woodpeckers, Treecreepers and tits are used to support the body when clinging to or climbing up a tree trunk: this is especially useful whilst drilling a hole in the tree trunk or, in tits especially, attacking their reflections in a window!

Plumage colours and markings may serve several purposes – to provide a way to recognise another of the same species, to be shown off in mating displays, or to provide camouflage. Often, as in the case of the Bullfinch (left), the male is more brightly coloured and may have elaborate elongated plumes that are shown off in a display before a female. The female is often drab so that she is well camouflaged on the nest, which is relatively exposed and easily seen. Males that share in the work of sitting on the eggs also tend to be well camouflaged and in species where the sexes are the same (such as Robin) the bright parts of the plumage cannot be seen when the bird is on the nest. When sitting quietly in the right hiding place, even a bird as brightly coloured as a male Pheasant can be extremely hard to detect while his mate may be virtually invisible at a distance.

Female Pheasant on nest – almost perfectly camouflaged.

## Other animals

In the UK there are only three native species of snakes, two toads, two frogs, three newts and three lizards. With relatively few species to choose between, identification is made simpler (though note that several other species of reptiles and amphibians have been accidentally introduced to the UK and have established small populations).

When we get down to the invertebrates (animals without backbones), some of the groups are amazingly diverse, and this makes identification all the more challenging.

Butterflies often have very bright distinctive colours and markings but there are some more difficult groups, such as the fritillaries and skippers. Are you sure it's a butterfly though? Or could it be one of our 2,000 or so species of moth? Sorting out the moths is a much bigger problem but telling them from butterflies is fairly straightforward. In general, moths have variable, often feathery antennae (feelers) and butterflies' antennae have clubs on the ends (very few moths do). Also most butterflies are active by day and moths by night, butterflies usually rest with their wings either closed above their backs or spread out while moths usually hold their wings flat and swept back, though there are exceptions to all of these rules.

A Green Hairstreak butterfly showing a typical wing resting posture compared with a Peppered Moth which holds its wings flat.

A Giant Wood Wasp which is quite different in form from a Common Wasp. It can reach 4cm in length and its most striking feature is the long ovipositor.

Wasp

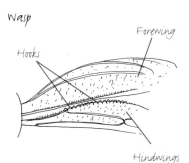

Forewing

Hooks

Hindwings

Butterflies and moths

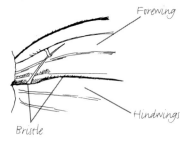

Forewing

Hindwings

Bristle

Detail of the wing hooks of flying insects.

All adult insects (and only insects) have six legs each, whereas spiders and their relatives (e.g. mites) have eight, and other 'creepy-crawlies' like centipedes and woodlice have many more. So, determining that you have an insect and not another kind of invertebrate is quite straightforward. From there, it's usually easy to recognise what general category of insects it belongs to, whether it is a grasshopper, dragonfly, ant, beetle or bee, but much harder to work out which species you have.

For example, there are about nine species of bumblebees that may be found in gardens, and in Britain as a whole there are well over 200 species of bees. Similarly with wasps: we mostly think of the Common Wasp with its striking black and yellow warning coloration, but there are great numbers of different parasitic wasps – often minute in size. And although we feel confident about bluebottles, greenbottles and houseflies, there are a great many flies that may even be confused with these – the name 'greenbottle' is applied to at least half-a-dozen different species.

True flies have only two wings (which is why their taxonomic order is called Diptera – *pteron* is Greek for wing). Other winged insects have two pairs and the hind wings are often hooked to the trailing edge of the forewings.

The classification of living things may seem dauntingly complex, or maybe just boring, but some understanding of how it works is invaluable if you want to identify what you see – especially when dealing with very diverse groups like insects and other invertebrates, so here is a short overview.

All animals are grouped together in the kingdom Animalia. This kingdom is divided up into a number of phyla (singular phylum). Our own phylum is Chordata – animals with a spinal cord. All the invertebrates (animals without backbones) so far mentioned belong to a different phylum called Arthropoda (which means 'jointed legs'). They have bodies that are divided into segments, and each segment bears one or two appendages (antennae, feeding appendages, legs or gills) on each side. This is why arthropods' legs are always in pairs.

The next division down from phylum is class. Insects (from the Latin *insectum* or 'cut into') form the class Insecta. They all have bodies that are clearly divided into three sections – a head, thorax and abdomen. Additionally, they have six legs, antennae and normally wings.

Another class in Arthropoda is Arachnida. Members of this group have eight legs and no antennae. Their bodies have two parts – a cephalothorax and an abdomen. They include the spiders, harvestmen, mites and ticks.

Other classes of arthropods include the Myriapoda (millipedes, centipedes) which have a distinct head, one pair of antennae and are terrestrial, and Crustacea (lobsters, crabs, shrimps, woodlice) which have a combined head and thorax, two pairs of antennae and are mostly aquatic.

If you find this helpful in putting some structure into the natural world, you could try the classification of insects. The class Insecta is broken down into a number of orders. For example, butterflies and moths form the order Lepidoptera, which means 'scale-winged'. The scales that cover their wings give them their colour, often by diffraction of light. The beetles belong to the order Coleoptera (*coleos* is Greek for shield).

Orders are divided up into families. Staying with beetles, there are some 500 families within the order Coleoptera, including the ladybird family Coccinellidae. The next level down is the genus (plural genera), and within the ladybird family there are about 360 genera. Most of the ladybird species that we know well belong to the genus *Coccinella*.

After the genus we reach the species level. Each species has a scientific name that is made up of two words. The first word is the genus name and the second the species. So with our ladybirds, the Seven-spot Ladybird is *Coccinella septempunctata*, while the rarer 11-spot Ladybird is *Coccinella undecimpunctata*. Both names are written in italics. This binomial system of classifying plants and animals was devised by the Swedish scientist Carl Linnaeus (1707–1778) and is still used today.

The Seven-spot Ladybird, Coccinella septempunctata.

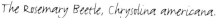

The Rosemary Beetle, Chrysolina americana.

A Red Admiral butterfly, showing the long proboscis typical of the Lepidoptera.

The order Orthoptera ('straight-winged') holds the grasshoppers, crickets and locusts. Mayflies form the order Ephemeroptera (from *ephemeros* – living a day). Other familiar insect orders include Hymenoptera ('membrane-winged') holding the bees, wasps and ants, Odonata ('toothed', referring to the insects' toothed mouthparts) which comprises dragonflies and damselflies, and Trichoptera ('hair-winged') – the caddisflies.

One of the advantages of knowing about orders is that some features are common to all the species within them. For example, nearly all members of Lepidoptera have no mandibles (jaws) and their mouthparts are modified to form a lengthy tube or proboscis, which is tightly coiled against the head when not in use (left). This tells you something about how they feed.

Caddisflies have an aquatic larval stage, when they make cylindrical cases of bits of weed, leaves, shells or small stones. If the adult insects had scales on their wings, they would be hard to distinguish from small, sombre-coloured moths, but instead of scales they have dense hairs – hence the name of their order. Also, caddisflies have licking mouthparts (they only take liquid food) but never have the coiled tongue characteristic of butterflies and moths.

The mayflies (order Ephemeroptera) all have very short aerial lives (one or two days), during which they mate and the females lay their eggs in water. The immature insect or nymph lives in the water for a year or more.

So it turns out that these complicated scientific names can actually be very helpful for the amateur who does not want to be bothered with all the different species but does want to identify the group it belongs to.

The Odonata order which comprises damselflies (right) and dragonflies have distinctive, toothed mouthparts.

# Galls

These are abnormal plant growths, produced in response to a tiny gall wasp laying an egg in the tissues of the leaf or stem. There are a great many gall wasps, all of them very small, around 1–8mm long, and they lay their eggs on a variety of different plants.

## Examples of galls caused by insects

| Insect Group | Species | Plant spp. | Nature of gall |
|---|---|---|---|
| **Hymenoptera** Gall-wasps and sawflies | *Rhodites rosae* (a gall wasp) | Rose | Bedeguar |
| | *Aulax glechomae* (a gall-wasp) | Ground Ivy | Pea-sized, reddish, on stems and leaves |
| | *Pontania proxima* (a sawfly) | Willows | Bean-shaped projection from both sides of the leaf |
| **Diptera** Gall-midges | *Perrisia ulmariae* | Meadowsweet | Numerous (30–200) reddish pustules on upper leaf surface with later some underneath |
| **Hemiptera** Aphids | *Capitophorus ribis* | White and red currants | Red, blister-like patches on underside of leaves |

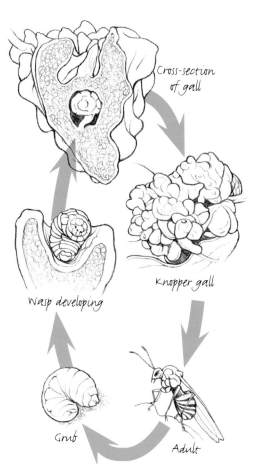

Cross-section of gall

Knopper gall

Wasp developing

Grub

Adult

The lifecycle of the Knopper Gall Wasp.

The easiest galls to see are on young oak trees, first in the late spring, then throughout the summer and a few persist into the winter. There are several very different kinds, which are described below.

The knopper gall (top right) is one of the most bizarre of all the galls. Caused by the gall wasp, *Andricus quercuscalicis*, it grows on the acorns of oak trees and often totally encloses them. These ridged growths can be found on the developing acorns at any time they are present. In the early stages of development they are red and sticky (see page 307), later they turn brown and become more woody in texture. A population explosion of the wasps in 1979 seems to have caused the abundance of knopper galls we see today.

Spangle galls appear on the underside of oak leaves, often in very large numbers (12 or more on one leaf) and appear first as more-or-less circular discs with a little bump in the middle. It is inside this bump that the wasp egg develops into a little grub, which eventually (but maybe not until next year) turns into an adult wasp. Because they are so small, they are difficult to open but, if you can manage it without damaging the occupant, you can find all these stages. Curiously enough, they remain on the leaves until they fall in the autumn and can be found on fallen leaves or on the ground under the leaves.

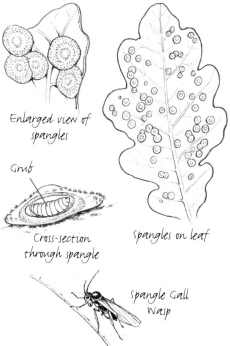

Enlarged view of spangles

Grub

Cross-section through spangle

Spangles on leaf

Spangle Gall Wasp

Formation of a spangle gall.

A series of Marble galls found on a single tree in my garden.

Marble galls are so-called because of their spherical shape, which starts on a twig as a small, green globe and gradually grows to become hard and brown by the autumn. At this time, the adults emerge and you can see the little round holes from which they have done so. Again, you can open them and find the grubs or adults in a small chamber in the middle or, later, the tunnel from the chamber to the outside. However, by the time they are brown and hard, they are very difficult to cut up (I use a hacksaw, holding the gall with pliers). These hard galls remain attached to the tree all winter, when they are easy to see in the absence of leaves.

Artichoke galls are bud-like growths on oak twigs and somewhat resemble artichokes. The wasp species responsible for artichoke galls also lays eggs in oak catkins at a different time of year, producing a different kind of gall.

The reason the tree responds in this way is to isolate the egg by growing a gall around it, so that the grub feeds on the gall and does not damage the leaf or the twig. The type of gall varies according to which part of the plant is attacked, so galls may be woody, leafy or take another form.

Artichoke gall formed on a Yew.

# Identification

Lots of people are put off attempting to identify what they see because they think, "Oh, I'll never learn *all* the species – there are so many of them." The truth of this is illustrated below.

| Group | Approximate number of species in Britain |
| --- | --- |
| Mammals | 75 |
| Birds | 600 (including vagrants) |
| Butterflies | 60 |
| Moths | 2,500 |
| Beetles | >4,000 |
| Spiders | 600 |

On the other hand, some groups are only represented in this country by a few species, for example:

| Group | Number of species in Britain |
| --- | --- |
| Bumblebees | 22 |
| Snakes | 3 |
| Frogs | 2 |
| Toads | 2 |
| Badgers | 1 |
| Foxes | 1 |
| Deer | 7 |
| Rabbits and hares | 3 |
| True mice | 3 |

Even within the most diverse groups, some are much commoner than others and, in any case, it is not necessary to try and learn them all. Sometimes, the sheer numbers cause people to specialise in one group: they become birdwatchers or butterfly specialists, but understanding a garden is most helped by knowing the most common species of each group. Once you have learned a few, it becomes easier to add one or two more. So, one should never be put off by the numbers.

Actually, in most groups, there are many species that all do similar things. Most butterflies feed on nectar, for example, most true bugs, including all the aphids, suck sap, most birds make nests, most wasps feed on liquids themselves but feed their grubs on little animals (bees, caterpillars, spiders) and most bees collect both nectar and pollen.

*An Elephant Hawkmoth.*

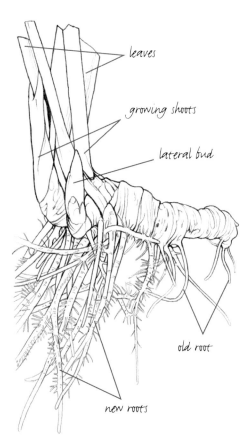

leaves

growing shoots

lateral bud

old root

new roots

Iris flowers and rhizomes.

The Red squirrel uses its 'hands' effectively to hold a nut while feeding.

Similarly, with plants, all legumes (peas, beans, vetches) have similar-shaped flowers (page 52), all sedges have triangular stems and all plants of the labiate family (mints, dead-nettles, page 53) have square stems, and all irises (above) have underground stems, called rhizomes, similar-shaped flowers and sword-like leaves.

So it's often possible to identify the group of species (whether it be genus, family or order) to which an individual belongs, but not by any standard method which applies to all cases.

## Legs and wings

A good starting point when attempting to identify a small animal is to count its legs. But are you sure that what you see *is* a leg? Some animals have antennae, or feelers, that are attached to the head, while caterpillars have stumpy false legs at their rear ends.

Typically, legs are jointed, making them suitable for walking, running and jumping. Some mammals also use their front legs as arms – just like us – and their paws as hands. Squirrels are good examples: they can use their 'hands' very skilfully to hold acorns and other nuts (left) and to dig holes in the ground in which to bury them for later use. Foxes, Badgers, Moles and Rabbits also use their front legs for digging.

But it's not only the larger animals that do this. Tiny solitary wasps and bees dig quite deep (up to 20–25cm) holes in the ground to lay their eggs in, though they also use their jaws to dig. Bumblebees cleverly store pollen in special 'pollen baskets' on their hindmost legs but it is put there by the front legs (see page 96).

All birds have their forelimbs modified to form wings and their (hind)legs and feet vary in all sorts of ways to suit their way of life. In bats, the leathery webbing between their finger-bones that forms their wings extends down to their hindlegs, meaning that all four legs are effectively wings (right). The hind legs end in hooked claws so that bats can hang upside down in their roosts.

So, in the case of bats and birds, we don't actually call the wings legs at all: we would say that birds have only two legs. In insects with wings, such as butterflies and beetles, the wings are not modified legs but quite separate structures: fore- and hindwings are often hooked together (page 62).

Some legs are used for swimming. In frogs and toads it is the hind legs (below), which have webbed feet, just like ducks. The front legs are used a bit like arms and actually grab hold of things. In the spring, male frogs grasp the females and stay on their backs until the spawn is laid, so that they can eject their sperm to fertilise it before the jelly swells up and prevents the entry of sperm (see page 78).

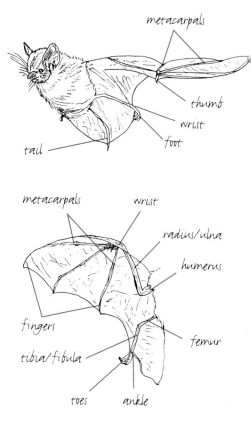

The structure of a bat's wing.

Frogs' hind legs with their large webbed feet are perfectly adapted for swimming.

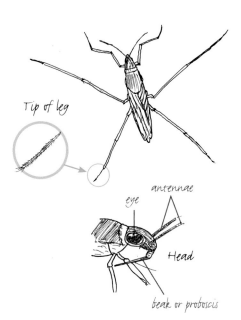

Tip of leg

antennae

eye

Head

beak or proboscis

The physical structure and head shape of a Pond Skater showing its 'beak'.

Fish have no legs but have fins to use in swimming. The tail provides the main propulsion though – this is also true for newts and tadpoles. In a few fish species, the fins function more like legs, supporting the fish when it is resting, and even providing enough power and control for the fish to jump about on dry land.

Besides walking, flying, jumping, swimming, crawling, climbing, running, digging and holding things, animals also use their limbs for grooming, scratching, fighting and kicking. The joints along the leg provide the means for a muscular 'push off' as the joint goes from flexed to straight. The structures at the end of the leg, whether they be paws, claws, pads, hooks, hairs, fingers or toes, fit the animal for the way it lives.

One example of very specialised leg-tip appendages can be seen in pond skaters, which manage to walk or 'skate' on water. This is partly because they are not very heavy and have widely-spaced legs to spread their weight. But the ends of the legs are very important (left). They end in curved hairs that rest on the surface film that covers all water surfaces. It is part of the water itself – not oil or anything like that (it has to do with the way the water molecules are arranged) – and creates a slightly resistant layer. This property is called 'surface tension'.

For very tiny insects that fall into the water, the surface tension is too strong for them to escape and they remain trapped on the surface, where they are attacked by pond skaters which are able to move about on their special feet. If you look carefully at pond skaters on the water, you will see that their hairy feet actually press down on the water, forming a small depression or dip in the surface film (below). When the sun shines down on these dips, their shadows can often be seen on the bottom of the pond (if it is not too deep) as dark circles. It is always worth looking closely at the feet of animals and thinking about how they help the animal in its daily life.

A Pond Skater literally appears to walk on the surface of the water due to the structure of its feet.

## Wings

As we have seen, most flying insects have two pairs of wings, which often hook together so they flap simultaneously. Dragonflies and damselflies are among those that have independently flapping wings. The true flies have small knobs called 'halteres' in place of the hind-wings (right). These are easily seen in crane-flies or 'daddy-long-legs', which can be found all summer but are especially noticeable in the autumn, resting on long grass prior to laying their eggs in the ground. When these hatch, they become grubs called 'leatherjackets', which live on the roots of grass (and farmers' crops). The crane-fly has long legs but it only uses them to hold on to its resting place – it can't run! Beetles, on the other hand, can often run very fast and are difficult to catch.

Some wings are hairy and some smooth: butterfly and moth wings are all covered with tiny scales, which overlap like tiles. These come off on your fingers if you touch the wings. Avoid touching the wings of live butterflies and moths, because losing the scales damages their wings.

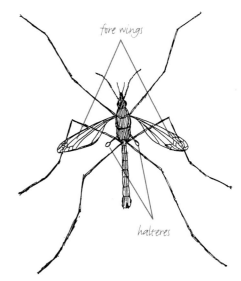

The tiny knobs that have developed instead of wings on a Crane-fly are known as halteres.

The scales on a butterfly's wings are very delicate and have a limited lifespan – this rather battered White Admiral has clearly had a long season.

So you can see that the kind of wings insects have can help you to identify them. Of course, it's not only insects that have wings – all birds have one pair of wings. Each wing has a row of long, strong flight feathers on its trailing edge, while nearer the body feathers become shorter and fluffier. Feathers are often dropped in the garden, especially from Woodpigeons, and it is worth looking at the way they are made and how the parts of the feather are linked together.

In many birds, like ducks and Moorhens, the feathers are highly waterproof as long as they are kept oiled. When you see a bird 'preening' its feathers, it is partly combing them to keep them clean and 'zip' the interlocking strands back together, and partly spreading oil on them, usually from a gland just above the base of the tail.

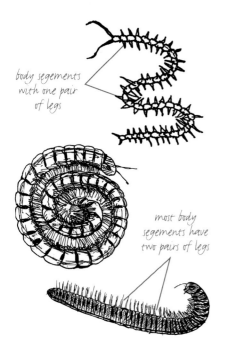

body segments with one pair of legs

most body segments have two pairs of legs

How many legs? Centipede (top) and millipede (middle and bottom).

## How many legs?

We know that mammals have four legs and birds have two, while most reptiles and amphibians have four. Snakes and Slow-worms have none, of course, and they get around by moving their ribs, using their large belly scales to grip the ground. We've also seen that all insects have six legs, but spiders and their allies in the class Arachnida have eight. But what about centipedes? They have a lot of legs – different kinds have anything between 40–120, with one pair to each body segment (top left). Millipedes, too, have many legs, but they don't move about as quickly as centipedes, so they're a bit easier to count. They have two pairs of legs to each body segment (centre left).

# The way insects grow

While adult insects all have six legs, in their immature stages things can be different. Insects undergo dramatic transformations as they pass from their immature to their adult stages. You and I simply get bigger as we grow and so does a caterpillar – but it doesn't just grow into a butterfly or moth.

When a caterpillar has finished growing, it stops feeding, leaves its food plant and goes to find a protected spot, sometimes buried in the soil or inside a shed, and pupates. This involves forming a hard case (below) that does not look like either the caterpillar or the butterfly it will become. In butterflies, this pupal case may be particularly attractive, and is called a chrysalis.

It remains like this for weeks or months, often over winter, during which time its whole insides change and then the case splits and out comes the fully formed butterfly or moth. Everything is packed close to the body, but the wings are not expanded – after all they wouldn't fit in. So the first thing that happens after emergence is that fluid (a sort of colourless, watery 'blood') is pumped into the veins of the wings, expanding them to their full size. Then as the veins harden the fluid is withdrawn and the wings dry out. As you can imagine, the insect is very vulnerable to birds at this time, so it benefits from the pupa being fairly well hidden, but, of course, those that are buried have to come out of the soil to emerge.

Peacock Butterfly pupa and the adult beginning to emerge from the pupa.

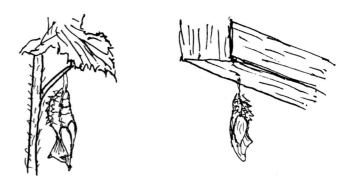

Butterfly chrysalides – under a leaf and suspended from a beam.

If you find a pupa, leave it where it is and, when the weather warms up, keep an eye on it and you can watch the whole process. The same thing happens with lots of insects, such as bees, wasps, houseflies and beetles.

But some insects grow rather like us, simply getting bigger but remaining much the same shape. Grasshoppers are a good example. In the long grass, in summer, you can find grasshoppers of all sizes. However, there is one big difference – they periodically moult, often about five times before reaching their full size. This is because they have their skeletons on the outside, so they can't just expand. We have our bony skeletons inside our bodies but insects don't have bones. Instead they have a hard skin or exoskeleton: you can see this easily in a beetle. So once a beetle or a butterfly has emerged, it doesn't grow any more, which is why, in any species, all the adults are about the same size (allowing for some differences between the sexes).

When insects moult (cast their hard skin) they expand suddenly, before the new skin hardens. When hardened, their exoskeletons are waterproof. In insects like butterflies and beetles, the young are called 'larvae'. Only in butterflies and moths are they called 'caterpillars', while larvae of beetles, bees, wasps and flies among others are often called 'grubs'. However, in insects that don't go through a pupa stage (like dragonflies and grasshoppers) where the young resemble the adults (except for their wings), they are called 'nymphs'.

# Observing animal behaviour

We often observe animals without actually interpreting their actions: sometimes we are only idly looking at them as part of the scenery or it simply does not occur to us to ask ourselves what they might be doing – and sometimes they may be apparently doing nothing. But quite often actions *are* interpretable and first assumptions may not be right. With a little practice, it is possible to deduce what they are going to do next and then to see things that would otherwise go unnoticed.

A simple example: if you see a bird with a billful of insects, it is clearly on its way to feed its nestlings. This tells you that its eggs have hatched and it may be possible to follow its route and see where the nest is. However, it is important to try and work out whether the bird has noticed that you have seen it, because, if it has, it will probably fly off in the opposite direction – but remain visible (so that it can also see you).

With patience, the bird can be reassured that you've gone or are harmless. Birds are very acute observers, however, and if you look away for a moment, they will be gone. In any case, the nest may not be in *your* garden at all. This is a rather obvious example: the following are rather less so and take as their starting point a particular location in the garden.

With time and care, birds such as this starling, may allow you to observe their lifestyle at relatively close quarters.

Young Carrion Crows at their nest.

## 1. In the trees

### (a) Crows

In the early spring, you may see Carrion Crows high in willow trees, trying to break off bendy twigs. This is quite a difficult operation – you can try it for yourself and you have two hands! This tells you that they have already started building a nest and have reached the stage where such flexible twigs are needed to weave together the rigid and often substantial twigs and small branches of which the nest is mainly built. The nest is more likely to be at the top of a tall tree, often a single-stemmed tree (like many Alders). However, oaks are often used too. The nest is substantial, and is built before the tree comes into leaf. It is therefore relatively easy to see at this stage and you can follow the birds and observe their weaving activities. This is a short phase during construction and is followed by some degree of lining with, usually, dead leaves.

### (b) Woodpeckers

In the early spring, often in February, you may hear rapid drumming in the tree tops. This is made by Great and Lesser Spotted Woodpeckers. The Green Woodpecker also drums but does so more quietly, and less frequently. The purpose is twofold, to establish a territory and to attract a mate.

The Lesser Spotted Woodpecker is really a very small bird, about the size of a sparrow, so it is easily distinguished although it has a similar black, red and white colour scheme to the much commoner Great Spotted Woodpecker. Because it is smaller and drums on thinner branches, the drumming sound is higher pitched, and it also stops abruptly while that of the Great Spotted fades away.

Later on, all three species start excavating nest holes. This is a quite different sound with separated pecks but is even harder to locate. The best way is to look for the fresh wood chippings at the base of the tree. When they rest on vegetation, they can be removed and the whole process followed by looking for fresh traces. If the tree trunk slopes, the hole will generally be on the underside; otherwise, it is more likely to be on the leeward side, for protection from the weather. The nests are not usually lined, so birds cannot be observed taking nesting material in or out.

A Great Spotted Woodpecker drumming on a tree trunk.

In general, they do not re-use old nest holes but other birds do, especially Starlings and the attractive Nuthatch. The latter often uses holes that are overlarge, and adjusts this by reducing the size of the hole to fit its body size exactly, using mud as a filler. Nuthatches can readily be observed doing this.

## (c) Tits

In the bushes, Blue Tits and Great Tits flit about collecting aphids and other insects but it is said that they change the size and shape of their bills in early spring by 'sharpening' them on the branches. So when you see a tit rubbing its bill on a branch, it looks as though it is cleaning its bill but this may not be the only objective. Sharpening the bill makes it more pointed, to suit the insect diet that it has to collect for its nestlings. Young birds commonly need a higher protein diet, for their early growth, than is needed by the adults and, in the case of the tits, than the much higher fruit and seed diet that they resort to in the winter.

Tits such as this Great Tit rub their bills on branches to sharpen them.

## (d) Wasps

On warm, sunny days, you will often see wasps on dead trees and stumps, where the bark has gone and the wood is exposed: the same applies to wooden cladding on buildings and fence posts. Very often they are collecting wood scrapings which they chew up and, with saliva, make into pulp from which they construct their nests. You can actually see and hear their jaws scraping at the surface.

If you look at the resulting nest, which may measure up to 45cm across, it seems that the amount of wood collected must be enormous. Well, it is, in relation to the size of a wasp but, in fact, it would crumble to quite a small heap for it is, literally, paper thin (in fact, much thinner than any normal paper). If you begin to look at a wasp in this way and see it working, you may then think, "If I watch it, it must lead me to its nest." However, I have never succeeded in this.

A wasp scraping wood in preparation for making a nest.

## 2. On the lawn

### (a) Green Woodpecker

This spectacularly coloured bird is often seen crouching on the lawn and one should certainly ask, "What is it doing?" Incidentally, they are not really crouching but give this impression because of their short legs (adapted for climbing up tree trunks). Also they look very alert (right) with their long pointed bills up at an angle to the ground. And so they are and are thus easily disturbed, although they can get used to you.

What they are doing is searching for ants. Many birds engage in a behaviour known a 'anting', picking up ants and placing them amongst their body feathers; this may be related to pest control or some other purpose connected to the acid bites of the ants. The Green Woodpecker is one of the few species that actually eats large numbers of ants. It digs circular holes in the soil where the ants have an underground nest and licks them up with its long sticky tongue. In fact, even if you don't see the bird at it, you may find these characteristic holes, often in groups, in the lawn. Smaller, round holes in the lawn are made by solitary bees or wasps.

A Green Woodpecker 'anting'.

*A Fox adopting this typical posture on a lawn at night is probably searching for earthworms.*

### (b) Foxes

Earthworms, of the kind that make casts, also leave holes but these are familiar to everyone. Less often seen are the Foxes that feed on these worms at night. The numbers of worms out on the surface on warm, humid nights is amazing – there may be a dozen large ones per square metre. The Foxes know this and regularly feed on them. The worms are very nutritious and, at times, form a large proportion of a Fox's diet.

This happens only at night, however, and there are only two easy ways of seeing them. One is by flashlight (which does not seem to disturb them) from, say, an already-opened upstairs window: the other is if you have security lights that illuminate the lawn.

### (c) Birds stamping their feet

Black-headed Gulls on grassland or mud flats often stand in one spot, alternately stamping their feet, then catching the worms that are stimulated to come to the surface. On the lawn, Blackbirds may occasionally be seen doing it – for the same reason. Running about on the surface may have the same effect.

It is thought that the stamping of light feet may fool the worms into thinking that rain is falling and thus conditions are suitable for their emergence to feed at the surface. If they are not stimulated by raindrops, how else would they know it was raining? And why should such worms want to come to the surface at all? They do feed on leaves at the surface, both dead and alive, and there is less danger of desiccation when it is damp: in general, there would be more organic food on the surface than underground and the worm does not have to process a lot of soil to obtain it.

## 3. At the water's edge

### (a) Birds

Of course, many birds come to the water's edge to drink, to bathe (especially Starlings and Blackbirds), to feed on aquatic creatures (ducks and Moorhens) or on insects on the vegetation (Wrens and tits), or to fish (Grey Herons and Kingfishers). All these activities are fairly obvious, but some come to collect mud – why? In all cases, it has to do with nesting but in different ways.

House Martins are the only ones to build their nests entirely of mud, although they also line them with dried grass and so on. The construction is readily observed, since they build under the eaves and will do it while you are watching. The mud is mixed with saliva and is puddled into small pellets that stick to each other and to the house in a remarkable way. Such nests take the weight of adults and several nestlings and may last for years. Nuthatches use the mud for a quite different purpose, to reduce the size of the nest-hole inherited from a larger woodpecker.

Two other birds that collect mud are Blackbirds and Song Thrushes, and both use it to line their well-built nests. They both create a smooth but quite thin cup of mud but the Blackbird then adds a further lining, of grass, which sticks to the wet mud and dries with it. It is not clear why they differ but when seen collecting mud, it is clear where they are going next.

*A group of House Martins collecting mud for nest building at a puddle.*

*A pair of Common Toads in amplexus, prior to spawning. The smaller male is on the back.*

## (b) Amphibians

All amphibians have to return to water to breed but spend most of the rest of the year on land, in moist places. The newts have a courtship ritual that ensures fertilisation of the eggs: frogs and toads behave differently. Both breed in the spring but the Common Frog is unusually tolerant of low temperatures and may be seen below the ice or on it, looking for a way into the water. Both frogs and toads are said to return to the same ponds, and even the same parts of the pond, every year and are able to find them from considerable distances. Toads, however, tend to spawn in deeper water, especially with weed in it: frogs generally spawn in shallow water, sometimes only a few inches deep and in ponds that may dry out in the summer.

In both frogs and toads, the male grasps the female tightly with his forelegs (called 'amplexus' - above) and remains in this 'piggy-back' position until spawning is over. Males will grasp anything of similar dimensions, including other males, but can identify a female by her passive acceptance of the embrace (other males understandably take a different view!) and, in the case of frogs, by the rough, lumpy granules on the skin of the females. The reason for all this is to ensure that the newly-laid eggs are fertilised immediately, before their surrounding jelly swells up by absorption of water and prevents the entry of sperm.

The spawn differs between frogs and toads. Frogs produce their spawn, maybe 1,000 to 2,000 eggs from one female, in a rush, resulting in the well-known floating mass. This looks like one continuous mass of jelly but, in fact, there are small spaces between the eggs that allow the circulation of water and thus oxygen.

*A Common Frog almost submerged by recent frogspawn.*

Toads, on the other hand, produce their eggs in a relatively thin, double chain, over several hours, during which they move about, so that the string of eggs becomes twined about the pond weed. The onset of the whole process is usually accompanied by much splashing about and, in the case of frogs, often by croaking. Toads, however, make very little noise but still splash about.

## (c) Choosing a nest-site

This may take place well before spring, when nest-building mainly occurs, but it is only readily observed in a few species, the most obvious being hole-nesting birds. In the latter, some knowledge of bird behaviour is needed to distinguish between exploring an existing hole as a possible nest site (clearly observable with Great Tits, for example) and simply looking inside to collect insects and spiders as part of a search for food.

Interestingly, after watching the behaviour of such birds for a while, it becomes possible to detect nest-choosing in other birds, too. Since I have a sizeable pond viewable from my office, through a large, double-glazed window (many species seem unable to see you through double-glazing), we regularly observe the behaviour of Mallards.

In the middle of December 2002, a pair arrived on the water and promptly started behaving in a way that we have previously found to be associated with nesting. Very often the drake stands guard, very obviously alert, in the middle of the pond, while the female starts to explore the vegetation round the pond edge, climbing out on to the bank and peering into sheltered positions. On this occasion, both birds started exploring and after a short time appeared to settle on one site at the base of a large Weeping Willow tree, where ferns and other plants grow later on.

Mallards had nested in this and one other place round this pond in previous years and it seemed possible that this pair had been involved. Certainly, the same two places were the ones that received most attention on this occasion. The female then proceeded to make a nest hollow – this is virtually all that happens initially, although twigs and leaves may then be rearranged about it. The hollow is made by sitting down and moving about to create a 'saucer' two or three inches deep.

Having completed this to their satisfaction, both birds, independently, flew up into the willow tree to look down on the nest site, perhaps to check how visible it was (or would become when leaves grew on the tree and on the ground). We have observed this several times before and found that Mallards rarely fly up into trees at other times (although some may nest in large tree hollows). They then retired to the middle of the pond and after a short time (and after the typical head-bobbing which often seems to precede departure) they flew away. This all took less than an hour on one day and the birds were not seen on the pond again until months later.

*The pair of Mallards that nested in my garden.*

## Nests

The nests to be found in a garden depend on its size and whether it has big trees, hedges and bushes, ponds or lakes and how it is managed. Only where there are tall trees will there be nests of Rooks and crows, only if there are sizeable holes and hollows in trees will there be owls, Jackdaws or Stock Doves, and only if there are smaller holes will there be nests of great and blue tits.

It is generally the case that the size, structure and location of the nest will tell you the species of bird that made it. Gilbert White pointed this out in his *Natural History of Selborne*: "It has been remarked that any species of bird has a mode of nidification (nest-building) peculiar to itself, so that a schoolboy would at once pronounce on the sort of nest before him."

The holes made by the three woodpecker species can be distinguished by their diameters (see page 123), the mud-lined entrance made by the Nuthatch is unique. However, other birds, such as starlings, may subsequently occupy holes used by these species. Rooks and crows build broadly similar nests (of twigs) but Rooks nest in groups or colonies, whereas crows are solitary.

Other big birds use mainly twigs, but the Magpie builds a roof on the top. The only other garden species that build roofs are the Wren, which builds a nest mainly of moss and feathers in roof timbers or dense hedges, and the Long-tailed Tit, which builds a domed nest of moss, spiders' webs and hair, covered with lichen and lined with feathers.

The Woodpigeon is generally described as putting together a simple platform of twigs but these are usually more closely woven together than at first appears and pigeons can be seen collecting dog hairs for a lining.

The commonest hedgerow-nesting birds are the Blackbird, Song Thrush (left) and Robin. The first two build nests of similar size, made mainly of well-woven dried grass, lined with mud. The main difference is that the Song Thrush leaves the mud smooth, whereas the Blackbird lines it with a thin layer of grass. The Robin's nest is a smaller, neat cup of grass and moss, often in an old kettle or other abandoned utensil.

The Mistle Thrush and the Jay build rather larger nests and often incorporate roots, earth and dead leaves. The Mistle Thrush favours a fork in a large tree. House martins, of course, make their nests almost entirely of mud (and saliva) stuck in the eaves of houses. Smaller cup nests are made by finches, Dunnocks, warblers and Nightingales which nest in quite low vegetation and even, surprisingly, on the ground.

Other ground-nesting birds are Pheasants, just in a hollow in long grass etc, and Mallards, though these may also nest in hedges and even hollows in trees. Moorhens and Coots construct a nest of twigs and water plants in rushes, water irises or in tree branches that trail in the water. Moorhens will often bend over rushes or iris leaves to form a roof.

A Song Thrush and chicks at its nest of mud and woven grass.

## Holes in the ground

It is fairly clear when Rabbits have been excavating their burrows and Badgers digging their setts. Rabbit warrens can comprise many entrance holes, often close together, while Badger setts have several large entrances, often many metres apart. Both species engage in a kind of spring cleaning and the remains of old bedding can be seen. Badgers are nocturnal, secretive and easily alarmed, so their activities are hard to observe. This is best done by putting transparent red (thin film) plastic over a torch. Most animals seem unable to see in red light but we can.

Rabbits, on the other hand, are relatively easy to see and, although most active at night, are frequently seen in daylight, when you may see them collecting fresh bedding for the nests. They use their chins to gather up dried grass and then carry it in their mouths, when they appear to have rather bristly moustaches.

Rabbit droppings are a familiar sight but Badgers establish latrines (shallow pits) at specific places in their territory. Since Foxes may occupy Rabbit burrows – they have a rather simple, gastronomic way of removing the owners – it is not always easy to tell who the current occupants are. One way is to look for tell-tale traces of hair stuck to the sides of the entrance. Badger hairs are quite distinct (right) and often offer the best way of working out whether a Badger is in residence in your garden.

*A young Badger at the entrance to its sett near dusk.*

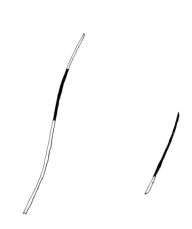

*Badger hairs have a typical tapering shape – look out for them close to where you suspect a Badger has made its home.*

A bumblebee covered in mites – an indication that it is still searching for a nest site.

Most bumblebees nest in holes in the ground, frequently taking over old Wood Mouse holes. Since they are so noticeable and some species are about very early in the year, you can easily see them searching the ground in woodland, in long grass or hedge-bottoms. These are the queens that are the only overwinter survivors of last year's colony and, while they are crawling about on the ground, you can watch them closely. Very often the back of the thorax is seen to be occupied by small brown mites (above). These appear to be harmless and are simply using the bee as transport to a new nest, where they can live on the detritus. So, seeing the mites tells you that the bee has not yet found a nest (or they would have dropped off).

The Common Wasp, however, frequently constructs its nest in roof spaces, attics and lofts, if it can gain access. This is most easily achieved in old buildings with tiled roofs. However, it will also nest in hollows in trees and logs and in holes in the ground. Wasps are efficient excavators and although they may start in, say, an old mouse hole, they will enlarge the space underground enormously. If you watch one of these holes, the wasps can be observed emerging carrying small granules of soil which they carry away for some distance; why?

This removal of the evidence is not uncommon in animals. Birds remove both the faeces of nestlings and egg-shells after hatching and drop them a considerable distance away. Cleanliness and hygiene in the nest would require removal but simply tipping them out would give away the location of the nest to would-be predators.

It is not so obvious why wasps need to be so secretive. When a strong colony is established, it is perfectly obvious from the regular comings and goings of the wasps exactly what is going on. And, in any case, not many animals attack a strong wasps' nest.

Another interesting feature of a wasps' nest in a hole in long grass, is that the wasps prune the grass around it. They can easily be seen sawing through the leaves that are interfering with their flight path, because it takes them some time to bite through the silica-encrusted leaves. Since the grass continues to grow, this activity also has to continue. You can actually observe a wasp at

A queen wasp starting to build a nest.

the entrance break off from what it was doing to deal with a leaf, as though it had suddenly got fed up with that particular obstacle. Others fly in and out whilst this is going on.

Several species of digger wasps make holes in bare ground. Hundreds of such holes are made every year in an area of about 6 square metres of brick path immediately outside my front door. They excavate a little mound of soil between the bricks and, on sunny days, are easily seen stocking their burrows with prey for their grubs to feed on. This has been going on for many years and the latest total number of holes was over 300!

In this particular case, the wasps, which are striped black and yellow but much smaller than the Common Wasp, prey on even smaller solitary bees which, perversely one would think, nest in holes within a metre of this wasp area. Other species of digger wasps specialise in catching spiders or caterpillars: they all sting their prey to paralyse it, so that it has the misfortune to stay alive and fresh for when needed.

The holes are surrounded by a little pyramid of soil and may be closed at night or during rain. On sunny days, the wasps' little yellow faces can be seen waiting just inside the entrance. The bees' holes are smaller but all are perfectly circular (top right): this distinguishes them from ant's nests, in similar positions, which have irregularly shaped entrances and a wider (flat) spread of soil.

A digger wasp (top right) emerging from its nest hole – you can just see the top of its head here.

Several other animals make holes in the ground in the course of feeding or related activities. Squirrels are well-known for digging holes in which to hide nuts and acorns but these are usually well-covered and, even if you see them doing it, it is quite hard to find what has been buried. Of course, sometimes, when a squirrel is seen digging it is recovering what it previously buried. So squirrels do not leave holes in the way that Rabbits do, in the lawn, for example. Incidentally, it has been found that, if squirrels see you (or anything) watching them, they pretend to bury acorns but leave the holes empty! Sometimes Rabbits are digging for roots but often there seems to be no purpose other than the joy of digging.

Rabbit digging its burrow.

The Smooth Newt needs to come to the surface quite frequently to increase its supply of oxygen.

## Animal behaviour in the water

The mating of amphibians has already been described and the activities of fish and invertebrates are usually fairly self-explanatory: they are feeding, hunting or breathing.

The last varies with the species. Quite a lot of invertebrates extract oxygen from the water by passing it over their gills, just as fish do. Fish do this actively by movement of the gills and some insects, such as caddisfly larvae, can create a current of water through their 'cases' or actually live in running water. Other insects simply rely on passive exposure to the water: in which case they may have expanded feathery gills with a large surface area. This is the case for damselfly and mayfly nymphs, both of which have three such appendages at their rear end (see page 221).

A wide range of other water animals have to come to the surface to renew their supply of air. Newts may do this and even fish may gulp air at the surface if the oxygen content of the water is low (due to rotting vegetation using it up or high temperature). Others, including beetles and water boatmen, *have* to surface in order to renew their supply. This they do by trapping a bubble of air, usually in stiff hairs at their rear ends or under their hard wing cases. So, if you watch the surface for long enough, you are bound to see which beetles and other air-breathing animals are living in the water – but it may take a very long time.

One of the more unusual sights is that of a Grass Snake swimming about at or under the surface (see page 219). These snakes are very good swimmers, quite fast, and are hunting for live prey. The vertical sides of some ponds defeat them but they are remarkably agile for creatures without legs. Their only purchase is by means of the scales on the underside of the body.

## Animal behaviour over the water

Many insects habitually fly over water. The most spectacular are the dragonflies and their smaller relatives, the damselflies. They may be engaged in one of three activities: hunting, mating or laying eggs. Hunting is a matter

As voracious hunters, many dragonflies, like this Azure Hawker, capture and eat their prey while on the wing over water.

of catching prey on the wing, at great speed. Dragonflies are actually a very ancient group of insects and their fore and hind wings move independently (see 'Wings and flight', Chapter 12, for contrasting features), giving them great manoeuvrability. Of course, they also hunt over areas other than water and can be seen zooming about between trees and over long grass.

Mating usually takes place over water, however, and egg-laying has to. Mating is an extraordinary business and often involves elaborate and contorted coupling. This is because the male produces packets of sperm in a reservoir in the ninth abdominal segment but transfers them to the second or third segment of the abdomen, just behind the powerful thorax. (The precise procedures and structures vary between species.) He then seizes the female behind her head with the 'claspers' at the end of his body – a position called 'tandem'. The female curves her abdomen under to bring her own genitalia (on the eighth or ninth abdominal segments) into contact with the male's body to receive the sperm, so the insects' long bodies form a 'wheel' shape. The tandem position is best seen in damselflies, which may actually fly about in this condition. Copulation itself, in the 'wheel' position, generally occurs when the pair are perched, however.

Oviposition also varies with the species. Some females simply drop their eggs on the water surface or dip their ovipositors just below it, but others have special equipment for slitting aquatic plant stems and leaves in order to deposit their eggs in the plant tissue. Indeed, some females actually submerge themselves completely in order to do this and need help from the still-attached males to lift them out again (overcoming the surface tension).

Blue-tailed Damselflies, Ischnura elegans, mating on a stalk.

## Aphids and ants

One final and very common scenario that should invite the question, "What is it doing?" or, "What is going on?" is when you see aphids on any plant, accompanied by black ants (right).

The ants touch the aphids with their antennae and suck up the drops of sugary fluid secreted by them. The ants protect the aphids from ladybirds and their larvae and from the larvae of hoverflies. The arrangement is often referred to as ants 'herding' their equivalent of cows and it is supposed that the aphids secrete the sugary solution as payment for protection. However, the aphids have no choice in the matter – they have to secrete the sugar whether the ants are there or not.

Incidentally, they do so high up in lime trees and the sticky drops will fall on you or your car, if either happens to be underneath! The reason flows from the way aphids feed. They are 'true bugs' of the order Hemiptera, and have that group's typical piercing stylet as a mouth, which they plunge into the plant tissue, even flexibly bending round cell walls to tap into the sap. This contains a lot of sugar and very little protein, so the aphids have to take in a great deal in order to get the necessary supplies of protein. The consequence is that they have to get rid of the excess sugar and water or they would burst (or starve). Of course, this does not in any way alter the fact that they do get protection from the ants, and that the association benefits both.

Black ants 'milking' aphids.

# Tracks and signs

Many of the animals in a garden are nocturnal or difficult to observe, so tracks and signs may be the only evidence of their activity. This is also true of trees in terms of *past* activity. For example, a deciduous tree in winter can be identified by its fallen leaves or fruits (such as acorns or beech mast), but this section is of most relevance to animals, especially large ones.

Deer, Foxes, Badgers, Weasels, Stoats and Hedgehogs are rarely seen in most gardens where they occur, unless special viewing or feeding arrangements are made. Some of them are more often heard, such as snuffling Hedgehogs on warm nights and vixens shrieking in late winter. Few birds are nocturnal and the owls are more often heard than seen, except when they are being mobbed by small birds in daytime. However, all these creatures may leave behind evidence of their activities.

Bird signs range from droppings below branches where Pheasants have roosted, to broken snail shells near a Song Thrush's 'anvil' and wood chippings beneath the newly excavated holes of woodpeckers. In fact, this last observation is often the easiest way to find such holes and, if the chippings fall on water or, say nettles, the daily progress of the excavation can be followed.

Mammals often leave characteristic excreta. Foxes and Badgers leave a strong smell as well as faeces: those of the Fox are often full of fur and end in a pointed curve and those of Badgers may be found in their latrines, shallow pits in the soil. Rabbits leave typical heaps of pellets (left) and bat roosts can be detected from the small black pellets (shaped like grains of rice) beneath them. Small nesting birds carry away the little bags of nestlings' droppings and deposit them at some distance, in order not to give away the location of the nest.

The scent of hole-diggers is most marked at the hole entrance and it is here (as well as on barbed wire, for example) that their characteristic hairs can also be found (page 81).

*Droppings of this shape and form are characteristic of Rabbits.*

*Animal hairs caught on barbed wire or branches are a good indicator of animals that have recently been in the garden. This is from a deer.*

House Mice use their scent to mark features of interest, but in Wood Mice this might give away their presence to predators, so they actually use 'signposts' made out of leaves and twigs. They use these to mark places where food can usually be found. Rabbit activity is mainly shown by the earth excavated from their burrows but they are probably the most readily seen in daylight, often on the lawn. Minor holes are signs of solitary bees and wasps or those of Green Woodpeckers looking for ants on the lawn.

The remains of food may also indicate the species of consumer. If you find a larger number of feathers, the bird was probably killed by a predator. The feather shafts are cut off neatly by Foxes but chewed by Stoats and Weasels, leaving ragged edges. Pigeons show this very well but they are also killed by Sparrowhawks.

Barn Owls and other birds of prey cough up pellets, containing the inedible parts of their prey (such as fur and bones). Thus with owls, as with Foxes, you can often tell what they have been eating by what they leave behind.

The way a Hazelnut shell is broken can indicate which animal has opened them (page 46). Leaves and shoots grazed off by Rabbits or deer are only too obvious, and both Rabbits and Badgers dig holes in the surface of a lawn, for roots and, in the latter case, earthworms.

An owl pellet that reveals evidence of the bird's most recent meal.

Moles are rarely seen but their 'hills' cannot be missed: they are made of the soil excavated by the Mole in its constant tunnelling in search of worms. So, it is sometimes argued, all you have to do is to slice off the heaps and remove the soil, they will not be renewed but, of course, new ones will appear as the tunnel system is extended. The soil from molehills is excellent for use in pots.

A rather different sign of past animal presence is the shed skin, most spectacular from the Grass Snake (centre right) but also the old nymphal casings of newly emerged dragonflies and damselflies.

The shed skin of a Grass Snake.

Damage to leaves is fairly easy to spot. Leaf-cutter Bees cut their circular or oval pieces (below right) from the edges of leaves (mainly of roses but also lilacs, laburnums and willows). They use these leaf sections to construct tubes in which to make the cells where they lay their eggs on stores of pollen. They even cut different shapes, according to whether they are making sides or ends of the cells.

Plant galls reveal the presence of gall-forming insects (see Chapters 4, 9 and 22). Leaves may curl up in response to aphid attack, and caterpillars (and some spiders) fold leaves and stick them together with silk. Both do it to protect themselves or, in the case of spiders, to protect their eggs and young. Some of the most spectacular leaf damage is caused by leaf-mining moth caterpillars, tunnelling between the epidermal layers of the leaf and leaving pale (translucent) tunnels (see page 229). These are very clear in the sow-thistle and if you open the widest end of a tunnel you can find the moth larva or pupa.

Signs of Leaf Cutter Bee activity on a rose bush.

Squirrel nests (dreys) are harder to detect than the animals themselves, but they do indicate the presence of squirrels (unless they are old and disused). Other signs of Grey Squirrels are bark stripped off tree trunks and branches.

The most bizarre signs of animal life are golf balls! I, like many people, regularly find golf balls where they could not possibly occur by human activity. I have generally suspected crows but, apparently, Foxes are the most common golf ball thieves: it seems they love playing with balls and golf balls are their favourites.

Moorhen tracks in fresh snow.

## Footprints

Most animal tracks can be really only be seen clearly in mud or snow. Not many gardens have a significant area of mud and these are chiefly at the edges of large ponds but, of course, even small patches of mud will hold a single footprint. Snow can give a picture of a whole line of tracks and it is often the pattern that identifies the owner.

Even snow is not always very helpful. In deep or soft snow the whole foot makes a rather blurred hole. Probably the clearest prints are found on ice covered by a thin layer of snow. The photo (above) illustrates the problems. The illustration opposite shows the tracks of mammals likely to be found in gardens and a few of the birds. Apart from those with webbed feet, bird tracks rarely enable you to identify the species, except by size.

One exception to all this is the trail of a slug or snail. The slime on which these animals move lasts for quite a long time and does not seem to be soluble in water. It shows up most clearly on paving slabs and bricks but you have to view the tracks from an angle, so that light is reflected from them. Interestingly, slugs and snails leave different tracks: those of slugs are continuous, whilst those of snails are broken (interrupted), as shown in below. The size of the culprit is indicated by the width of the trail (left).

The tracks made by snails (top) and slugs (bottom).

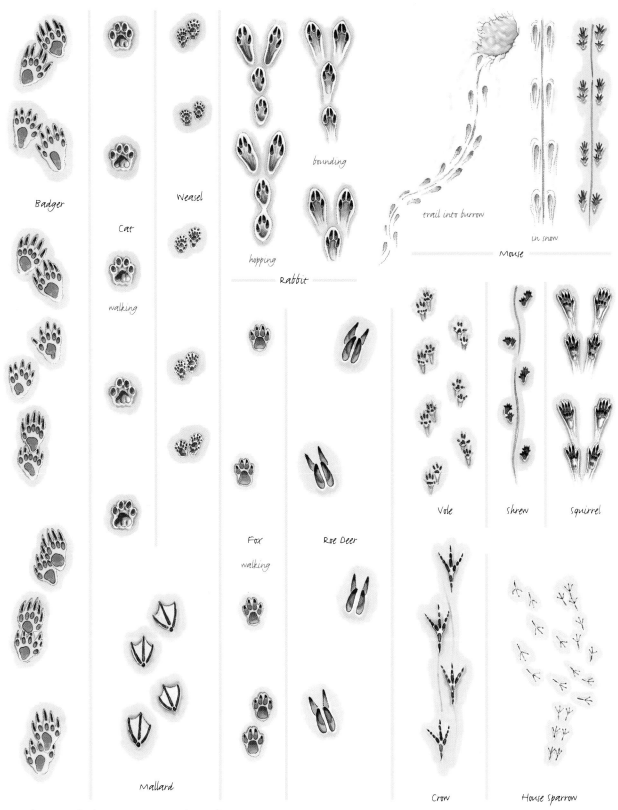

Badger

Cat

walking

Weasel

Rabbit

hopping

bounding

trail into burrow

Mouse

in snow

Fox

walking

Roe Deer

Vole

Shrew

Squirrel

Mallard

Crow

House Sparrow

Tracks made by birds and mammals in the garden.

# The garden at night

Many interesting things only happen at night. Nocturnal animals (most garden mammals, amphibians, moths and other invertebrates) are active and flowers such as honeysuckles and night-scented stocks give off their scent. A flashlight may not only be necessary, revealing the illuminated eyes of a Fox, the extraordinary number of earthworms on the surface of a damp lawn, the activities of newts in a pond, slugs and snails at work, and other wonderful sights that might not otherwise be seen.

Ponds are especially fruitful, partly because reflection makes observation difficult in daylight. Newts, frogs, toads, diving beetles and dragonfly nymphs can be clearly seen and most of them appear to be quite undisturbed by torchlight. Bats may be observed but are too fast for a torch to be of any help: many flying insects are nocturnal and bats do not depend upon sight to capture them.

Few birds are about, apart from owls, though pigeons and ducks may fly off noisily if disturbed. A few birds sing in the dark, notably the Nightingale and the Robin. Otherwise, the characteristic night sounds are the hooting of Tawny Owls, the shrieking of Barn Owls and the barking of vixens (most noticeable in the autumn and early winter), and the croaking of frogs for a short time in the spring.

In many ways, the garden looks different at night. Pale flowers stand out in what light there is, and Dandelion seed heads look like little lanterns. There are now several aids to observation at night, from simple light-enhancing devices to expensive night-vision goggles.

Watching at night, I have seen events in the pond that I didn't even know were occurring, such as Great Diving Beetles preying on newts. The beetles stab their prey with mouthparts that inject digestive fluids and then suck everything out, leaving just the newt's skin. This is so flimsy that you would not even know what it was the next day.

You may think that this last rather grisly sighting is an argument for *not* looking at the garden at night, but it does illustrate the point that some things can only be observed after dark.

There is a remarkable story about the famous 18th century naturalist Carl Linnaeus, wanting to show his gardener a flowering Birdsfoot Trefoil in late evening. He couldn't find the plant, although it had been quite obvious that day. After repeating this for three days he eventually found that the trefoil, at night, surrounded the flower with its five leaves, rendering it invisible! He went on to study other specimens and concluded that the garden looked quite different at night.

A Tawny Owl on its perch at night.

A Brown Long-eared Bat emerging from its tree hole at night.

# 5 Cultivated plants

What is the function of flowers? For the gardener, the answer is obvious: flowers are mainly for attractive colour and shape but also for scent and, sometimes, for butterflies. Other insects can be attracted by flowers, sometimes rather particular flowers. For example, bees are especially drawn to blue flowers and bumblebees especially to flowers with trumpets; all kinds of beetles, including Soldier Beetles, and flies are attracted to umbelliferous flowers, like Cow Parsley and Wild Carrot, and many moths are drawn to pale, scented, night-flowering plants, for example the Tobacco Plant.

## Scent

Gardeners are also attracted to scented flowers but, very often, our reaction – whether a scent makes us feel good or bad – is greatly affected by past associations. Although, it has been pointed out, we draw about 23,000 breaths every day, the extent to which we use our olfactory senses is very variable and tends to be most developed in people who have lost other senses.

Some scents add to the pleasure of a garden at night, especially the Tobacco Plant, Night-scented Stock, honeysuckles, night-blooming jasmine, verbena, syringa and evening primrose. During the day, lilies (the Madonna Lily is said to be the easiest to grow) are notable but there are many other powerful scents, such as jasmine, viburnum and daphne (see Table, right).

However, it is a mistake to think that scent only comes from flowers. Many parts of plants may be scented, especially the leaves. Some pelargoniums have scented leaves and Rosemary, mint, Basil and lavender leaves all release powerful scents when crushed.

The plant did not develop flowers to please us but quite generally to attract the insects that pollinate them. However, the insects have to be attracted either by supplies of sugary nectar or by the pollen. Bees are generally interested in both, while most flies, wasps, butterflies and moths are just after the nectar. Modern varieties, bred solely for appearance, may lack these attributes.

The glorious scent of Tobacco Plants is particularly strong in the garden at night.

### Scented flowers

Grass-leaved Flag Iris

Lavenders

Lilies

Pinks

Purple Heliotrope

Roses

Sweet Rocket

White Lilac

A great avenue of scented plants including lavender and roses in a grand country garden.

# Pollination

Fertilisation of flowers is achieved by pollination, the transfer of pollen from the anthers (where it is produced) to the stigma, where each pollen grain forms a tube that travels down to the ovule. In many plants, especially trees and grasses, the pollen is carried on the wind and pollination is said to be anemophilous (see Box, left).

Most garden plants are pollinated by insects, however, especially bees – Honey-bees, bumblebees and solitary bees. This is largely due to the fact that they all collect both nectar and pollen and so are obliged to visit many flowers. The amount and quantity of nectar varies with the species of flower, the time of day and how often the flower has already been visited. Some flowers, such as Meadowsweet, lack nectar and only produce pollen.

Self-pollination occurs among some plant species – each flower can fertilise itself – but most are cross-pollinated – obligatory for plants that bear male and female flowers on different plants (for example hollies, Gingko and yews).

Flowers that are not fussy and don't mind being self-pollinated do not make such elaborate reception arrangements as those that need their own pollen taken to another flower whilst receiving pollen from the last flower the insect visited. The most elaborate arrangements are made by plants like Lords-and-ladies, which traps small insects inside its flower until its own stigma is pollinated and releases them in such a way that they collect pollen on the way out (see below and left). Several species may be involved: I have found small non-biting midges and a dung fly within the flowers, but I have no idea whether more are trapped or whether they all act as successful pollinators. The Common Fig is another example, pollinated by a gall wasp that breeds among the female flowers.

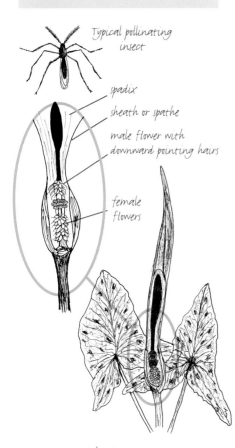

Typical pollinating insect

spadix

sheath or spathe

male flower with downward pointing hairs

female flowers

How Lords-and-ladies attract and trap insects to aid in pollination.

The Lords-and-ladies plant has an elaborate arrangement with the insects it entices in for pollination.

Flowers like those of the Foxglove combine colour, 'honey-guides' (lines on the lower petals that guide the visiting bee) and clever arrangements for dusting the back of the visitor: this is usually a bumblebee because it may be the only pollinator long-tongued enough to reach the nectar. If a sufficiently heavy insect, such as a bumblebee, lands on the lower petal (often specially shaped as a landing stage) its weight presses it down and opens up the way in to the nectary, commonly depositing pollen on the back of the bees from above (below). Such devices are aimed at keeping out undesirable creatures. Bumblebees' long tongues make them the only insects able to pollinate crops such as Red Clover and field beans.

A bumblebee inside a flower and covered with deposits of pollen.

| Pollen colour | |
| --- | --- |
| **Plant species** | **Colour** |
| Dandelion | Bright orange |
| Lime | Greenish-yellow |
| Great Willowherb | Grey |
| Crocus | Orange |
| Snowdrop | Yellow |
| Charlock | Yellow |
| Fuchsia | Primrose yellow |
| Willow | Yellowish-white |
| Pear | Greenish-yellow |
| Blackberry | Greenish-white |
| Buttercup | Orange |
| Horse Chestnut | Crimson |
| Lilac | Yellow |
| Hazel | Yellow |
| Poplar | Greenish |
| Ragwort | Deep gold |
| Yew | Cream |
| Daffodil | Creamy yellow |
| Bluebell | White |
| Hyacinth | Pale yellow |

It takes a lot of energy for bees to collect and transport their loads, so they work hard at the efficiency of the operation. In general bees prefer old varieties to new ones, many of which have been bred with no regard to their production of nectar. They also often prefer blue flowers – bees are red-blind – and Honey-bees go for radially symmetrical flowers while bumblebees prefer irregularly-shaped flowers (symmetrical from left to right – like our faces!) such as antirrhinums and aconitums, often called bumblebee flowers.

Bumblebees, like other bees, collect the nectar in their honey-stomachs, which can hold between 60 and 200 microlitres of fluid, and regurgitate it into empty wax cells for storage. Nectar is the only source of water for both adults and young and supplies energy: protein comes from pollen.

Only bumblebees have long enough tongues to reach the nectar in long, tubular flowers like Foxgloves: tongue length varies with species, from 7–10mm. Furthermore, only bumblebees can perform 'buzz pollination' by clinging on to swept-back flowers (like Tomato and Borage) with their legs and vibrating their wings at twice flying speed – hence the 'buzz'. The flower responds with a puff of pollen.

Many garden flowers, vegetables and fruit trees have to be pollinated in order to produce and set fruit but it is even more important for large-scale food production: bumblebees pollinate Oilseed Rape, field beans, Sunflowers, peas, runner beans, raspberries, strawberries, apples and currants. Wild flowers depend upon pollination to set seed, which is the key to their survival.

Bumblebees are regarded as particularly important because they can fly at lower temperatures than others and thus work over longer days (in summer, for example it may be from 4.30am to 10pm). This is in part due to the fact that they can warm themselves up by shivering, the wing muscles repeatedly contracting whilst uncoupled from the wings.

The thorax (mostly filled by wing muscles) is normally maintained at 30–40°C during flight, and if it drops below 27°C the bee can only crawl. However, they also have an ingenious biochemical mechanism for generating heat without muscle contraction! Remarkably, it has recently been found that a few flowers can actually warm up themselves, and their nectar, by chemical reactions within the plant, and the bees can exploit this

It has been known for a long time that some plants, notably the Arum Lily *Zantedeschia aethiopica*, can raise their temperatures to 35°C above ambient, but the warming of flowers in order to attract bees is a relatively new idea. Many flowers warm up by facing the sun and even following its movement (known as heliotropism): this is most noticeable in Sunflowers. Dark-coloured flowers are very effective at trapping the warmth of the sun and warm flowers may also produce more nectar. The effect of all this is to make such flowers more attractive, especially to bumblebees, which are warmed both by the flower and by the nectar. This saves the bees significant amounts of energy.

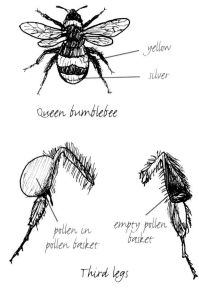

Queen bumblebee

yellow

silver

pollen in pollen basket

empty pollen basket

Third legs

How bees collect pollen in their pollen baskets.

Pollen is collected by combing it off the hairs to which it sticks and, sometimes moistening it with honey or nectar, storing it in special pollen baskets. These, called corbiculae, are hollows on the hind legs of bumblebees and Honey-bees (page 96). Pollen grains are, of course, minute, but a bee can trap and hold as many as 15,000 at one time! In Leaf-cutter Bees and other solitary bees such as the Red Mason Bee, pollen is stored on the underside of the abdomen, held in place by flanges of long hairs.

Indeed, although they are less noticeable than bumblebees and Honey-bees, there are many species of solitary bees and they are of enormous importance for the pollination of wild flowers and for some crops. In the USA, for example, colonies of two solitary bees (the Alfalfa Leaf-cutter Bee and the Alkali Bee) are placed in the alfalfa (called lucerne in the UK) crop to ensure pollination.

There are lots of ways in which flowers can be protected from undesirable invertebrates, by waxy or sticky coverings of the stem that prevent crawling creatures from gaining access, by hairs, and by the secretion of latex (the milky-white fluid present in many species of lettuce and also Dandelions) in special delicate cells which, when broken by marauding insects, solidifies in a gummy mass. Other plants, like water lilies, are protected from non-flying insects by the water in which they grow and some plants (for example bromeliads) collect water in the lower leaves, which also has this effect.

There is thus much to explore and wonder about in the structure of flowers. If some of the protective features sound bizarre, consider how the gardener does exactly the same with sticky pads round fruit tree stems, prickly bands to deter slugs and snails, traps of various kinds and standing pots of seedlings in water.

One simple protective measure adopted by some flowers is to close their petals, at night, at low temperatures or in the rain. Lesser Celandine is a very easily observed example. Its eight to ten bright yellow petals are fully open in warm sunshine but close up tightly when in the cold (see Chapter 22). Of course, many flowers are structurally unable to do this, including daffodils. Foxglove, Bluebell and lungworts don't need to because their downward facing flowers do not expose pollen to the elements.

One very unusual group of species are the evening primroses (see Box, right). The space devoted to these plants is exceptional, mainly to illustrate the fascinating story associated with any particular plant, once you examine it in detail.

**Evening primrose**

There are actually four species of evening primrose, of the genus Oenothera (all biennials). There are the Large-flowered Evening Primrose which is distinguished by its size, growing to a height of about 150cm, and by tiny red spots on the stem (and red spots or stripes on the sepal-tube). The other species, the Common Evening Primrose, the Small-flowered Evening Primrose, and the Fragrant Evening Primrose, all have smaller flowers and no red spots (although the Small-flowered may have faint ones). They are all part of the willowherb family (Onagraceae).

## Nutrition and growth

Plants derive most of their substance from photosynthesis (see Box, page 32), creating carbon compounds (cellulose, lignin), sugars, fats and proteins from carbon dioxide, oxygen and water, using solar energy to power the process.

Garden plants usually have a high water content (varying with species and stage of growth), absorbed by the roots: this is the only source of the minerals required, which can only be taken up dissolved in water. The major minerals are nitrate, calcium, phosphorous, potassium, sulphur and magnesium, but a range of minor minerals are also needed (iron, manganese, copper, boron, molybdenum and zinc) and many others occur (sodium, chlorine, aluminium, silica, selenium and cobalt) which may not always be essential.

All these, however supplied to the soil (perhaps as compost or manure) have to be taken up by the roots in solution. The only exception is nitrogen which can be absorbed from the air by bacteria in the root nodules of legumes (see Chapter 6) and trees like alders. However, these minerals do not actually make up much of the plant and the major part of its dry weight is usually made up of carbon compounds.

This is well illustrated in a tree. The wood is made of cellulose, hemicellulose and lignin (sometimes with tannins) and you can see how small the mineral content is by burning the wood – the minerals are all in the little heap of ash!

As is well known, trees accumulate all this material in annual rings, the thickness of which reflect the growing conditions at the time. So an annual ring is thicker in the part grown during the spring and summer; little growth occurs in the winter. That part of the annual ring grown in spring is paler and that grown in summer much darker (below).

*Annual rings on Alder which turns orange when cut and exposed to air.*

The whole plant is composed of cells of various shapes and sizes, with varying thickness of the typically cellulose walls (left). These cells form the main tissues, such as phloem for the transport of the products of photosynthesis and xylem for the transport of water.

Since trees can be very tall and we believe that water cannot move upwards, how do the leaves receive the huge amounts of water they require? One key to the answer is capillary action. In a very narrow tube, water does move

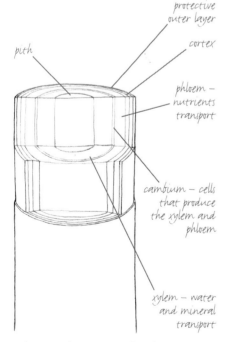

pith

protective
outer layer

cortex

phloem –
nutrients
transport

cambium – cells
that produce
the xylem and
phloem

xylem – water
and mineral
transport

*The typical structure of a plant stem.*

upwards and the xylem consists of very narrow tubes, lined with special cells and formed of lignified fibres. Water is, of course, continually evaporated through the stomata (right) of the leaves and continually absorbed through the huge surface of the root hairs, provided that there is water available to them. Root hairs themselves also need oxygen and nutrients.

The stomatal guard cells can close, to limit evaporation and the evaporative loss is, in any case, dependent on the temperature and humidity of the air surrounding the leaves.

Plants grow mainly by the addition of new cells, although buds in the spring expand rapidly by the absorption of water. Leaves form in buds and subsequently expand but stems elongate by the addition of cells from the growing tip. It is very noticeable that stems (including those of leaves and flowers) generally bend towards the light. This is achieved by growth of the cells on the side away from the light source and it is in response to chemical 'messengers' from the tip. These chemicals are called 'auxins' and they also control how much 'cytokinin' is made, which travels up the stem and has a reverse effect.

Most garden plants are not trees, however, and their stem growth is less woody, but they have the same need for transport of water upwards and transport of nutrients to all parts of the plant, including the roots.

The main factors affecting plant growth are light, water, nutrient flow and temperature. The last imposes limits but these vary quite a lot with the species of plant. Lawn grasses, for example, will grow at anything above about 4°C but the optimum is between 13 and 18°C. Legumes, such as clovers, prefer higher temperatures (at around 24°C) and, as is well known, the main flowering plants tend to have distinct seasons. Growth is limited at very high temperatures but these are very often also associated with drought.

# Seasonality

All gardeners are familiar with the fact that there are more-or-less well-marked seasons, although some of the differences are less marked than they were (see Chapter 21), and they are always varied according to where you live.

Many plants exhibit seasonality in the form of annual cycles of leaf appearance, flowering, seed-setting and senescence, but in many others (perennials), leaves are present all the time (for example the lawn, Rosemary, conifers, holly and ivy) and just vary in the amount of growth or the appearance of new leaves. Trees that are always in leaf still shed them, just not all at once, as happens with deciduous trees.

Some plants even flower over most of the year (such as Dandelion and lungworts) but others have very sharply defined flowering, seed-setting and fruiting seasons (including Bluebell, apples and pears, and Lesser Celandine). Many gardeners plan their gardens to produce a sequence of flowers, and most cultivated fruit trees and bushes have well-defined fruit-bearing seasons.

## Stomata

Stomata are very small holes in the leaf surface, about 15µm x 35µm, surrounded by (usually) slightly curved guard cells (see below). There may be as many as 10,000 stomata per square cm of leaf surface.

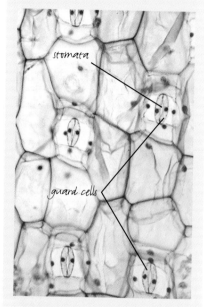

Hardy snowdrops are one of the earliest plants to flower, often blooming at the height of winter.

All this has an impact on the animals that feed on plants and their products. So aphids are seasonal in terms of their appearance as pests but have stages that winter on other plants (for example, Black Bean Aphids winter on the Spindle Tree). Slugs and snails are active whenever it is warm enough (unless it is extremely dry) but don't confine their feeding to any one plant species – many feed on decaying vegetation anyway. Indeed, under rotting logs, slug eggs can be found in January and February.

Ants withdraw to protected underground nests, snails hibernate, butterflies and moths overwinter in various forms (eggs, caterpillars, pupae, adults) and their caterpillars are wholly geared to the life-cycle of the plant they feed on. Most plant-eating mammals simply change their diet to fit the seasonality of food supply but their breeding seasons may be restricted.

In lean times, Jays make use of food stores that they have created months earlier.

Some birds (such as Coal Tits and Jays) and mammals (including voles and squirrels) store food in protected places to cover times of shortage or inaccessibility. Water birds can forage on land if their water course is frozen. Even animals that hibernate (like bats and Hedgehogs) may wake up whenever it is warm enough, though they may have difficulty finding food.

Invertebrate pond dwellers are exposed to a much narrower temperature range: water does not fall below about 4°C below the ice and large bodies of water (as sea-bathers know) take a long time to warm up significantly. Even so, pond snails, water boatmen and pond skaters all exhibit seasonal cycles. Very markedly, so do Cyclops and Daphnia, but they are most numerous in January/February.

Plant galls (pages 65, 162 and 306–307) are seasonal in origin, because the 'gallers' are, but some galls remain throughout the winter. The solitary bees and wasps and all the social bee and wasp workers all die off before the winter and the egg-laying of the Red Mason Bee, for example, lasts for only a few weeks in April and May. Only the year's new generation of digger wasps survives the following winter, living underground and emerging in early July. Spiders can survive over winter but breed seasonally. Nursery Web Spiders build their nests in July.

However, seasonal cycles should not be confused with other overlapping cycles. The cycle of predator/prey numbers, with good years often alternating with poor ones is at least easy to understand but others are not. I am regularly puzzled by cases where I can find something in numbers every year for years and then, suddenly, no trace at all, for one or more years, sometimes for quite a long time and then, as suddenly, they reappear. This has happened with Smooth Newts, caddisfly larvae, Water Starwort and Grass Snakes. In some cases, such as frogs and Rabbits, disease is often the cause of local disappearances (fungal infections in frogs and myxomatosis in rabbits). There is thus a problem in suggesting when and where a given animal may be found: sometimes for no apparent reason, it is absent.

There are also daily cycles, between day and night, between sunshine and showers and in relation to temperature. There are also surprises. For instance, the evening primrose is said to flower at dusk (hence the name) but I have photographed it in full bloom at 8.30am and it stayed like that all day! Bird activity comes and goes and I have not been able to work out why. Some days, all the small birds seem to be active and on another, apparently similar, day there are none to be seen. Perhaps gardens would be less interesting if things were more predictable: there is a lot to be said for not knowing what you are going to find.

The slow worm is a lucky sighting amid leaf litter.

# Reproduction

Plants reproduce in many different ways, both sexual and asexual. Many primitive, flowerless plants have quite complicated methods of reproduction and may demonstrate sexual differentiation (see Chapter 8). Liverworts, found as green, ribbon-like structures on damp ground, are quite small and are rarely noticed: they reproduce by spores. Mosses, ferns and fungi produce minute spores – usually single cells with few food reserves, but produced in vast numbers.

Most garden plants, however, are able to reproduce by seed, produced as a result of fertilisation of an ovule by pollen. They are not all limited to this method, however, and gardeners regularly take cuttings for vegetative production. This results in a true reproduction of the original and is the only way of replicating most fruit trees, for example, where cuttings from the desired tree are grafted on to quite different rootstocks (top left). This not only produces a fruit tree that is genetically identical to the parent but combines these with the special qualities of the selected rootstock (which has to be off a related species). The planting of tubers plays a similar role in the growing of potatoes.

Vegetative reproduction, as seen with the rhizomes of irises, the stolons of White Clover and some grasses and the runners of strawberries (below) is very effective at producing dense patches of plants but limits the distance that they can spread in the short term. Over a longer period, however, it is astonishing how large an area can be covered in this way by, for example, lungworts (below left).

Over short distances, buds on stems and roots can generate new individuals by gradual separation from the parent plant. This may happen with trees that have been cut down and the stump left in the ground. Elms only reproduce in this way and do not set seed at all.

Grafting new cuttings onto an existing rootstock.

Lungworts are one of the most effective groundcover plants.

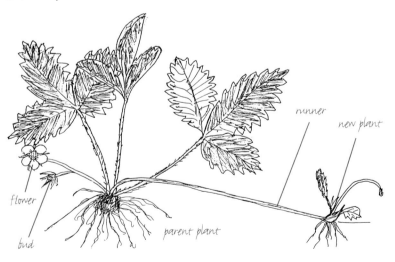

runner

new plant

flower

bud

parent plant

Vegetative reproduction in the Wild Strawberry using runners.

Many of the best known flowers in a garden regrow from bulbs, for example daffodils, tulips, snowdrops, hyacinths and lilies. The bulbs remain in the ground the whole year and multiply by splitting off new bulbs. Bluebells do this very vigorously, quite deep in the soil (often more than 15cm), producing dense clumps. In the spring, these may completely cover the ground but, of course, they die down equally completely by June.

Bulbs and corms, like tubers, allow plants to survive an adverse season (in our case, the winter), providing mechanisms for storing nutrients during the growing period, in their fleshy scales or swollen stem bases. This gives them a rapid start in the spring. Many wild plants do the same, such as White Bryony with its substantial, pale, swollen root, which like the berries is poisonous.

Plants that are grown from seed may be perennial, as with trees, Ground Elder and couch grass, annual (only lasting one season), or biennial, flowering in the year after they were sown (for example evening primrose). Trees grown from seed take a long time to mature and somewhat faster progress can be made by 'layering', whereby a branch is bent over and covered with soil (this can be in a box), where it will root and can be detached in due course.

Altogether, the most effective method of reproduction is by seed, partly because of the vast numbers produced (right) – unfortunately by weeds as well – partly because of their longevity and partly because of their ease of distribution.

## Seed production (typical examples)

| Species | No. of seeds per plant* |
|---|---|
| Poppy | 17,000 |
| Dandelion | 180 per head |
| Ground Elder | 500 (20 florets each with 25 seeds in one flower head) |
| Dock | 4,000–30,000 |
| Toadflax | 29,000 |
| Mullein | 700,000 |
| Foxglove | 750,000** |
| Honesty | 2,000 (6 stems x 9 stalks x 10 seed pods x 4 seeds) |
| Rosebay Willowherb | 100,000 per plant in one season |
| Yellow flag | 700 on one stem |
| Evening primrose | 40,000*** |

*All these figures are very variable – for seeds per pod, number of pods etc.

**One plant I counted had six branches on one stem, with 10–80 pods per branch, each pod with c.600 tiny seeds! (i.e. c.180,000 on one stem).

***I counted 200 seeds per pod and 200 pods per plant (with six stems).

*A carpet of bluebells at the peak of their spring flowering.*

# Spreading the seed

All living things are designed to reproduce and if they do not produce enough progeny to maintain their numbers, the species will obviously become extinct. When this happens, it is usually because their environment has become unfavourable to their survival in some way, including adverse changes in their food supply, or some other organisms (non-native predators, parasites or diseases) have arrived on the scene.

Plants are no exception and reproduce in a great many different ways. Simple, usually microscopic, plants may simply split into two and literally multiply. The ferns produce spores in vast numbers. The Male Fern (see Chapter 8) is quite a large plant and in the summer under every frond, small round, orange-brown discs develop which, in the autumn, give rise to vast numbers of minute spores. As with all ferns, the recognisable plant is the asexual phase and the spores give rise to relatively insignificant, free-living, sexual phases.

Fungi also reproduce using spores. Puffballs appear in the autumn (see Chapter 8), usually on the ground, as near-spherical, pale brown globes, which grow up to 4cm in diameter. They are well-named and, if burst, shoot out a cloud of fine brown spores.

Most plants, including most garden plants, produce seed, sometimes embedded in hard cases which enable them to survive for many years in 'seed banks' in the soil (left) and sometimes in soft fruits. For wide dissemination, seeds and spores excel. Spores and some seeds are light enough to be carried on the wind. In some water plants, even quite large seeds may float and be carried away on river currents, for example.

Heavier seeds that are to be wind distributed have structures designed to help this process. These may be 'parachutes' of fluff, as in Dandelions, narrow 'wings', as in ash and lime or the double-bladed 'helicopters' of Sycamore (below).

## Seed banks (examples of seed banks in the soil)

| Species | No. of viable seeds per sq m |
| --- | --- |
| Grass (*Poa annua*) | 31,300 |
| Poppy (*Papaver rhoeas*) | 34,200 |
| Gorse (*Ulex europaens*) | 10,000 |

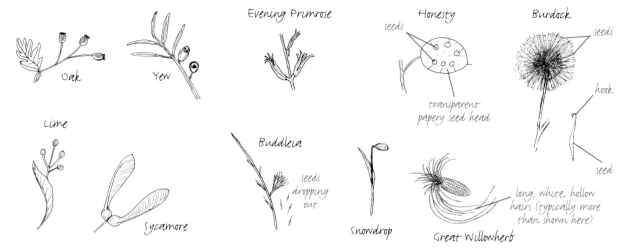

A variety of seeds showing dispersal mechanisms.

Some very small seeds are sprayed short distances by their containers swaying in the wind, such as poppies (top right). The same applies, incidentally, to catkins on trees, which spread their pollen from swaying branches and thus directly on to the wind. Others are brushed by passing animals: others are shot out by spring-loaded structures (for example Himalayan Balsam).

But a great many of the larger seeds are embedded in fruits that are attractive to animals, which may carry them off to eat, store them for later and sometimes forget them or do not survive to collect them, or eat them with the fruit. In this last case, the seeds may be passed out in the droppings, either unchanged or actually improved as far as germination is concerned. It is extraordinary how long ago this was observed in mistletoes. Pliny the Elder (32–79AD), agreeing with Theophrastus, commented, "But universally when mistletoe seed is sown it never sprouts at all, and only when passed in the excrement of birds, particularly the pigeon and the thrush; its nature is such that it will not shoot unless it has been ripened in the stomach of birds."

You will have noticed that, in many cases, berries remain on the bushes over the winter rather than falling (notably rose hips and hawthorn berries): this means they avoid being eaten by small mammals, which eat the seeds, and ensures that they are only taken by birds, which eat just the fruit.

Then there are the nuts, mostly with quite hard outer coats. In most cases, including acorns and conkers, these contain a single seed, usually made up of two cotyledons (the first leaves that a seedling may produce) acting as storage organs. Cotyledons often emerge, as in Sycamore seedlings, but with acorns and conkers for example, they remain where they are within the seed case. These hard, outer casings may help the seed to survive or ensure that animals like squirrels and Jays carry them off to a food store at some distance. This would help distribute the seedlings away from the parent tree (where they are really not wanted) but there is little point if they are then completely consumed.

Some plants, like hellebores and nasturtiums, just drop their seed where they are, so you find their seedlings close by. Honesty is similar, with the seeds encased in the papery 'pennies' (called 'silver dollars', I believe, in Canada) The umbelliferae have exposed seeds on the large heads and only shed them if these heads are shaken, in the wind or by animals. Geraniums, such as cranesbills or Common Storksbill, have ejection mechanisms (opposite) for propelling the seed away from the plants. Many seeds have hooks that cling to passing animals (or the mention of humans!). They include Cleavers and burdocks (whose seeds inspired velcro).

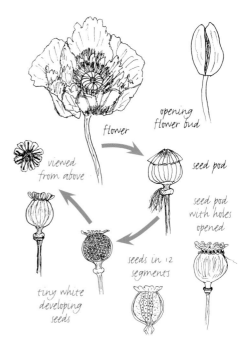

A poppy – from flower to seed dispersal.

This Mistle Thrush – feeding on a Mistletoe – will spread the seed after it has passed through its system.

Dried seed pods of Honesty – when the outer casing breaks the seed will disperse.

If you want to collect seeds, wait until they are ripe: in general, the darker the seed, the riper it is, but many seeds benefit from being spread out on a tray to dry. Those embedded in fruit or berries need to be extracted first.

When the seed/nut germinates, the growing tip of the root is really fairly delicate: how does it get through the shell? Some of these hard-coated seeds will only germinate if they can absorb moisture: how does this get in? It used to be thought that this was direct from wet soil but it now seems that most of it comes from water vapour in the surrounding air. This may be why some of them need the outer coat to be broken (scarified) and small animals, like voles, often do this and eat part of the contents.

The conker is a good example. The inside (the cotyledons) is very substantial and probably more than the seedling needs to get going. So, as long as the embryo is not damaged, loss of some of these reserves may not matter. It is very difficult to remove the outer case of a conker (unless you are a vole) but, if you do, there does appear to be an extension of the inner (furry) part of the coat that protects the growing point of the embryo (below).

The losses of seed are enormous but, on the other hand, so is the production. Trees may take many years before they produce any seed at all – 30 years for the Common Beech tree, for example, but they may then live for 100 years or more. In its life, a birch tree may shed a million seeds (10,000 per year) and only one is needed to replace the original and maintain the population. A sow thistle can produce 15,000 seeds a year and one Fat-hen plant as many as 70,000.

Furthermore, seeds can lie dormant for long periods and only germinate when disturbed: in the case of docks this may be 100 years.

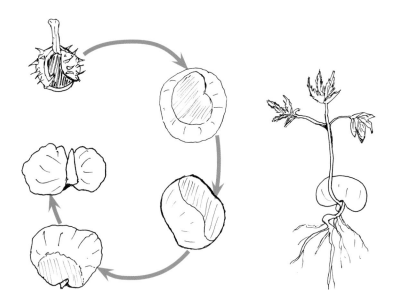

The development of a conker.

# Competition for light

Plants compete for light in various ways and angle their leaves to optimise the amount of sunlight received. In general, most plants grow towards the light because the shaded side is stimulated to grow faster. The most common form of competition is to grow taller than others but some plants that cannot do this, simply climb up others.

## How do plants climb?

Did you know that some plants climb up others in order to find a place in the sun? Why can't they just grow straight up like most of the others? Often it is because their stems are not strong enough for that and certainly some of them, even with strong stems, could not support by themselves all the leaves they can produce.

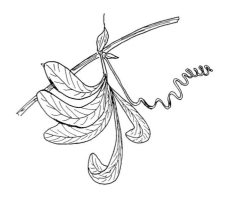

A Passion-flower – a typical example of a climber that uses springs to cling on.

Here are some climbers to look at, to see if you can see how they do it – ivy, clematis, honeysuckle, convolvulus (bindweed), Hop, Dog-rose, White Bryony, peas, Runner Bean, Cleavers, Passion-flower. (top right) Most of these are easily found.

Ivy grows mainly up walls and trees. Honeysuckles also grow up trees and bushes. So do convolvulus but they will also grow up any other plant they encounter, including nettles. Dog-roses grow up within hedges but also around tree trunks and branches. White Bryony climbs up hedges of all kinds (below right). Peas and runner beans grow where they are planted, in the vegetable garden, but have to be supported by stakes. Their relatives, the vetches, however, can be found in rough grass growing among the grass stems and leaves. Cleavers will grow up almost any vegetation. But how do they all do it?

spring mechanism on White Bryony.

Some, like Blackberry, simply grow amongst the twigs and branches of other bushes, or even trees, but other plants have developed special features and methods. The main methods are: twining by itself; twining aided by rough hairs or thorns; holding on by small roots; and holding on by leaf-twisting, or by tendrils.

Hops climbing up the trunk of a tree.

### Ground cover plants

| Species | Type |
| --- | --- |
| *Alchemilla mollis* (Lady's Mantle) | Herbaceous |
| *Cotoneaster* spp. | Prostrate or dwarf shrub |
| *Euonymus* spp. 'Darts blanket' | Prostrate shrub |
| *Geranium macrorrhizum* | Semi-evergreen herbaceous |
| *Hedera helix* 'Hibernica' | Woody climber or trailer |
| *Juniperus communis* subsp. *alpina* | Prostrate shrub |
| *Lonicera pileata* | Shrub |
| *Pulmonaria officinalis* (Common Lungwort) | Short spreading plant |
| *Rubus tricolor* (Chinese Creeping Bramble) | Scrambler |
| *Vinca major* (Large Periwinkle) | Spreading plant |

Which species use what methods? Some have dense hook-like hairs that effectively stick on to things (including you in the case of cleavers). The same technique is used by many plants in order to use passing animals to distribute their seeds (e.g. burdock). The Hop plant (left) is an excellent example of using stiff hairs on the stem to climb up other plants. If you pass your fingers down the stem (from the tip), it feels quite smooth: the other direction feels sharp enough to cut you.

The climbers that use tendrils may just twine, quite tightly, round their chosen support but, in some cases, after attaching itself, the tendril then coils up like a spring, along its length, tightening up the anchorage in such a way that the 'spring-loading' absorbs wind and other disturbance. This is well illustrated by White Bryony (page 107) – be careful when touching this plant as it is poisonous.

## Ground cover plants

Almost any ground left bare will eventually become covered by vegetation, which may not be wanted, because it is of undesirable species, plants that are too tall or ugly, that spread vast numbers of weed seeds, that have to be cut or that look a mess at certain seasons of the year. None of this is relevant to a lawn (which does, of course, cover the ground) or to cultivated flower beds, but there are some areas where low-maintenance ground cover is required, mainly to prevent colonisation by other species.

These may be understorey areas beneath trees or shrubs or simply uncultivated areas that are full of nettles, thistles and umbellifers. In these circumstances, several species can be planted that grow close to the ground and form very dense cover. Examples are listed in the Table, left.

The dwarf shrubs, such as cotoneasters, need occasional pruning if they are to be kept low; otherwise they cover the ground all right but form a shrubbery up to a metre in height. Some of the most attractive wild plants cover the ground very densely but only for a relatively short period of the year. Lesser Celandine (page 50) is a good example, with early flowers and attractive leaves, but it dies down completely for the summer and winter.

Bluebells are much the same, becoming extremely dense, very attractive in the spring but die down completely for the summer and most of the winter. Periwinkles will fill a bed with tough, dense growth but are very difficult to remove if they get out of hand. I have found the most useful to be Common Lungwort (opposite), which covers the ground with attractive vegetation for the whole year, flowers for most of the year (it is very attractive to bumblebees) and forms such a dense canopy that everything else is excluded. This includes Stinging Nettles and I have planted it by dumping rooted clumps on top of the nettles: in a year or two, without further intervention, the nettles have been eliminated. Occasional removal of isolated nettles speeds the process.

Common Lungwort spreads by creeping stems and is shallow rooted. It is therefore easy to remove if not wanted and to transfer to fresh sites. A few scattered clumps soon spread to form a very dense canopy that does not grow more that half a metre in height. Gardening magazines also recommend a range of attractive species, such as bergerias (which tolerate dry shade) *Sarcococca humilis* (whose fragrant flowers appear in early winter), *Reineckea carnea* and *Liriope mascari*.

Common Lungwort (left) and Bugle (right) will both thrive in shady sites.

## Plants for shady areas

Some plants require full sunlight, others can survive under shade and yet others actually prefer shady areas, such as under trees, and will thrive there. Notable examples are: Yellow Archangel; Betony; Bluebell; Bugle; Foxglove; Ground Ivy; Lily-of-the-valley; Lords-and-ladies; Nettle-leaved Bellflower; Primrose; Sweet Violet; Wild Daffodil; and Woodavens.

Lily-of-the-valley.

# 6 Grass

Grass is a characteristic of British gardens, mainly in the form of a lawn which is kept trimmed and offers a soft surface, ideal for garden picnics, family games and so on. Some gardeners also cultivate wild flower meadows, with grass that is allowed to grow and flower.

## The lawn

The finest lawns, such as are admired at Oxford colleges, are maintained by frequent cutting. As they are said to remark in such establishments, when asked the secret of such fine lawns: "There's nothing to it, just cut it short every day – for about a hundred years." The reason for this is that grass cut frequently grows by lateral branching of stems (called 'tillers'), creating a very dense foliage. The growing point is placed very low down, so is protected from cutting – many plants with higher growing points are destroyed by cutting.

Grass that is cut infrequently grows tall and lacks density. If this occurs in the spring, the grass flowers at the top of quite tall stems. If it is cut after that, especially under drought conditions, the individual plants may die off and the grass takes weeks to recover. Indeed, the original plants may not in fact die, but other species will invade the bare ground from wind-blown or buried seed.

Most agricultural grassland – and in the UK some two-thirds of the agricultural land is in grass – grows different species from those used for lawns (right). The grass crop grows taller and is grazed when 10–15cm high or cut for silage when even taller or for hay when it is about 30–45cm. However, grass grazed closely by sheep, as on the Romney Marsh, is very short and dense and resembles a lawn in many ways.

Lawn grass, usually a fine-leaved fescue, is a major component of the lawn but other species occur, not always sown. A common component is a legume such as White Clover (see overleaf).

Typical fine-leaved lawn grasses.

### The main grass species used in agriculture

Perennial Ryegrass *Lolium perenne*

Italian Ryegrass *Lolium multiflorum*

Timothy-grass *Phleum pratense*

Cocks Foot *Dactylis glomerata*

Meadow Fescue *Festuca pratensis*

Tall Fescue *Festuca arundinacea*

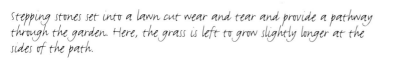

Stepping stones set into a lawn cut wear and tear and provide a pathway through the garden. Here, the grass is left to grow slightly longer at the sides of the path.

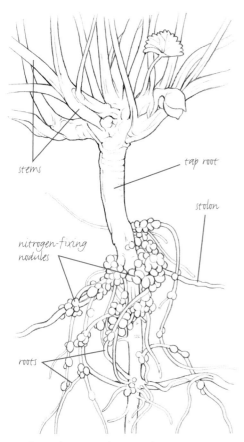

stems

tap root

stolon

nitrogen-fixing nodules

roots

*White Clover root showing the nitrogen-fixing nodules.*

## Legumes

White Clover is a typical legume, with trifoliate leaves and flowers of a characteristic shape but the most distinctive feature of all legumes is the development of nodules on the roots, containing nitrogen-fixing symbiotic bacteria of the genus *Rhizobium*. When effective, these nodules are large, few and pinkish-red: when ineffective they are small, numerous and whitish (left). The nodules make legumes independent of soluble nitrates, most of which are in the upper layers of the soil.

In a drought the upper soil layers dry out, and grass roots, 80 per cent of which (in ryegrass) occur in the top 10cm, cannot supply the plant with nitrogen. Legumes also have about 80 per cent of their roots in this surface layer but they have their own source of atmospheric nitrogen. Their leaves therefore tend to remain green in dry conditions, whilst the grasses go brown, in spite of the fact that their deeper roots still supply water (but without nitrogen).

Wild legumes are also common in lawns, especially Birdsfoot Trefoil (below left), so-called because its leaves superficially look as though they have three leaflets, although they actually have five, and their flower-heads dry to a shape reminiscent of a bird's foot! Naturally, the legumes that thrive in a lawn have a creeping growth habit, so avoid severe defoliation.

Other species found in lawns include those where the leaves form flattened rosettes (e.g. Daisy, Dandelion, Self-heal, Common Catsear (*Hypochaeris radicata*) and Mouse-ear Hawkweed (*Pilosella officinarum*).

# Inhabitants of lawns

Few of the animals in a lawn are seen, since they live mostly underground (such as earthworms, see Chapter 2). Ants may appear on the surface if the grass is left uncut for a week or two. Visiting birds hunting invertebrates in the grass or topsoil include Blackbirds, Mistle Thrushes, Green Woodpeckers, Starlings and Pied Wagtails.

*Birdsfoot Trefoil.*

*A starling may search for earthworms amidst the grass.*

# Growth in grasses

The most important factors governing grass growth are light, temperature, water and minerals. Photosynthesis is carried out by the green parts of the plant (that contain chlorophyll) but only the 0.4 to 0.7 $\mu$m wave region of sunlight is important for this. The narrow ribbon-like shape of the grass leaf makes it a good receiver of sunlight whatever its direction. Grasses can grow over a wide range of temperatures: it is rarely too hot in the UK and growth takes place at anything above about 4°C.

Water is important for several reasons. It is a major constituent of the plant: grasses contain some 70 to 80 per cent of water, depending on their stage of growth. All the minerals required by the plant have to be taken up in water by the roots: they all, therefore, have to be in soluble form. The flow of water required for this is far greater than the water held in the plant, so the excess has to be evaporated from the leaves, through minute openings called stomata. This constant evaporation has the effect of cooling the plant, especially when the weather is hot and dry. This is when the need for water is greatest and the evaporative rate is highest.

*Frequent access to water is essential for healthy growth in grasses.*

## The cycle of grass growth

Since light levels, temperature and available water vary round the year – very markedly in some parts of the country – grass growth follows a seasonal curve. The actual growth curve varies with the species and the level of nutrition (mainly nitrogenous fertiliser) as well as the season.

In the UK, there is relatively little growth in the winter, though this is already changing noticeably (in some winters!) as global warming takes place. Most growth takes place in the spring: as much as two-thirds of the annual total may occur in two or three months in the spring, with May as the most common peak (below right).

Grass that is not eaten or cut and removed will senesce and die, and most of it will be recycled by earthworms (pulling it down into their burrows), fungi, bacteria and countless other tiny organisms in the soil. This also applies to the substantial amount of roots which, like the leaves, only live for a matter of weeks before dying.

The only major loss is that of carbon, expired as $CO_2$ through the stomata, along with water vapour. However, there are pests of grass, notably nematodes (roundworms) and crane-fly larvae, mainly affecting the roots.

In plant photosynthesis, carbon dioxide is absorbed and oxygen given off during daylight, with respiration reversing the process at night but only to a small extent, outweighed by photosynthesis in the light (since the $CO_2$ produced is used within the plant).

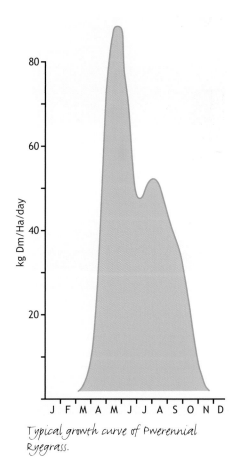

*Typical growth curve of Pwerennial Ryegrass.*

The Meadow Grasshopper (*Chorthippus parallelus*) feeding on thistles that thrive in longer grasses.

## Long grass

Where grass is allowed to grow tall, a wider range of flowering plants occurs and, in warm summers, grasshoppers appear (left). This is partly because lack of cutting allows taller plants to survive, but also because they can flower and set seed, thus reproducing themselves. This 'meadow' flora attracts nectar-seeking invertebrates (moths, butterflies, hoverflies, bees, bumblebees and many kinds of beetles) and seed-eating birds.

Not cutting the grass also has less obvious effects, such as the change in behaviour of the Yellow Meadow Ants. In cut lawns, these ants are rarely seen, though they are regularly collected by Green Woodpeckers, living entirely underground, but even after a few weeks without cutting, little patches (a few centimetres across) of earth granules may appear here and there. This is the start of mound building and, if cutting is totally stopped, these mounds will be built up, often reaching a height of over 40cm and a width of, say, 30cm or more (below). These become covered with grass and maybe other plants, although these can be covered up if the ants continue building.

The lawnmower, of course, prevents all this – and this illustrates another feature of mowing. When the grass is cut and removed, it is also a cleaning process. Those who would like a non-growing grass (such as a lawn made of Camomile) that doesn't have to be cut, would find that the lawn needed cleaning, to remove animal droppings, leaf litter and so on. Heavy rain, and perhaps wind, are the only other ways in which grass is kept clean.

Uncut grass soon develops a different flora and fauna, harbouring taller-growing grass species and a wide range of invertebrates, including grasshoppers in the summer. It also becomes a refuge in which larger animals can hide, such as Grass Snakes, voles and mice. These may be very difficult to see, as they can move easily through the foliage – which is less dense than lawn grass – using tunnels that are not readily visible to us. Voles, mice and some bumblebees may nest amongst tall grasses, weaving balls of grass, moss and dead leaves. Ways of observing such animals are described in Chapter 4.

Of course, grass also occurs as a weed in flower beds, driveways and paths, and patches of woodland, usually mixed with other species, including tree seedlings.

Ant mounds built by Yellow Meadow Ants when the grass remains uncut.

# Wildflower meadows

Meadows can take many forms but one of the most common is based on the old hay meadows that were found on most farms before more productive methods of preserving grass for winter feeding, such as silage and grass drying, were introduced.

This allowed a wide range of grass species to grow unharvested until about June, when it was cut for a big hay crop at a time when (it was hoped) it could be sun-dried. This allowed field-nesting birds and small mammals to breed undisturbed and a variety of spring flowers to bloom and seed. After cutting, it is best to leave the cut grass in place for a few days to allow the seeds to be shed, but removal of the grass is often recommended, as is the absence of fertiliser, as it leads to the low soil fertility that avoids dominance by grasses.

The species that appear depend greatly on the location and the site: they would be different in different parts of the country and on different soil types and aspects. The area can be cut again in late September. In gardens, large meadows are rarely practicable but the same idea can be reproduced even on quite a small scale. There are two ways of achieving this.

The first is simply to allocate a grassy area and treat it like a hay meadow. Gradually, wild flowers will appear; the advantage claimed for this hands-off approach is that the native plants of that locality will dominate. These are often drought-resistant and require little or no fertiliser. Indeed, heavy fertiliser use will result in such massive grass growth that other plants are shaded out.

Scattering seeds on to an established lawn is said to give disappointing results in many cases. An alternative is to raise small plants in seed trays and transplant them into the lawn. Attractive additions are Birdsfoot trefoil, Thyme, Self-heal, Eye-bright and violets. Where grass can be left uncut for most of the summer, taller plants can be used, including umbellifers, knapweeds, Marjoram, scabiouses, Teasel and mallows. These are not only attractive but provide food for bees and seed-eating birds. The value of the wild meadow has been claimed to include the best pest control as it is full of hoverflies. It may also attract colourful butterflies (see Chapter 13).

The above description applies to what are often called 'Spring Meadows'. 'Summer Meadows' are cut fortnightly from mid-April to mid-June and left for the remainder of the year to allow plants to flower and set seed. Diversity can be encouraged by cutting different parts at different heights.

*Though the desired effect is casual, wildflower meadows need a fair amount of planning to give a display as appealing as this one.*

# 7 Trees and shrubs

In general, it is considered that the best conditions for wildlife in gardens are provided by those trees and shrubs that occur naturally in this country. English Nature suggest the following selection of trees and shrubs (right). However, there are others, including cultivated varieties, that are very attractive, including many conifers, Rowan (or Mountain Ash) and sycamore. (Here's an interesting observation: sycamore aphids feed by tapping into the leaf veins!)

## Trees

Quite apart from their appearance and their accompanying wildlife, trees are of considerable biological interest in their own right. In some species (such as Gingko and yews), individual trees are either male or female but not both. This can be seen even in yew hedges, which often consist of a row of different individuals.

Only the pinkish-red fruits are really noticeable. They are eaten by birds but the highly poisonous seeds within them are passed out in their droppings. The female flowers are quite small and, like the equally small male flowers, cream-coloured, but the males, which can occur as early as March, stand out more because of their pollen (below). Walnut is unusual in having male catkins on last year's branches and female flowers on the new branches.

*Male flowers on a Yew.*

*A Grey squirrel may have a nest much higher up in the branches of a large tree such as this.*

### Trees and shrubs

#### Large trees

| | |
|---|---|
| Ash | *Fraxinus excelsior* |
| Beech | *Fagus sylvatica* |
| Elm | *Ulmus procera* |
| Oaks (Pedunculate and Sessile) | *Quercus robur* and *Q. petraea* |
| Small-leaved Lime | *Tilia cordata* |
| White Willow | *Salix alba* |
| Wild Cherry | *Prunus avium* |

#### Medium/small trees

| | |
|---|---|
| Alder | *Alnus glutinosa* |
| Aspen | *Populus tremula* |
| Crab Apple | *Malus sylvestris* |
| Field Maple | *Acer campestre* |
| Holly | *Ilex aquifolium* |
| Rowan | *Sorbus aucuparia* |
| Silver Birch | *Betula pendula* |
| Yew | *Taxus baccata* |

#### Native shrubs

| | |
|---|---|
| Blackthorn | *Prunus spinosa* |
| Dogwood | *Cornus sanguinea* |
| Elder | *Sambucus nigra* |
| Guelder Rose | *Viburnum opulus* |
| Common Hawthorn | *Crataegus monogyna* |
| Common Hazel | *Corylus avellana* |

*Great trees play host to a huge range of wildlife – both easily seen – and much more elusive.*

There is another phenomenon common to all trees: they raise water from the ground right to the highest leaves. Yet we are all convinced that water cannot move uphill! So how does this happen? The water travels up the narrow vessels (the xylem) beneath the bark, at a rate of around 45m per hour, by capillary action (which can only happen in very narrow tubes). The total amount of water transpired is enormous because of the vast total leaf area on a big tree, but the same process occurs in all living vegetation, dependent on water moving against gravity. So, since nearly all life, and certainly ours, depends ultimately on green plants, our lives actually depend on water moving upwards, a proposition we generally reject because it is contrary to common sense!

The Pedunculate Oak is the British tree with the most insect life, including the gall-forming wasps: 56 different types of gall have been recorded on a single tree!

## Hedges

A hedge can be defined as a close (or dense) row of woody plants managed to form a barrier. It may be designed to protect, by keeping people and animals out or by deflecting the wind, or to confine, by keeping animals in (generally the case in agriculture). In gardens, hedges serve all these purposes, confining pets but keeping others out, and protecting plants, people and property from the weather.

The constituent woody plants may be bushes or trees, or mixtures, may be natural or planted, of various heights and, within limits, widths, but all hedges have to be managed. If they are just left to themselves they generally become a line of trees with major gaps between them: they then serve none of the functions listed.

In wild hedges, an estimate of their age can be made from the number of different tree and/or shrub species over a given length. In general, a 100-year-old hedge has only one or two species of shrub per 30 metres, a 200-year-old one has two or three, and a 1,000-year-old hedge may have 10 or 12.

As is well known, the most managed hedges, such as privet, yew or cypress, require frequent cutting (at least annually) and respond to this by branching and producing a very dense, usually impenetrable, barrier. The densest hedges have no trees, because trees need more light to produce the typical thick development of leaves. In wild hedges, several hundreds of species of plants have been identified but typical garden hedges that have been deliberately planted use a more limited number.

Sometimes, a typical wild or farm hedge plant, like hawthorn, is used because of the dense array of thorns presented to an intruder. Other wild plants, such as Common Hazel, may be planted for their attractive leaves, fruits and catkins. Roses, Blackberry, ivy, Blackthorn and elms are also common. Blackberry presents special problems because of the extensive runners that develop in the autumn, growing to several metres in length and rooting at the ends. A whole host of herbs may develop in the hedge bottom (see Table right).

*The most ancient hedgerows are likely to host the widest variety of shrubs.*

## Hedgerow herbs and weeds

| | |
|---|---|
| Cleavers | *Galium aparine* |
| Bindweed | *Convolvulus arvensis* |
| Cow Parsley | *Anthriscus sylvestris* |
| Dog Violet | *Viola reviniana* |
| Elder | *Sambucus nigra* |
| Ground Ivy | *Glechoma hederacea* |
| Hedge garlic | *Alliaria petiolata* |
| Herb Robert | *Geranium robertianum* |
| Hogweed | *Heracleum sphondylium* |
| Lords-and-ladies | *Arum maculatum* |
| Primrose | *Primula vulgaris* |
| Stinging Nettle | *Urtica dioica* |
| White Bryony | *Bryonia cretica* |

There are also characteristic animals living in or under hedges, or making use of them in some way. The larger ones are mammals and birds. In big, mature hedges, bats may roost in hollow trees, badgers and rabbits burrow in hedge-banks, Hedgehogs nest in the base of the hedge and deer shelter under hedge overhangs.

Hedgehogs, Moles and shrews may hunt snails, slugs and other invertebrates along hedges, while voles and mice nest in the undergrowth. Mice and voles may climb hedges to harvest fruits, such as rose hips. Both species sever the stalks with a clear diagonal cut but mice discard the flesh and the opened carpels from which they have extracted the seeds, whereas Bank Voles eat the flesh and leave the carpels. Hazel nuts are also opened differently (see page 46 while birds, such as the jay, chip away at the apex until it splits open.

Birds use hedges for several purposes. Some species nest in hedges, notably Blackbirds, Song Thrushes, Robins, Dunnocks, Wrens and several finches. The nests are quite different from each other, some made of moss, horsehair and willow fluff, while others are more substantial, using twigs and leaves.

Birds also find much food in most hedges, invertebrates at all times and fruit, berries and nuts in season. One of the surprising sources of berries is from ivy, these contain two to four seeds each and appear to be relished by Blackbirds and, especially, Woodpigeons.

*Woodpigeon on an ivy hedge – they frequently enjoy the berries.*

## Pests and diseases of apples and pears

### Apples

**Pests**

Aphids
  Rosy Apple *Dysaphis plantaginea*
  Apple Grass *Rhopalosiphum insertum*
  Apple Woolly *Eriosoma lanigerum*
  Green Apple *Aphis pomi*

Apple Sucker *Psylla mali*

Winter Moth *Operophtera brumata*

Apple Rust Mite *Aculus schlechtendali*

Apple Sawfly *Hoplocampa testudinea*

Red Spider Mite* family Tetranychidae

Codling Moth* *Cydia pomonella*

Fruit tree tortrix* genus *Pandemis*

Summer fruit tortrix* genus *Pandemis*

**Diseases**

Powdery mildew

Apple scab

Canker

Storage rots

### Pears

**Pests**

Dominated by the Pear Sucker *Psylla pyricola*. However, several of the pests of apples also occur on pears (see * above).

*Red spider mites – a frequent pest of apple trees.*

Amphibians are usually associated with ponds but they actually spend most of their lives away from water. Frogs and toads only go to water to breed, so it is a matter of a few days in the spring. Their tadpoles, of course, spend longer in the water but even these few weeks represent only a small part of their lives. Adult newts take longer over their breeding, spending several months in the water, and females continue to lay eggs over quite a long period. The 'newtpoles' grow up in the water but don't return to it for some two years.

When amphibians are not engaged in reproduction, they hide away in long grass or other vegetation, under logs and stones, in hollow logs and ditches: but they do require moisture, which also tends to attract their prey, slugs, insects of all kinds and other small creatures. Hedge bottoms provide suitable conditions, especially for hibernation in the winter.

This country has few reptiles and many of them find much of their food and shelter in hedges, where they may also burrow for hibernation. All three species of lizards feed mainly on insects and spiders whereas the three British snakes feed on vertebrate prey (frogs, newts, young birds, mice, shrews).

The populations of invertebrates in hedgerows can be very large and varied, depending, of course, on the nature and composition of the hedge. Aphids and their predators are very common, weevils and their leaf-mining larvae, moth caterpillars, beetles, spiders, harvestmen, many species of flies, gall wasps, shieldbugs, millipedes, centipedes, slugs and snails.

# Orchards

Fruit trees are planted on a commercial scale but in gardens consist mainly of apples and pears. Most fruit trees are grown as separate individuals but there is no reason why they should not be grouped, including apples and pears, stone fruits (cherries, plums, greengages) and nuts (hazel, almond, walnut).

Pests tend to be worse when the same kinds of tree are grouped and on a large scale but there are now so many varieties that this situation may be avoided. Apple pests are numerous (see Table left) but they vary in the damage they do, partly with their abundance and whether they affect leaves or the fruit. Fewer insects and mites occur on pear trees.

The existence of distinct varieties (now called cultivars) is not a modern phenomenon. In the 1540s, at least 31 apple cultivars and 50 pear cultivars were known and described in a book published in 1562. Even earlier Roman writers on horticulture were well aware of the existence of varieties. Indeed, pomology – the study of fruit and fruit trees – was derived from Pomona, the Roman goddess of fruit trees (just as Flora came from the Roman goddess of flowers).

Control of orchard pests can be achieved by pesticides but, in some cases, by biological control (see Chapter 15). The natural enemies of apple and pear pests include mites, lacewing larvae and earwigs which, although responsible for some minor damage to fruit, can consume large numbers of aphids and Pear Suckers. There are also a number of useful parasites.

Orchard trees mostly need to be insect-pollinated and depend upon bees (Honey-bees and bumblebees) to achieve this in the relatively short period available (see Box below). Many other insects are attracted to the fruits, whether on the tree or fallen. Once the juice is accessible, whether by senescence on the tree or because of attack by birds and wasps, it will attract butterflies and a range of other insects.

Some fruit trees seem to be generally grown as isolated trees, notably mulberry, fig, damson and quince (although most are used as a rootstock for pears). Plums, greengages and the other stone fruits, notably cherry, also tend to be grown as individual trees. Many fruit trees, such as apples, can grow very large, which are difficult to harvest, but they can, of course, be kept small by pruning. Modern varieties (cultivars) are bred to remain small and easily harvestable. Garden apples and pears may be grown for eating or cooking but fruit for juice, cider (apples) or perry (pears), are normally grown commercially.

## Pollination in orchards

Many animals pollinate crops of all kinds, garden and wild flowers, but bees are the world's dominant pollinators. In orchards, the Honey-bee is the most important. Incidentally, its scientific name (*Apis mellifera*) means 'honey-producing bee' and most bees are kept for this purpose.

It has been estimated that (in 2006) there were about 274,000 colonies of Honey-bees in the UK, kept by about 44,000 bee-keepers, but only about 40 of these are 'money-making enterprises', including those providing pollination services to commercial growers. However, numbers have since been drastically reduced, largely due to disease.

It is well known that the queen is the centre of the hive, laying about 150 eggs a day, but it is less well known that she mates some 9 metres above the ground with drones from miles around, thus ensuring 'cross-breeding'. Orchard trees may also need this genetic diversity. Most apple varieties, for example, are self-incompatible and commercial orchards include enough 'polliniser' trees blooming at about the same time as those to be pollinated.

Bees visit trees for nectar as well as pollen but achieve pollination in any case. The nectar varies between species of tree, both in colour and content. For example, pears have, on average, 15 per cent of sugars in the nectar (ranging from 7 to 37 per cent!), apples 25 per cent (up to 35 per cent), and cherries between 21 to 60 per cent. Pollen grains are pale green in pears, pale brown in cherries and pale green/yellow in apples. Pollen from fruit trees provide protein, while legume pollen provides fats, minerals and vitamins.

Poor pollination may result in poor crops and, in some cases, misshapen fruit. Apple blossom contains 10 potential seeds in each flower and if only some are fertilised misshapen fruit results. Assessing the importance of pollination by Honey-bees is difficult, because it varies with the year. In three years out of four, hives may not be necessary: in any case, bees work a radius of about 3km from the hive. Furthermore, it is only some 5 to 10 per cent of the flowers that need to be successfully fertilised to produce a full crop. More than this results in very small fruit.

However, the effective pollination period for any one flower is only about 24 hours. Fortunately, not all trees blossom at the same time: roughly speaking, there is a succession from cherries to plums, then pears to apples, so the bees' efforts can be spread over a longer period of time.

# Dead wood

Many gardeners automatically remove dead wood and it is hard to argue that it is beneficial to leave it but, in terms of wildlife, it can add great interest. Dead standing trees may take years to rot away and in the meantime they may harbour all three species of woodpeckers and the Nuthatch. I have all of these nesting in my trees but they clearly prefer dead trees. In fact one dead willow has been occupied simultaneously by Great Spotted Woodpeckers, Nuthatches and Starlings, nesting in holes one above the other. Such trees are also used by wasps, bees and hornets to nest in hollow branches and old woodpecker holes, and by wasps to collect wood pulp to make their nests.

Fallen trees are used as shelter by snakes and toads and all dead wood may grow interesting and attractive fungi. Logs that are rotting retain moisture and provide a relatively safe, humid, refuge for centipedes (which are very vulnerable to drying out), millipedes, slugs, small snails, ground beetles, woodlice and, occasionally, newts and even small toads. From a gardening point of view, many of these creatures are useful and, aesthetically, the site for logs can be chosen – they don't have to be left as untidy litter.

Among the most spectacular occupants of dead wood are the larvae of Stag Beetles (left). These striking beetles (below) only live for a few weeks but their larvae will spend three or four years in or under dead wood. I regularly find them, up to 3cm long, under large logs, in a log-pile but in contact with the ground. When revealed, they disappear surprisingly quickly, burrowing into the earth.

Log piles – especially if undisturbed – provide homes for a wide range of animals.

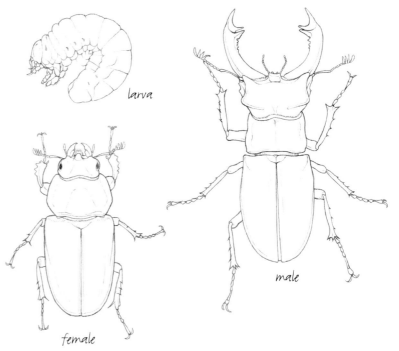

larva

male

female

Male and female Stag Beetles and a typical larva – all of which can be found in dead wood.

# Tree-dwellers

Birds use trees and shrubs for feeding, perching at night and nesting. They eat the insects found living on the leaves and in the bark but pigeons, particularly, also eat the flowers and buds of many trees in the spring and many species feed on the seeds and fruits in the autumn.

Nests are of three main kinds: large visible structures, smaller, woven, well-hidden nests and nests in holes. The large, highly visible nests are in colonies (Rooks) or solitary, usually very high up (crows). Magpies do not usually nest so high, often in bushes, and build a large nest with a roof on it (top right). Pigeons' nests are also usually lower down but less obvious. They are often described as mere platforms of twigs but, if you lift one up by an edge, you usually find that it stays together and is, in fact, more skilfully constructed than at first appears. Jays and doves also make nests of twigs but they are usually extremely well hidden.

The tightly woven nests tend to be hidden in dense hedges (Blackbird, Song Thrush, Robin, Dunnock), at the ends of leafy branches (mainly finches) or in ivy covered trunks (Wrens – a ball of mainly moss with a hole at one side – and Treecreepers).

The hole-nesting birds choose hollow branches or cavities in decaying trunks (owls, tits, and Jackdaws which also nest in old woodpecker holes and chimneys), old holes (Great and Blue Tits, and Nuthatches, which use mud to make the entrance hole smaller) or excavate new holes (all three species of woodpecker – Green, Great Spotted and Lesser Spotted). These three woodpeckers differ greatly in size and so do their nest holes (centre right). They generally use the underside of a sloping branch or the less exposed side of a trunk.

Although woodpeckers seek out weak or rotten spots to start excavating, they still have to absorb considerable shocks. They do this by having a cartilage shock absorber and a (5cm) long tongue wrapped round the brain. The holes made by these woodpeckers can be distinguished by their sizes. Measurements I have taken are as follows: Green 8cm x 7cm; Great Spotted 7cm x 7.5cm; Lesser Spotted 4.4cm x 5cm. A Nuthatch nest hole was 2.5cm x 3cm, narrowed down from a woodpecker hole measuring 7cm x 5cm.

No birds can be said to 'live' in an individual tree, even though they nest there, since feeding and other activities (such as bathing, foraging and courtship) make use of quite large areas and are not even confined to trees.

A Magpie nest with a 'roof'.

Juvenile Great Spotted Woodpecker in a nest hole.

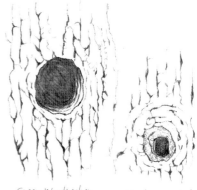

Green Woodpecker          Mud-encrusted by Nuthatch

Nest holes made by the Green Woodpecker and Nuthatch to the same scale.

Nest holes of the Great (left) and Lesser Spotted Woodpecker (right).

*Adult treecreeper.*

## Treecreepers

These little birds (left), as their name implies, creep up the trunks of trees, clinging to the bark with their long-clawed feet. They can cling to quite smooth surfaces, as can be seen in the picture, but usually climb up tree trunks, whereas the Nuthatch is as happy going down.

Normally, Treecreepers nest in crevices in the bark or in ivy but in the example illustrated (below left, they chose to nest in the eaves of my garden shed, only about 20cm from a regularly used door.

Here they reared three chicks and I was fortunate enough to be present with my camera when they fledged and was able to photograph their first efforts at creeping and flying. Less than two hours later they dispersed, which illustrates the fact that observations of wildlife are often very chancy and have to be seized. I happened to notice the first fledgling popping out of the nest just for a moment and stayed to see the whole sequence. Just hours later and I would not have known that anything had happened.

As I was photographing the three chicks and their 'training' flights, one of them flew straight at me and perched on my head! It seemed quite happy there, while I tried to take a picture of it by stretching out my right hand and pointing the camera at my head. Unfortunately, I could not focus it and the picture was very blurred. Since the bird showed no signs of departing, I put my camera in my left hand and picked the bird off with my right, where it also seemed quite content. I then realised that cameras are right-handed and I could not take a picture with my single left hand. I had originally photographed the adults on their feeding visitsbut was able to get much closer to the newly emerged young (below right).

*A Treecreeper bringing food to its nest on a shed.*

*A newly-fledged young Treecreeper from the same nest.*

## Squirrels

The few garden mammals that dwell in trees, Grey Squirrels being the most widespread, do not confine themselves to one tree, or even one garden. They nest in trees, building their 'dreys' of twigs, dead leaves and ivy high up in big trees, often in the angle between the trunk and a major branch, but also embedded in thick ivy. In my garden, they regularly nest in an owl box placed in a weeping willow tree but can use nest boxes intended for smaller birds too (right).

## Invertebrates

The only animals that can be said to 'live' in a particular tree are invertebrates, but most of these spend only part of their lives in one tree. The Pedunculate Oak is host to more species (up to 400!) than any other tree, varying from beetle larvae living in dead parts or in crevices in the bark, to butterfly caterpillars feeding on leaves and the gall wasp larvae within the widely differing galls on the leaves, stalks or acorns.

One of the most interesting of the caterpillars is that of the Green Oak Tortrix moth. These feed on the first crop of new leaves, commonly 'sewing' the edges of a leaf with silk to form a protected little enclosure. These are easy to spot, as curled leaves or as two leaves stuck together. Thousands of these caterpillars, with those of the Winter Moth and the Mottled Umber moth (both of which have wingless females), may virtually defoliate the tree, which then grows a second crop of leaves. It is these caterpillars that form so much of the feed for Blue Tit nestlings, and Blue Tits time their egg-laying so that the chicks' arrival coincides with the greatest abundance of caterpillars. Sparrowhawks may time their nesting to feed on young Blue Tits. It is this sort of behaviour pattern that global warming might disrupt (see Chapter 21).

A Grey squirrel making use of a nestbox.

A Blue Tit takes advantage of a glut of caterpillars.

*Bright seed balls of the Strawberry Tree.*

The London Plane tree, which is not native to Britain, is apparently avoided by both birds and insects, whereas the native hawthorns can support over 200 species. The London Plane is one of the few trees whose reproductive cycle overlaps from one year to the next. In the early spring, the young balls of flowers are quite small but can be seen developing alongside the previous year's seed-heads, which do not fall and distribute their seeds until about May. The Strawberry Tree is similar in that it flowers at the same time as the red seed balls from the previous year are at their brightest (top left).

In dead stumps (of oaks and other species, see 'Dead Wood' above) may be found the larvae (page 122) of our most spectacular beetle, the Stag Beetle. These large and rather fierce looking insects are fairly harmless, although, if carelessly handled, both sexes can seize your finger with their sharply pointed jaws. It is often said that only the female can do this, but I have experienced a male actually drawing (a very small amount) of blood. The males use their 'antlers' to try and overturn rival males (below left).

Another large beetle that flies about in the tops of trees but may blunder into you is the Cockchafer, also known as the 'May Bug' (below right). It is completely harmless and feeds on the leaves of trees (mainly oak and lime) but its larvae live in the soil on the roots of grasses (for two or three years).

Most of the vast number of insects on trees are rarely seen, as most of the tree is rather inaccessible to the human observer, and they are, in any event, rather small. They provide food for many species of birds but also for spiders (see Chapter 11).

*Male Stag Beetles jousting on a tree stump.*

*Newly-emerged Cockchafers feeding.*

# Diseases and disorders of trees

It is not possible to describe, or even list, all the diseases – bacterial, viral and fungal – that affect the leaves, seeds and trunks of trees, much less all the disorders caused by parasites and pests. Here are two examples, one of mainly past importance and one of current concern, both affecting major tree species, characteristic of British gardens.

## Dutch elm disease

This devastated our elm population from the early 1970s onwards and, although new trees continue to grow from suckers, they generally become infected after about 20 years and die off. The disease is caused by a fungus (*Ceratostomella ulmi*) which spreads just beneath the bark and destroys the water-carrying tissue, hence death often occurring in dry weather.

The fungus is carried from tree to tree by a beetle (*Scolytus destructor*), which tends to fly only at relatively high temperatures (about 26°C), laying its eggs beneath the bark. The larvae radiate out in tunnels that can easily be seen when the bark falls off (top right), as can the flat, dark sheets of the fungus, which also has a characteristic smell.

## Horse Chestnut disorder

When vast numbers of Horse Chestnut leaves started turning brown and withering (in 2008), disease was suspected, but it turned out to be caused by a leaf-mining moth (*Cameraria ohridella*), which first appeared in Britain in 2002. If the brown patches are held up to the light, the leaf-mining larvae (or their silken pupae) can be seen and, with care, taken out for closer examination.

The moth lays its eggs on the leaf and the larvae burrow in between the epidermal layers producing empty, transparent patches (brown patches caused by a fungus are not transparent). The damage can be quite spectacular, affecting every leaf on the tree (below right) and presumably affecting that year's growth. The tree is not otherwise damaged, though the conkers may be smaller, and control can be exercised by burning the dead leaves to prevent the next generation of moths hatching out.

The 'gallery' created by Dutch Elm beetles on the tree's bark.

Typical signs of Horse Chestnut disorder.

# 8 Fungi, lichens, mosses and ferns

This chapter deals with a group of superficially similar but unrelated organisms. Mosses and ferns are both simple plants, whereas fungi are not plants at all but form a separate biological kingdom. Lichens bridge the gap, being a symbiotic fusion of a simple plant and a fungus.

## Fungi

Unlike plants, fungi possess no chlorophyll, so they cannot engage in photosynthesis. This means that they are dependent upon existing organic matter and are therefore either saprophytic (living on dead or decaying matter) or parasitic on other plants or animals.

To the gardener, fungi are largely invisible. The familiar mushrooms and toadstools are simply the fruiting bodies (akin to an apple on an apple tree), for producing and disseminating spores. The main part of each fungus consists of masses of fine filaments spread out in the substrate on which it is growing (leaf-mould, rotting wood or living tissue), none of which is normally visible to the naked eye. An illustration of this can be seen in dried-out filaments under the bark of an elm that has died of Dutch elm disease. Many of the moulds (such as you find on old bread) are visible because they grow on the surfaces of their source of nutrients: they tend to have spore capsules on the end of aerial threads.

### Mycorrhizal fungi

The word 'mycorrhiza' means, literally, 'fungus root' and it refers to a symbiotic relationship between a particular fungus and the roots of a particular plant species (some fungi, however, associate with many species). Some grow inside the roots, while others are mainly found on the outside.

As in all symbiotic relationships, both partners benefit, and many of these fungi cannot grow in the absence of a host plant. The main benefits to the plant are more efficient nutrient uptake and utilisation of soil nutrients, but there are also benefits in a greater tolerance of environmental stress and of diseases.

Indeed, it has recently been found that some diseases are suppressed (in ways not yet understood) by the presence of mycorrhiza. This is so for tomatoes grown hydroponically, where the addition of the mycorrhiza fungus *Glomus intraradices* leads to suppression of phytophthora root rot. This is most useful in growing media that are sterile and have no natural mycorrhiza.

*Slime mould on wood.*

*Tiny toadstools may spring up overnight given the right growing conditions.*

## Examples of diseases caused by fungi

| In animals | In plants |
|---|---|
| Facial eczema in sheep | 'Rust' in herbage |
| Aspergillosus in poultry | Powdery mildew on grasses |
| Ringworm in rabbits | Ergot in grasses and cereals |
| Fungal epidemic in frogs | |

Above: A Death Cap (Amanita phalloides), one of the most deadly toadstools. Below: Fly Agaric (Amanita muscaria). Though considered poisonous, it is far less dangerous than the Death Cap.

None of the fungi need light but they do need water and will not usually grow on or in completely dry material. Many of them are responsible for common diseases of plants and animals (see left), many are poisonous (see Table, page 38) and many are edible: there is no reliable way of distinguishing between the last two, except to identify precisely the species involved.

Poisoning from mushrooms of the genus *Amanita* has been responsible for more than 90 per cent of all mushroom fatalities, but silybinin extract from milk thistles has reduced these fatalities by 80 per cent over the last 40 years.

Apart from those responsible for diseases of plants, the main species that are likely to be encountered in a garden are listed below: categorised by location.

## The lawn

The Fairy-ring Fungus (below) forms the familiar ring-shaped colonies. The mushrooms have a pinkish tinge, a tough, elastic stem and are edible, but this species is not the only toadstool to form rings on lawns. The reason for the ring formation is due to the way the fungus grows. When spores arrive on the lawn, the hyphae (fungal threads, also called the mycelium) grow out in all directions gradually from the organic food source at the centre. So the hyphae continue to grow outwards, with toadstools periodically forming at the periphery. Those within the circle die off and the grass may grow greener in consequence.

Grassland generally harbours the smaller species of fungus. The 'fairy clubs' of *Clavaria* species often appear as white or yellow, sometimes with banded tufts. Marshes and boggy ground also have their own characteristic ring-forming species. However, 'puffballs' (*Hycoperdon* species) may also appear (though not confined to grassland). These brownish, almost spherical fungi produce clouds of minute spores when ripe, in most cases ejected through a hole in the top (called the apical mouth) when the ball is touched.

Fairy Ring fungi forming the classic circle in a lawn.

Another spectacular, common fungus of roadsides and other grassy places is the Shaggy Inkcap. This starts off egg-shaped and whitish with shaggy fibres. As it grows and ages, it expands and, together with gills, the cap blackens and liquefies. Many fungi are capable of lifting up paved surfaces but the Shaggy Inkcap probably holds the record for lifting up a paving stone (75cm x 60cm) by 4cm in 48 hours (in Basingstoke in c. 1820).

## Tree trunks

A great variety of fungi grow on tree trunks or stumps. The Candle Snuff fungus (bottom, right) is common in deciduous woodland throughout the year. The flattened, antler-shaped stems, arising from dead wood start off white but gradually blacken. The many species of bracket fungi stand out like semi-circular shelves from the living tree trunk or on dead branches. The upper surface is concentrically zoned (with brown or grey) and the underside has white pores (top right).

Candle Snuff and bracket fungi can be found all the year round and grow very hard and difficult to remove. Some species can be used as a way of carrying the means of starting a fire. The fungus is lit from the last fire and will continue to smoulder for many hours: it can thus be safely carried and blown into a glowing ember when required. (This can be demonstrated on common species found in English woodland.)

## Woodland fungi

As you would expect, particular fungi may be associated with certain soil types, but many of the common woodland ones seem to be indifferent to soil type and even to the dominant trees. However, some are characteristic of the leaf-mould under oak trees, or beech or pine, whatever the soil. There may be competition for nutrients between fungal hyphae and herbaceous roots, which is probably why few fungi are found in dense patches of Dog's Mercury, Blackberry or Bracken.

The tree canopy tends to produce a higher relative humidity than is found, for example, on a lawn, which is a major reason why the two habitats' characteristic fungi are so different. Many of the woodland fungi are toadstool-shaped but others are funnel-shaped or 'antler-shaped'.

A different group, the mycorrhizal fungi (see page 129) form a close physical association with specific tree roots, their hyphae entering the rootlets and colonising the area around the roots, creating a 'rhizosphere'. It is thought that the tree benefits by gaining access to organic nitrogen from a wider area of nutrient-poor soil. Benefits to the fungus may be plentiful sugars from the tree roots.

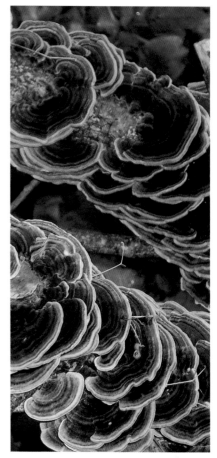

Bracket fungus colonising a tree.

The Candle Snuff fungus (Xylaria hypoxylan).

## Fungi in biological control

It is now possible to harness fungi in the biological control of insect pests; examples are as follows:

| Fungus | Organism controlled |
| --- | --- |
| *Verticillium lecanii* | Aphids |
| *Metarhizium flavoviride* | Vine Weevil on strawberry and blackcurrant |
| *Zoophthora radicans* | Diamondback Moth on vegetable crops |

## Contents of fungi

Fungi, like green plants (and especially vegetables) are composed mostly of water (84 to 92 per cent), with a similar range of minerals. They are low in structural carbohydrates, such as cellulose and chitin, but, on a dry basis, have rather more protein than vegetables (except nuts).

# Lichens

There are about 1,500 species of lichens in Britain and they are found in a variety of situations, on trees, posts, walls and rocks (left and below).

One of their fascinations is that they are regarded as 'litmus plants', because they are good indicators of air quality and pollution. Curiously enough, one lichen (*Rocella*) actually produces the litmus dye used to measure acidity and alkalinity! Lichens are actually associations of fungi and algae (green or blue-green). The main body of the structure (the 'thallus') is tough, fairly rigid and opaque, with a range of fairly dull grey-green/brown/orange colours, often differing between the upper and lower surfaces.

Lichens are extremely slow growing and very hardy, surviving both very hot and very cold temperatures but not polluted air. They reproduce vegetatively but the fungus component can also produce spores. A group of common garden lichens are the 'pixie-cups' (*Cladonia* sp), growing on walls, rockeries and tree stumps.

*Lichens on a wall and a tree.*

# Mosses

Mosses belong to the bryophyte group of plants, which also include the liverworts. The latter are not very noticeable and will be mentioned briefly later in this chapter: by contrast everyone is familiar with mosses. They occur mixed with grass in a lawn, on brick paths, in damp areas, on tree trunks and on roof tiles if you have an old house.

They are small, mostly green plants that produce no flowers, seeds or fruits. They can reproduce vegetatively and as they grow to form a dense clump on a roof, for example, they accumulate dust and dead moss around them to form a kind of soil where otherwise there can be none.

They also reproduce by minute spores which are contained in a capsule (belwo right) atop a stalk. These capsules, each of which may contain hundreds of thousands of spores, are so constructed that they will only release their spores in dry weather. Mosses like moist places but some species survive on bare, exposed surfaces, even in dry weather, trapping moisture in their clumps when it rains. They do not possess any penetrating roots, so they do not damage the walls or tiles on which they grow (below).

Gardens are homes to many different species of moss but some are more common, or more conspicuous, than others. The Silvery Threadmoss (*Bryum argenteum*), very common on putting greens, has a shiny appearance and the Grey Cushion Moss (*Grimmia pulvinata*) although green looks grey because each leaf ends in a long white hair. It actually thrives on warm, sun-scorched tiles, trapping dew.

The most prominent on walls is the Silky Wall Feather-moss (*Homalothecium sericeum*) with its feathery golden-green leaves. The Rough-stalked Feather-moss (*Brachythecium rutabulum*) also invades lawns but raising the height of the cutter in the mower usually allows more vigorous grass growth to crowd it out.

*A Chaffinch on a lichen covered branch with mossy growth to the right.*

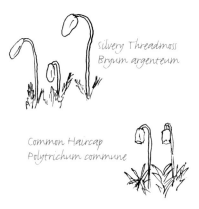

Silvery Threadmoss
Bryum argenteum

Common Haircap
Polytrichum commune

Willow Moss / Antifever Fontinalis Moss
(Fontinalis antipyretica) an aquatic moss

undecorated

capsules

*Moss growing thickly on old roof tiles.*

*Moss capsules.*

# Ferns (or pteridophytes)

The structure of ferns is very different from that of most other plants. The stem is in the form of a swollen rhizome, commonly underground or close to the surface, and the leaves, or fronds arise from this.

Each leaf has a stalk and a lamina or blade, which is sometimes undivided but very often highly divided. An example of the former is the Hart's-tongue (*Phyllitis scolopendrium*), while examples of the latter include the delicate maidenhair ferns and the massive Male Fern (*Dryopteris filix-mas*). Bracken is another example, but not usual in gardens (below).

Reproduction is by spores which develop in little sacs on the underside of the fronds. The fern itself is the asexual phase and the spores produce ephemeral, insignificant, free-living sexual phases: this is quite different from mosses and liverworts (see opposite for life-cycle).

The Male Fern (Dryopteris filix-mas).

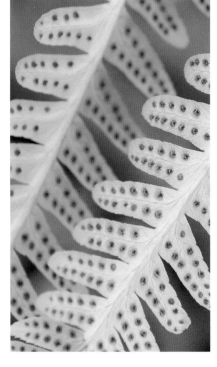

Spores on the underside of fern fronds.

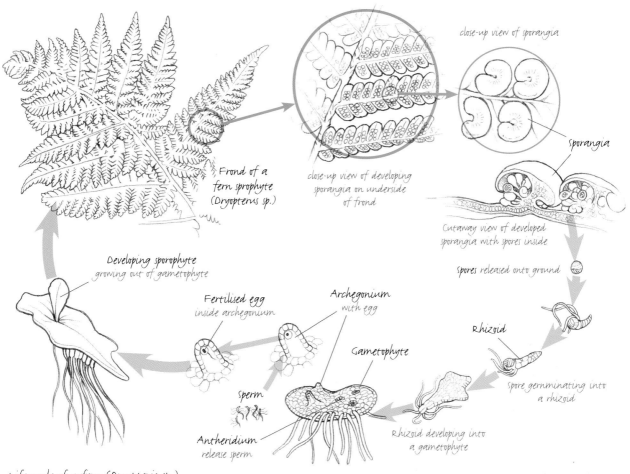

Frond of a
fern sprophyte
(Dryopteris sp.)

close-up view of sporangia

close-up view of developing
sporangia on underside
of frond

sporangia

Cutaway view of developed
sporangia with spores inside

Spores released onto ground

Developing sporophyte
growing out of gametophyte

Fertilised egg
inside archegonium

Archegonium
with egg

Gametophyte

Rhizoid

Sperm

Antheridium
release sperm

Rhizoid developing into
a gametophyte

Spore germinating into
a rhizoid

Life-cycle of a fern (Dryopteris sp.).

# Liverworts (Hepaticae)

These simple plants are of little importance in gardens but may be found on damp, usually unvegetated surfaces. They are small (a few centimetres long) and are attached to the ground by delicate, colourless rhizoids (akin to the root hairs of higher plants). Like mosses, they have two distinct stages in their lives – a green vegetative stage and a dependent (non-green) stage which produces and sheds spores. They differ from mosses in not being differentiated into stems and leaves, the latter are deeply lobed and usually green on both upper and lower surfaces.

Liverwort in its green vegetative stage.

# 9 Interactions between plants and animals

It is not always appreciated that all animals are ultimately dependent on plants. How can this be, when some animals eat no plants at all? But what do their prey feed on? If it's yet other animals, what do these eat? Follow the food chain down far enough and you will always come to plants.

## The plant eaters

So, we start with the larger grazing and browsing animals (like rabbits, voles or deer) and those that feed on leaves, nuts, seed and flowers (such as pigeons, Pheasants, Wood Mice, leaf beetles, weevils and caterpillars). Then there are the nectar and pollen feeders (bees, butterflies and moths, pollen beetles) and those that eat wood (such as some beetle larvae). What about roots? Large roots, especially storage organs, like bulbs, corms, rhizomes and tubers, may be dug up by the larger animals (Badgers, squirrels, Rabbits), especially to provide food in the winter.

But, unseen, below ground, there are smaller root feeders. Gardeners may find them when they are digging but no-one normally looks under the lawn. However, some of these root-feeders are quite well-known, such as leatherjackets (larvae of craneflies of the genus *Tipula*, the familiar daddy-long-legs) and slugs. The latter, of course, not only feed on grass roots and potato tubers but also above ground.

Wireworms are also common: these are the larvae of click beetles (their name derives from their ability to get off their backs by stretching and then jerking themselves 7–10cm into the air: this is accompanied by an audible click.) Wireworms are serious agricultural pests. If there were only about 300,000 per acre, it was reckoned to be safe to grow almost any farm crop. Only 300,000!

Many of the beetles (such as the chafers) are root-feeders as larvae and there are even a few caterpillars, such as that of the Garden Swift moth, that frequent herbaceous borders feeding on delphiniums, lupins and peonies. As with the aquatic insect larvae, the larval stage may last considerably longer than the life of the adult.

*The caterpillar of the Elephant Hawk Moth prefers to feed on willowherb and bedstraws although it may eat fuchsias if available.*

*Bullfinches have bills specially developed for cracking hard seeds although they will make the most of a glut of berries in autumn or new leafbuds in spring.*

## The animal eaters

There are vast numbers of animals that eat other animals, from the outside as predators or, as it were, from the inside, as parasites. But sooner or later, all the prey are dependent on plants for their food, whether live leaves, flowers, stems, roots and fruits or dead and decaying organic matter derived from plants. Thus without plants there would be no animals. What about the reverse?

## The dependence of plants on animals

This is a less obvious proposition since few plants actually eat animals: the exceptions are the insectivorous plants, such as the sundews. But plants don't eat horse manure either, so what happens when we apply it to the soil in order to 'feed' the plants?

Plants have two sources of nutrients. The green parts of the plant use sunlight as a source of energy to convert carbon dioxide and water into carbohydrates such as starch and to produce proteins and fats. This process (photosynthesis) uses water from the roots and carbon dioxide absorbed from the atmosphere through pores (stomata) in the leaves (usually on the underside). Water vapour is evaporated through these pores (transpiration) and oxygen is both taken in during the night and given off during the day. Oxygen is needed by plants, just like animals, for respiration, but an excess is produced in the light as a product of photosynthesis.

All the minerals the plant needs come from the soil and are taken in by the roots, but most of them can only be absorbed in solution (the exception is the fixation of gaseous nitrogen by bacteria in root nodules). So the horse manure, and all other manures and fertilisers, have to be rendered soluble before the plant can make use of them.

This conversion of organic matter is undertaken by soil micro-organisms, including vast numbers of tiny animals. And they only work on small organic particles, so animal excreta and plant remains (such as dead leaves) have to be broken down by earthworms, woodlice, beetle larvae, millipedes, the larvae of dung flies, and slugs, as well as bacteria and fungi. Before that, large lumps are broken up by other animals. Birds scatter cowpats looking for insects and burying beetles bury carcases before their larvae consume all the tissues, and carrion eaters (such as crows and Magpies) tidy up larger carcases.

*A Dung Beetle rolling a ball of waste matter.*

*Flies will start to colonise the body of a dead animal such as this stoat, within hours of its death. The complete animal will eventually be recycled back into the soil.*

And, of course, all the animals, whether they eat plants or other animals, digest their food and produce excreta, which is then further processed by smaller animals. Although we only see a few of the droppings of the larger animals, the total amount must be phenomenal, but it will be vastly exceeded by all the excreta of the myriads of invertebrates.

If nothing was actually eating the living plants, they would still eventually die and, if nothing fed on the dead plants, we should accumulate vast quantities of useless litter. As it is, all the organic matter, even tree trunks, is eventually turned into humus that helps to give soil its structure and soluble nutrients, without which plants could not grow.

There is thus complete interdependence between plants and animals, except for the role of bacteria and fungi in the decaying process. As it is, both animals and plants continually interact and gardens depend upon animals to recycle plant remains. But without plants there would be no animals, including us.

## Areas needed by plants and animals

Every individual plant and animal needs a given area of land to support it, with more required to maintain a healthy population. If it is a species that has separate sexes, at least one of each has to be present in the same area (at least some of the time) so reproduction can occur. Very large animals in arid environments may mainly live alone, mating briefly in widely separated meetings. Polar Bears and most of the big cats are examples of this, although females with cubs form family groups, often for several years.

In the case of garden animals, Foxes, Hedgehogs and rodents tend to be solitary, but Rabbits, Badgers and deer live in social groups. Reptiles and amphibians live mostly solitary lives, with brief mating spells, although they may come together in groups for wintering.

Bats live in colonies and some birds flock together – either just with their own kind or in mixed flocks – for feeding (for example, Fieldfares join up with Redwings when foraging) or for protection against predators. Some species nest in colonies (such as Rooks, but not crows or Jackdaws) or roost communally (like Starlings).

Where an animal will only thrive in a social group, the area needed is obviously greater, though not per animal. Some animals have well-marked territories, which they may defend, in order to protect them, their offspring or their food supply.

Whatever these patterns of behaviour, there are genetic reasons why a critical population size has to be maintained, in order to avoid excessive inbreeding. Again, clearly such populations may require much larger areas. In general, the critical area required is determined first by the food supply: it may therefore vary with the productivity of the area (dependent on climate, soil type, aspect and other topographical features).

*A starling roost at dusk. Sometimes their colonies can number into the hundreds of thousands.*

*Red Admirals' (top) primary source of food is nectar from flowers.*

If the animal lives for more than one season (and many species must do so), account has to be taken of seasonality. Food supplies can vary enormously from year to year and within a year.

For example, an animal that eats acorns cannot rely on an oak tree producing the same number each year – this varies greatly. Common observation shows the same thing for berries (notably holly and hawthorn). Most animals feed on many different things and are thus less vulnerable to these factors than the specialist feeders.

Examples of the latter are common amongst the larvae of invertebrates. Red Admiral butterflies (above) feed almost entirely on nectar, supplemented by rotting fruit juices, some muddy water (supplying minerals) and even moist animal faeces. The nectar may come from several different flowers – after all the appearance of flowers is seasonal.

However, their eggs are laid mainly on Stinging Nettle leaves, so the larvae have little choice but to feed on them. It is true that there don't seem to be any bad years for nettles and perhaps this is a clue – the specialist feeder rely on plants that are rarely in poor supply.

It is also the case that only a small proportion of what is available is actually consumed. Similarly, the larvae of gall wasps are highly specialised: they only feed on the characteristic gall produced by the tree (commonly) used by that species of gall wasp. It may well be that not every egg produces a gall but once produced it is enough to feed the larva (or, in some cases, larvae) inside.

Birds and mammals rarely feed on only one plant species or even on a small group of species (the eucalyptus-eating Koala of Australia is an exception) or, indeed, on only one animal species. The most omnivorous eat leaves, shoots, fruits, dead animals and some living ones. Badgers are true omnivores, eating fruits, roots, carcases, earthworms and many other offerings that come their way.

However, some species, such as the Barn Owl, do feed predominantly on a limited number of species (voles and mice) and, when these are scarce, the owls rear fewer offspring. Thus the numbers of predators fluctuate with the number of prey: but the area the Barn Owl uses for hunting has to be sufficient in an average year to support the bird's needs without depleting the population to the point that hunting becomes inefficient.

Since the Barn Owl, especially when feeding its young, can consume very large numbers of prey (one owl is said to catch as many mice as 20 cats), the area needed is considerable. It has been estimated that one young Blue Tit will consume about 100 caterpillars a day and there can be up to 10 in a brood, so one pair of Blue Tits has to find up to 1,000 caterpillars per day! Remarkably, it has been found that, regardless of the species of predator or prey, approximately 10,000kg of prey supports c.90kg of predator. The Table, right, illustrates the areas required by different garden species.

It may seem that the same questions cannot sensibly be asked of plants but there are some similarities. Each plant needs a certain amount of light and its structure reflects the ways in which it achieves this. Some, like those used by gardeners for 'ground cover' (see page 108), do actually spread over a measurable surface area but this is a way of increasing the number of plants rather than meeting the needs of an individual. Of course, those that require cross pollination do need to have relevant neighbours not too far away.

Photosynthesising species obtain the light they need by the shape or orientation of their leaves. The lanceolate leaves of grasses are very efficient light collectors on open grassland, but shaded undergrowth usually leads to the development of large, flat leaves. Pond plants (see Chapter 14) illustrate the whole range of solutions to the problem, from flat waterlily leaves to submerged milfoil, with amphibious bistort bearing two different designs for its submerged and aerial leaves.

Two common solutions to the fight for light are to grow tall, as trees do, or to climb up other plants (fences or walls). The trees (see Chapter 8) share a basically similar structure but the climbers exhibit great variety (see page 107).

A Barn Owl with one of its main sources of prey – a vole.

## Examples of areas required by different animals

| | Areas needed by animals (very approximate) |
|---|---|
| Badger | 30–50ha |
| Bumblebee | c.500m |
| Fallow Deer | 50–90ha |
| Fox | 20-600ha |
| Mole | 3–400m² |
| Rabbit | 0.4-2ha |
| Red Squirrel | 2-10ha |
| Shrew | 400–600m² |
| Vole | 100–1,000m² |
| Wood Mouse | 2,000+ m² |

All these figures are very variable, depending on sex and abundance of food. Small invertebrates, such as woodlice, may not wander more than a few centimetres if the food supply is adequate.

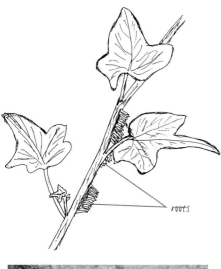

How ivy roots adhere to walls and trees.

Close up of White Bryony showing sprung tendril.

Ivy is perhaps the most familiar climber, growing upwards by supporting itself against a wall or tree trunk, adhering by densely packed, short roots (top left). The plants are not parasitic and so the roots themselves do not damage the supporting tree, although they may cause flaking of brickwork, because, like many plant tissues, they can penetrate cracks and then expand with remarkable force (centre left).

Damage to trees from ivy usually results from competition with the tree's own leaves or by adding to the top weight (especially in winter because ivy is evergreen), directly or as a platform for snow and a surface for wind blow. Trees may then be blown over.

Other climbers, such as honeysuckle, convolvulus, hops and blackberry, simply twine round their supports, so they do not go up walls, for example. Blackberry does not twine as expertly as the others but its thorns help to secure the position of the growing shoots – and they grow at phenomenal rates. Blackberries also colonise the ground, especially in the autumn, by sending out ground-hugging shoots, for as much as 10 metres, and developing a clump of roots at the end, thus starting another bush.

Hops are different: their stems are covered with stiff, backward-pointing hairs (or bristles) that make forward growth easy but prevent any backward movement. These stems feel quite smooth to backward stroking but are quite sharp and abrasive if stroked forwards. The leaves also have these stiff hairs on the underside.

One of the most interesting of the climbers is White Bryony (which is poisonous, even to the touch for sensitive skins). This species has tendrils, but unlike those of peas, passion flowers and vetches, which simply coil their tips around supports, they develop an additional coiled-spring in the middle section of the tendril (below left). This coiled spring allows the plant to move away from its support and back, in the wind, without putting a breaking strain on the tendril. White Bryony grows up the surface of hedges, such as cypress, and will easily cover 3 to 4 metres. Like many other plants, it has a thick rhizome from which it sprouts each spring. This enables it to make an early start, which is another way that plants compete for light. Others do the same from food reserves in bulbs, tubers and corms.

Of course, light is not the only resource that plants compete for, and some of these have implications for the area needed. The main resources are water and mineral nutrients: they are closely related since minerals can only be taken up by the roots in solution in water. If the concentration of minerals is low, more water may have to be transpired in order to take up sufficient minerals. This must apply to plants that grow in water, in ponds or bogs, and even to those submerged.

For plants with aerial parts, however, evaporation from the leaves is largely governed by the microclimate (temperature and humidity) of the leaves. The plant exercises control by its ability to open or close the stomatal pores on the leaf surface.

Alternatively, plants can extend their root systems to explore more soil. This is generally done laterally as, although water can be obtained at depth, minerals tend to be concentrated in the top few centimetres. This gives rise to interesting phenomena in lawns (see Chapter 7), due to the fact that one groups of plants, the legumes, can fix their own nitrogen (in gaseous form) by virtue of nitrogen-fixing bacteria in nodules on the roots (page 112).

There are two more resources that plants need, oxygen and carbon dioxide, obtained from the atmosphere. They tend to be ignored because the supply appears not to be limited. These gases are exchanged through the stomata, so they are linked with temperature and humidity.

Plants are obviously relatively fixed, although the seeds, spores and fruits may travel considerable distances. However, the gaseous part of their environment is not static and winds can move it past the plant to a remarkable extent. Take a tree as an example and bear in mind that most of the tree is made of carbon compounds, from carbon dioxide derived from the air. As pointed out in Chapter 2, if the tree has a circular cross-section from all sides, with a radius of 10m and a cross section area of 300m$^2$ and the average wind speed is 10m per second, the oak tree will sample 260,000m$^3$ air per day. As has been said: not bad for a stationary object.

So although plants are fixed, they do require a minimum area of land defined by that covered (a) by the canopy and (b) by the root system. Some plants spread by vegetative growth and occupy as great an area as they can. Many of these will crowd out others, especially if they stay green and grow during most of the year. These are used by gardeners as 'ground cover' plants (page 108). Such a plant community will also define the area occupied by many small creatures, especially those that feed on them.

Similarly, the oak tree defines the area of the creatures that occupy it – but few occupy it all. The 400 or so organisms that can only exist on or in oak trees live on quite small parts of the tree, such as a leaf (although sexual generations may move to other trees as part of their life-cycle). However, birds and mammals (such as squirrels) that nest in oak trees are far from being confined to them and the areas needed to support them may vary with the size and density of the trees.

Since animals do not necessarily have a monopoly over an area, that required by an individual or a pair may depend on the numbers of other animals present – of the same species, of competitors, of predators and prey.

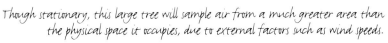

*Though stationary, this large tree will sample air from a much greater area than the physical space it occupies, due to external factors such as wind speeds.*

This Field Vole was enticed under a dustbin lid by the gift of an apple.

# Numbers of animals and plants

Absolutely every living thing in the garden is eaten by something else, sooner or later, whether it is parasitised or predated while it is still alive, or just consumed after it has died. And just as well, too. After death, carcases are scavenged (by crows, Magpies, Foxes, Badgers, beetles and the larvae of insects). This is fortunate for us – although no-one seems very fond of scavengers, we should be grateful for their activities.

The astonishing thing is how little we see of all this. Larger carcases (such as Rabbits, Hedgehogs and Pheasants) are most often seen on the roads. But how often do you find a dead animal in your garden? Yet the numbers can be enormous. It has been estimated, for example, that the number of Short-tailed Field Voles – the commonest mammal in this country (how often do you see one? have you ever seen one?) – born each year is about 677 million (equal to 13,500 tonnes!). In 2002, it was estimated that 2 billion were born.

Weasels, owls, Foxes, Adders, Kestrels and cats are beneficiaries of this abundance. One of the reasons why we don't find dead voles lying about is that most of them don't die of old age: most are killed and eaten by predators long before that. And, of course, animals suffering from disease or injury are easily picked off by predators.

Even if they die 'naturally', as we might see it, they tend to hide away to do it. Few mammals come out into the open to die, with the possible exception of Rabbits suffering from myxomatosis. Unfortunately, in nature, there is no realistic way to express the rate of mortality or, indeed, longevity.

The Wren, for example, is a very vulnerable species, being very small and, although aggressive, quite unable to fend off predators, such as larger birds (like owls and Sparrowhawks), and often nests quite close to the ground where its eggs and young are easily destroyed. As with most animals, mortality is highest amongst the young but even most adults do not live many years.

The Woodpigeon also has by far its highest mortality when young and the adults mostly die of disease or food shortage (apart from shooting). The average longevity has been calculated at 38 months for adults, but including juveniles brings it down to 25 months.

For small birds, cats are one of the major causes of death, though birds such as Blackbirds may be plucked off their perch at night by owls. Availability of food, which is highly variable, is usually a major factor, even for squirrels, especially when combined with exposure to severe cold weather. Young squirrels may be taken by hawks but the adults have few effective enemies in most parts of Britain (except humans) and may live for three to four years.

Although populations can be maintained with only a modest survival rate, most populations tend to fluctuate markedly from year to year, sometimes, as is claimed for voles, on a four-year cycle. When you come to think about it, this is quite likely, since, if a prey species becomes numerous, its predators

Cats are one of the main predators of songbirds.

will gradually increase in numbers also. At some point the number of predators greatly reduces their own food supply, predator numbers collapse and the prey population can recover. This can happen with any predator species that has one main source of prey, such as the ladybird feeding on aphids, but most predators do have several different prey species.

Not all, however. Parasitic digger and mason wasps are usually highly specialised and different species take only caterpillars, or bees or spiders to feed their young (right). Gall wasps are also highly specialised, but do not damage their host plant (which may be an oak tree) as to affect its availability the following year. Clearly, the numbers of animals and, to a lesser extent, plants, vary in very complicated ways.

Two points are important in observing life in a garden. Variations can be enormous from year to year and within years. I commonly find, for example, that one year I see, let us say, caddisfly larvae almost whenever I look (in water) and in the next year can find hardly any. So this kind of variation is to be expected. Secondly, numbers of progeny – seeds, spores, eggs and young – are usually way in excess of any conceivable need and something will be feeding on the surplus. The balance of nature depends on this but it is never a constant ratio of one species to another. The expression is quite misleading, making you think of some harmonious constant state: this is a myth.

Strangely, this mythical state seems to be conjured up about animals, not about plants. Yet the same struggle for survival goes on, with plants also producing even greater numbers of progeny and with consequent enormous losses. Common plants produce large numbers of seeds per plant (for example, docks produce up to 25,000; Foxglove in the region of 750,000). These are usually very small seeds, containing little in the way of food reserves but easily dispersed. Of course, annuals do not need to achieve wide dispersal but trees do – there is little point in a tiny oak growing up in the shade of its mighty parent. Many plants have therefore developed special mechanisms for ensuring dispersal.

A parasitic wasp (Anoplius viaticus) attaching a wolf spider.

Though sparrowhawks kill large numbers of small birds, their overall impact on numbers is not significant.

Puffballs in autumn primed ready to burst and release their spores.

## Seed and spore spreading

All living things are designed to reproduce and if they do not produce enough progeny to maintain their numbers, the species will obviously become extinct. When this happens, it is usually because their environment has become unfavourable to their survival in some way, including adverse changes in their food supply, or some other organisms (predators, parasites or diseases) are destroying most of the offspring.

Plants are no exception and reproduce in a great many different ways. Simple, usually microscopic, plants may simply split into two and literally multiply. The Male Fern is quite a large plant and in the summer under every frond, small round, orange-brown discs develop which, in the autumn, give rise to vast numbers of minute spores (see page 134).

The same is true of fungi. Puffballs (above) appear in the autumn, usually on the ground, as near-spherical, pale brown globes, which grow up to 4cm in diameter. They are well-named and, if they are burst, shoot out a cloud of fine brown spores (see page 297).

But most of the higher plants, including most garden plants, produce seed, sometimes embedded in hard cases and sometimes in soft fruits. Of course, this is not the only way in which higher plants reproduce, even those that produce seed. Many have bulbs (such as daffodils, tulips and hyacinths) or corms (like crocuses), while others send out runners (strawberry), stolons (clover and some grasses) and rhizomes (iris) or form tubers (potato, Jerusalem artichoke). All these methods only spread the plants relatively slowly and in the immediate neighbourhood.

For wide dissemination, seeds and spores excel. Spores and some seeds are light enough to be carried on the wind. Water is also a means of dispersal – some water plants have quite large seeds that nevertheless float and are carried away on river currents, for example. Heavier seeds that are to be wind distributed have structures designed to help this process, such as 'parachutes' or 'wings' (see page 104).

Some very small seeds are sprayed short distances by their containers swaying in the wind (such as poppies). The same applies, incidentally to catkins on trees, which spread their pollen from swaying branches and thus directly on to the wind. Other seeds are brushed by passing animals: others are shot out by spring-loaded structures (such as storksbills).

*Poppy seedpods – these just need the right conditions and they will explode and spread their seeds (see also page 103).*

But a great many of the larger seeds are embedded in fruits that are attractive to animals, which may carry them off to eat, store them for later and sometimes forget them or do not survive to collect them, or eat them with the fruit. In this last case, the seeds may be passed out in the droppings, either unchanged or actually improved as far as germination is concerned. Some seeds are poisonous. Yew seeds are poisonous to mammals – but not to Nuthatches!

Then there are the nuts, mostly with quite hard outer coats. In most cases, including acorns and conkers, these contain a single seed, usually made up of two cotyledons (the first leaves that a seedling may produce) acting as storage organs. Cotyledons sometimes emerge, as in sycamore seedlings, but with acorns and conkers for example, they remain where they are within the seed case.

These seeds' hard outer casings may help the seed to survive or ensure that animals like squirrels and Jays carry them off to a food store at some distance. This would help distribute the seedlings away from the parent tree (where they are really not wanted) but there is little point if they are then completely consumed.

*Yew seeds are surrounded by enticing berries which attract the beeds which spread the seeds..*

*A fully developed conker inside its capsule.*

Seed losses are enormous but, on the other hand, so is seed production (see page 103). Trees may take many years before they produce any seed at all – 30 years for the beech tree, for example – but they may then live for 100 years or more. In that time, a birch tree may shed a million seeds (10,000 per year) and only one is needed to replace the original and maintain the population.

When the seed or nut germinates, the growing tip of the root is really fairly delicate: how does it get through the shell? Some of these hard-coated seeds will only germinate if they can absorb moisture: how does this get in? This may be why some of them, such as conkers, need the outer coat to be broken (scarified) and small animals, like voles, often do this and eat part of the contents – but not enough to affect the seed's successful germination.

It is very difficult to remove the outer case of a conker (unless you are a vole) but, if you do, there does appear to be an extension of the inner (furry) part of the coat that protects the growing point of the embryo (see page 106).

## Animal numbers

No animals live for ever, although some may live for many years (see Box, page 154), so the species survives by reproducing. Birds, insects, most reptiles and amphibians lay eggs, while virtually all mammals give birth to live young because their eggs are retained inside the body of the mother until they are ready. So, in mammals, the young look a bit like their parents, the young of frogs and toads (tadpoles) look very different and, in most birds, newly hatched young only resemble their parents in very general ways, such as legs and beaks, but they do not have developed wings or feathers.

Most animals produce more than one young at a time (see page 167) and some produce vast numbers, but when averaged out each individual only needs to replace itself to maintain the population. Of course, most young animals will not survive to breeding age. They may die of cold, lack of food, disease or, most commonly, are killed and eaten by some other animal (predation). To compensate, animals try to produce and rear as many young as they can.

However, some species are not able to produce very large numbers, due to limited available resources. They compensate by investing more time in protecting the youngsters that they do have in various ways – defending them or hiding them. But, if the weather is bad, there may not be enough food, especially in the winter.

*Large mammals, such as Roe Deer, produce well-developed young that can move along with the herd.*

Voles, for example, may rear lots of litters each year but owls and Foxes may eat most of them. This provides lots of food for the owls and Foxes, which then produce lots of young of their own. Then there are more owls and Foxes and fewer voles so, eventually, the owls and Foxes may be short of food (of course, they also eat other things, too).

Often this results in cycles, lots of food leading to lots of voles, leading to lots of owls and Foxes, leading to fewer voles and then fewer owls and Foxes, as prey becomes harder to find and they can produce fewer young. It is therefore not possible under normal circumstances for a predator to completely exhaust its food supply. People think this 'balance of nature' is a good thing: what the voles and owls think about it is not known.

# Life-cycles

Plants and animals are usually observed as individuals but, of course, they grow, develop, reproduce and die. These life-cycles represent the way the garden works but they cannot be observed in the same way as individuals. You either have to follow the whole sequence, often in suitable containers in order to be able to see it all happening, or connect up your observations of individuals at different stages of development. Here are some easy examples.

## Tadpoles

Everyone knows the tadpoles of frogs; those of toads and newts (so-called 'toadpoles' and 'newtpoles') are much less familiar. Their life cycles are broadly similar. In all three the eggs hatch to produce tadpoles and, because the jelly covering the eggs is transparent, their early development can be readily observed. The tadpoles grow at a rate dependent on the food supply (what do they eat?) and the temperature of the water and, in contrast to that of many insects, development is virtually continuous once the eggs have started to develop.

In all three, the tadpoles grow external feathery gills (to absorb oxygen from the water). Frog and toad tadpoles grow hind legs first and then forelegs (this is reversed in newts). Eventually, the tail is absorbed, except in newts, and they all emerge from the water for a life on land as small versions of the adult.

In terms of observing all this, the only real difficulty is in finding the eggs of newts. These are not laid as masses of free-floating spawn but are stuck to vegetation. If suitable leaves of water plants are available, the eggs are laid singly within the folded leaf (see page 187), which the female folds over using her hind legs. If no suitable plants are available, the eggs may simply be laid in a tangle of blanket weed.

Mating is also less obvious, though more interesting in the newt, the crested male courting the female with arched body and then depositing a packet of sperm that the female picks up. All this is most readily observed at night. Male frogs and toads clasp the females from behind and ride piggy-back until the spawn is deposited, releasing their sperm before the jelly swells up by absorption of water (this would prevent the entry of sperm so no fertilisation would occur).

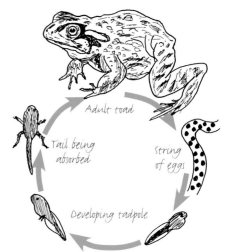

The life cycle of the Common Toad.

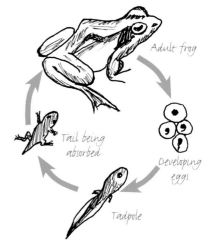

The life cycle of the Common Frog.

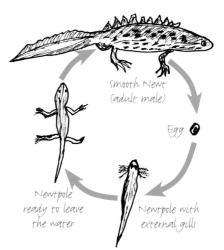

The life cycle of the Smooth Newt.

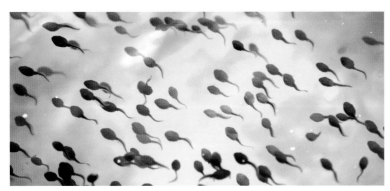

How many of these tadpoles develop into adults is dependent on a host of factors.

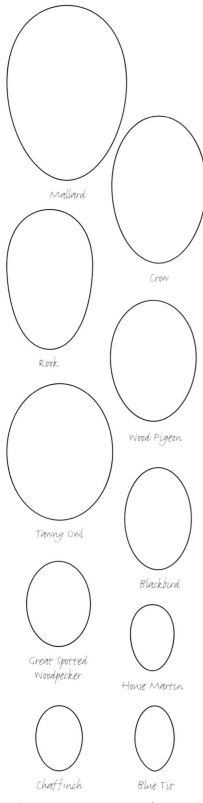

Mallard

Crow

Rook

Wood Pigeon

Tawny Owl

Blackbird

Great Spotted
Woodpecker

House Martin

Chaffinch

Blue Tit

Relative sizes of a variety of birds' eggs
(shown actual size).

## Birds

All birds lay eggs, but of a great variety of shapes and colours. The shape may serve an obvious purpose (see left) but what is the purpose of the differing colour patterns? After all, who sees them? Well, since they're not all laid on one day, some of them may be visible before incubation begins, and in birds like the Pheasant that incubate without the help of a partner, the nest must be left unattended from time to time. Camouflaged eggs may have some protection from egg-stealers that hunt by sight (squirrels, crows and Magpies). The Cuckoo is a rather special case. It only parasitises a few species, and each female Cuckoo specialises in a single host species, laying eggs that closely resemble the host's own eggs.

Eggs have to be incubated for several weeks and the sitting bird is very vulnerable, so camouflage is vital. When the eggs hatch, there is a huge difference in the degree of development, with 'single parent' species having more developed chicks that require less intensive care. In general, ground-nesting birds and those nesting on or near water usually have chicks well-covered in down and able to run, and in some cases, swim, within a short time after hatching.

Birds that nest in bushes, trees and holes, may have chicks that are bald, helpless, unable to move much and often blind. Such chicks usually require the care of two parents. They have quite large mouths outlined by brightly coloured (usually yellow) soft skin. When opened, this colourful 'gape' stimulates the parent to provide food: the chicks open their mouths when they feel a parent bird land.

Chicks that leave the nest almost immediately after hatching find their own food, although the parent (usually the female) may show where it is by pecking at it. In some cases (such as Moorhens and Coots), the parents may

Dunnock parent feeding a Cuckoo chick.

present some food, like pond weed, to the chicks but most often young chicks feed on animal tissues (commonly insects and other invertebrates) to provide the concentrated protein needed for rapid growth. Eventually, the chicks develop feathers and become largely independent. They may then have to learn to fly and perch, including in high winds.

## Dragonflies

These spectacular insects (spectacular in colour, speed and manoeuvrability) are commonly seen over water – even over quite small ponds. This is because they lay their eggs in water: females can be seen dipping the tips of their abdomens into the surface but it is normally impossible to see the eggs themselves, although the largest may be up to 1mm long. Many are inserted in slits made in plant tissue. Males and females of some species fly coupled together in a curious (tandem) fashion because the male clasps the thorax of the female with the end of his abdomen.

Methods of copulation vary with the species but commonly the male transfers his sperm from the rear abdominal segments to his own second segment, where the female can get access to it by curving her abdomen tip under her own body.

Adult dragonflies may only live for a few days and, at most, for a couple of months, but when the eggs hatch the nymphs may take up to three years (in the water) to reach the stage when they emerge as adults. To do this they climb up a vertical surface, such as the erect leaf of a yellow iris or a rush (though, in the absence of such plants, they may climb on to a lily leaf, for example).

Here the old nymphal skin splits and the adult emerges to pump up its wings and dry out, during which period it is extremely vulnerable to predators like birds and frogs. The cast skins (exuviae) can be seen for some time after emergence.

During the years in which the larvae are aquatic, they become among the most voracious predators in the pond and, since they may grow to several centimetres in length and do not move very quickly, they may easily be observed.

An adult Southern Hawker dragonfly (Aeshna cyanea) emerging.

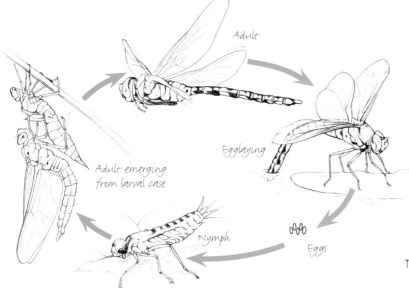

Adult

Adult emerging from larval case

Egglaying

Nymph

Eggs

The life cycle of an Emperor Dragonfly.

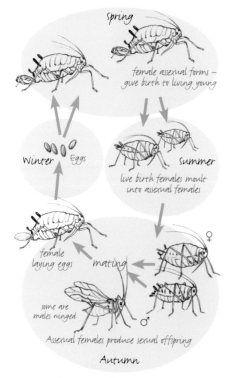

Life cycle of an aphid.

## Greenfly

Aphids of various colours (mainly green or black) are a common and generally unwelcome sight in both flower and vegetable gardens Their life-cycles, however, are rather more complicated than at first appears. First of all, there are two different generations, wingless aphids that give birth to live young (viviparous) and, later in the year, winged females which migrate to a secondary host plant, where they produce both winged and wingless progeny (see left).

Towards the end of the summer, winged females are produced which leave the secondary plant host and migrate back to the primary host. These produce, without fertilisation (i.e. by parthenogenesis), a single generation of wingless females which mate with winged males from the secondary host. The eggs are laid in the autumn and overwinter on the primary host.

This is a typical life-cycle. Thus the Black Bean Aphid survives during the winter on woody hosts such as the spindle tree. However, the Grass Aphid found only on grasses and spends its whole life cycle on them. Incidentally, aphids do their damage not only by sucking plant juices but also by spreading viruses. If these life-cycle seem complicated, compare them with those of some of the gall wasps (see page 65).

## Mammals

By comparison, most mammals have a relatively straightforward life-cycle. This is illustrated for the Wood Mouse below.

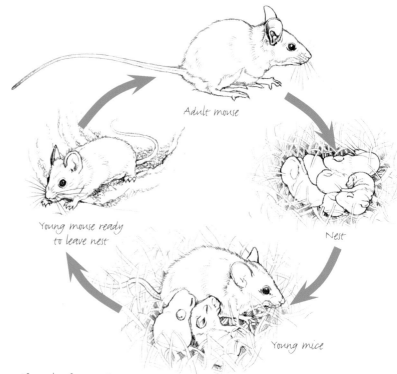

Life cycle of a Wood Mouse.

# Plants

Plant life-cycles are straightforward and well-known, pollinated flowers producing seed, the seed overwintering and germinating in the spring to produce a seedling that steadily develops into the mature plant. But what happens to seeds in the wild? Where and how do they survive?

Take two well-known examples of seed, the acorn and the conker. Everyone knows that they are produced, often in large numbers, by oak and Horse Chestnut trees, respectively, and they fall to the ground. What happens then? Well, of course, some of them eventually grow into trees.

However, as with all the animals we've considered, if they all survived, the earth would be smothered with the results, we would not have room to move and most animals would not have anything to feed on. This is one of the problems with life-cycle diagrams: for simplicity they rather give the impression that each stage develops into the next. But, in fact, only a very small proportion do so: the rest are lost, in a great variety of ways, to parasites, bacterial and fungal decay, or animals that feed on them, including predators of animals. And very often an animal is both a predator of those of smaller size and the prey of someone bigger. That is why I have often argued that after, 'What is it?' the next most sensible questions about an animal are, 'What does it eat?' and 'What eats it?'

So a more accurate life-cycle would show where they all go to and the lines indicating the losses would be thicker than those showing the survivors. This is best illustrated by a tree, such as an oak (right) indicating what happens to acorns and seedlings. Acorns are mainly lost in the autumn and winter and survival is progressively higher as the seedlings develop. This is also true of conkers but the reasons for losses tend to differ.

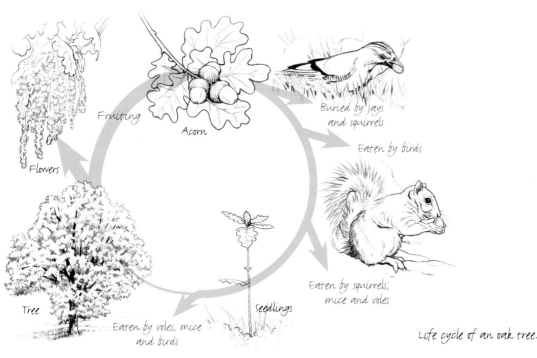

Life cycle of an oak tree.

(The figures given are for animals that survive to adulthoood – early mortality can be very high and averages mean very little.)

| | Typical life-span |
|---|---|
| **Mammals** | |
| Squirrel | up to 6 years |
| Fox | up to 8 years |
| Rabbit | up to 8 years |
| Vole | <15 months |
| House Mouse | <18 months |
| Rat | <18 months |
| Shrew | c. 1 year |
| Bat | c. 4 years |
| **Birds** | |
| Robin | c. 1 year |
| Blackbird | <2 years |
| Swallow | up to 15 years |
| Wren | c. 1 year |
| Pigeon | c. 2 years |
| **Amphibians** | |
| Frog | up to 12 years |
| Tadpole | 2–5 months |
| Newt | c. 4 years |
| Newtpole | 3.5–4 months (up to 20 years) |
| Toad | up to 40 years |
| **Reptiles** | |
| Grass Snake | 4–5 years |
| Slow-worm | up to 30 years (one recorded at 54 years!) |

| Invertebrates | Adult | Larva |
|---|---|---|
| Butterfly | <1 year | some weeks or up to 1 year |
| Bumblebee | Queen <1 year | |
| | Worker 2-3 months | |
| | | <2 weeks |
| Wasp | Queen c. 1 year | |
| | Worker 2–3 months | |
| | | 4–6 weeks |
| Honey-bee | Queen 2–3 years | |
| | | c.3 weeks |
| | Active worker 6 weeks | |
| Mayfly | <1 day | c.1 year |
| Dragonfly | 4–8 weeks | 1–2 years |
| Cranefly | 2–3 days | c.11 months |
| Ant | Queen >5 years; worker up to 7 years | |
| Snail | 2–3 (up to 10) years | |
| Earthworm | up to 6 years | |

# Longevity

Plants may live for one season (annuals) or for many years (perennials) and everyone knows that many tree species can live for hundreds of years and, furthermore, continue to grow during that time. Seeds can also survive in a non-growing state for even thousands of years (when dry).

Even the largest animals do not usually live for more than tens of years, but they do tend to live much longer than the smaller ones. Fish can live for many years and continue to increase in size but mammals and birds all have final size limits, which they may reach quite quickly. Garden mammals such as squirrels, Foxes and Rabbits may live for half-a-dozen years but the majority die long before this. Indeed, the vast majority of progeny, whether seeds or animal offspring, die early, providing food for many others.

High reproductive rates are more of a compensatory response to high early mortality than to the need for new mature animals or plants. After all, how many acorns are needed to replace an oak tree that lives for 100 years? Smaller mammals, such as voles, mice and shrews, may live for a year or even two but frequently for much less. In theory, it has been calculated that one female vole could give rise to 90 individuals in a season but, of course, most of the young voles get eaten before they themselves are able to breed.

*small rodents, such as rats, produce large and frequent litters.*

Birds vary quite a bit but most Robins, Blackbirds and Wrens do not survive for more than about a year. However, these small birds' maximum potential lifespan is much greater than that of small mammals – the British longevity records for the three species mentioned above are, respectively, eight years, 14 years, and nearly seven years. Amphibians, like fish (also cold-blooded), can live for 10 years or more, but very few survive the tadpole stage.

Invertebrates vary greatly. Snails and earthworms may live for several years but insect adults rarely last for more than a year. We have already seen that adult dragonflies live a couple of months at best, after up to three years as nymphs.

Bumblebee workers and males live for only a few months: only the new queens survive the winter and these are already fertilised by the short-lived males. This is just as well, since, when the queen emerges from hibernation in the spring, there are no males. These are only produced later, when the queen lays non-fertilised eggs – the fertilised eggs produce workers. The same is true for wasps: only the (larger) queens survive the winter – often in your house!

## Survival over winter

The problems of survival over winter are very varied. Cold-blooded species do not have the option of remaining active, and there is little point anyway, since food would be very scarce.

So they either hibernate (are inactive or deeply asleep with greatly slowed-down metabolism) as do a few mammals, or operate in very protected environments. When they hibernate, it is not necessarily as adults. Butterflies use all phases of the life cycle: some overwinter as eggs, some as caterpillars, some as pupae and others as adults. Of course, some butterflies, like some birds, simply migrate to more suitable climates. Those mammals that hibernate have to lay down stores of body fat and the metabolism of this fat also provides water.

Many mammals, however, manage to remain active. Moles can manage – as do their earthworm prey – underground and the same is true for ants, many insect larvae and, to a lesser extent, Rabbits and voles, which can retreat down their burrows. Squirrels and voles store food – nuts, seeds and, in the case of voles, cut grass. Shrews have to remain very active because they need to eat every few hours. That may be one of the reasons why they eat snails, which they can easily find congregated in groups in sheltered spots but above ground (below). Snails provide substantial meals compared to small insects.

It helps to be omnivorous and many birds that mainly eat insects in the warmer months, live to a great extent on berries and other fruits during the winter.

Because it lives mainly underground, the Mole does not hibernate in winter.

A Fieldfare may search without luck for insects on frozen ground.

A stash of snails is a veritable feast in winter for birds and small mammals.

The ladybird's vivid coloration is offputting for potential predators.

# Avoiding danger

All animals and plants are at risk from some direction. The least vulnerable to total destruction are mature trees. They can be blown over, struck by lightning, their trunks can be drilled by woodpeckers and their leaves eaten by innumerable invertebrate pests (the oak has about 400 such species) but they rarely suffer total destruction during their active growing life.

Causes of tree death include fire and extreme drought, and fungal attack. The latter can wipe out whole forests and is often more common in older trees. The best UK example has been Dutch elm disease, caused by a fungus blocking the xylem (tubes carrying water and nutrients up the trunk). This fungus is transmitted by the Elm Bark Beetle which lays its eggs under the bark. The larvae tunnel through the wood just below it.

So it is that the greatest are likely to be brought low by the least. There is a parallel in large animals, all of which have internal parasites, such as the roundworms (nematodes) that infest their stomachs and intestines. This is a major problem for cattle and sheep which pick up infective larvae while grazing, the eggs having been passed out in their excreta. But exactly the same happens with rabbits and probably no animals are free from minute parasites of one sort of another.

Plants, too, have their pests and parasites and, very importantly, viruses: these can be transmitted by sap-sucking insects, such as aphids. Fit organisms may be to an extent resistant and parasites and pests are more prevalent when the same species is present in large numbers and crowded together in a confined area.

But plants cannot move about or hide, as animals do. Small animals hide away from large predators but can be pursued even underground by those of similar size. Short-tailed Field Voles, however, travel in tunnels just under rough grass and rarely appear on the surface. But owls can hear them and Foxes can probably both hear and smell them. Owls can even see the urine that often marks their tunnels.

Bats, also hunting in the dark, find moths by echo-location – which some moths can detect and take evasive action! Other animals depend upon camouflage and, indeed, virtually all animals use it, except for those (like wasps and ladybirds) that have bright warning coloration. This tells predators (and people!) that they either sting, bite or are unpleasant to eat.

Plants may protect themselves passively, by containing toxins, often in their most colourful parts. They may also have to protect themselves from drought or, more generally, from water loss, because a reduction of water loss (by evaporation) is the only way a plant can adjust to drought. They cannot go and find water, as many animals would do: indeed this is also true of many small animals. Flying insects will visit ponds but crawling creatures cannot. So earthworms and snails may retreat to protected areas and snails seal over the entrances to their shells – this is called aestivation but it is very similar to the hibernating state in winter.

Some invertebrates have hard outer casings, for example beetles, millipedes and woodlice. This greatly reduces water loss, and they also seek out damp places (under stones and logs). Plants may also have hard waxy cuticles but their nutrition depends upon water flow, up the roots and out through the leaves. Water loss from leaves is generally through minute pores, the stomata (page 99), which have guard cells that can swell to close the apertures. However, no flow of water means no mineral nutrition and therefore a reduced rate of growth.

Grass may suffer doubly because, in a drought, it can still obtain water from considerable depth but not from near the surface where most of the minerals (such as nitrates) are. So it may cease growth and still lose water but I suppose by this means it stays alive and does not wilt. It may not, therefore, affect longevity.

# The balance of nature

Many people, on learning more about the diversity of plants and animals interacting with each other, are impressed with what they call the 'balance of nature'. But this is often a romantic over-simplification, sometimes expressed as all species 'living in harmony' with each other. Now it seems unlikely that the Rabbit being eaten by the Fox – or even the other Rabbits not being eaten (at the time) – regard this as a 'harmonious relationship'. And, of course, it would never occur to the Fox to see it that way either.

There is, naturally, a balance of numbers between them, or there would be if the Fox only ate rabbits and the Rabbits were only eaten by Foxes: neither is the case. Where a predator is largely limited to one prey species, numbers tend to go in cycles. A well-known example is the cyclic fluctuation of Snowy Owl and lemming numbers in the high Arctic. When the numbers of prey are high, the predators raise more young (unless something else is eating those) and, with a lag, predator numbers increase to the point where the prey become scarce again.

So, even where a balance of numbers is achieved over time, it tends not to be constant and such 'harmony' as exists is between species and not individuals. All this stems from the evolution of species to fill all available niches. Thus, whatever exists is likely to be the food of something else and to suffer from diseases and parasites.

However, not everything requires food in the form of other species and most plants do not. There are non-animal disease organisms and parasites that live on other organisms or tap into their food source and there are lots of (small) animal species that live on decaying matter, both vegetable and animal.

So we have mistletoe growing on apple trees, woodlice living on rotting wood, burying beetles and fly larvae living on the dead bodies of animals and dung beetle larvae feeding on animal excreta. All of which, however unpleasant or unsavoury we may consider it, is a vital part of the ecological cycles on which life depends.

*Though it may appear to take large numbers of animals, the impact of a bird of prey, such as this Kestrel on total numbers is minimal.*

## Carnivorous plants

There are very few carnivorous plants in Britain and both of the commonest species are associated with water. The Common Sundew (*Drosera rotundifolia*) thrive in boggy areas and Bladderwort (*Uticularia vulgaris*) is aquatic. Both catch invertebrates, with Common Sundew mostly insectivorous.

*Common Sundew*

*A Song Thrush eating a snail having smashed the shell on its 'anvil'.*

Where do plants fit in? They don't go about eating each other or (with limited exceptions, see left) eating animals, so how does the concept of 'balance' apply to them? Plants only do battle with animals in a few limited ways, the most obvious of which is by containing poisons that make their tissues inedible. Some of these poisons, such as the galitoxin in milkweeds, may be tolerated by certain animals. For example they may accumulate in the bodies of feeding caterpillars, protecting them from predation. But for the most part, plant constituents undesirable to animals are, like thorns, stinging hairs, prickles and secretions, mainly protective – they are a means of defence.

Plants compete with each other, however, mainly for light but also for nutrients in the soil, more rarely for oxygen or carbon dioxide. They do this chiefly by timing (growing earlier in the season), speed of growth (to gain light and shade others), climbing ability (using others as scaffolding), occupation of space (crowding above ground or below) and root competition (for nutrients or water).

Balance among plants thus comes from a structure of species of different heights, leaf shape, tolerance of sunlight or shade, and degrees of resistance to drought, insect attack and disease. Animals may control some plant species' population size and structure, but plants control animal numbers and diversity by their mere presence – or absence.

So, over evolutionary time, we arrive at a situation where we can marvel that, in nature, 'nothing is wasted' and some sort of ecological balance is preserved. In most cases, looked at from a human or humane point of view, it is not very pleasant and not a model one would wish to copy or set up. When we keep pets or zoo animals, therefore, we do not arrange any of these 'harmonious' balances but contrive artificially to avoid direct involvement with the unpleasant killing, dismembering and ingestion (not necessarily in that order) that occurs naturally – though of course our cats and dogs still need to eat meat!

Even so, much of this is valuable in the garden, in the control of pests, weeds and diseases, but, quite often, we don't want a balance of Rabbits and flowers, snails and plant leaves or aphids and ladybirds – we want, as near as possible, total elimination of the pests. Very often, this is neither possible nor desirable. Attractive and interesting balances can be struck but it requires a fair understanding of, and interest in, what's going on. The purpose, of course, is to intervene in these interactions to produce the result we want, an attractive and/or productive garden with the plants we want, but without the pests we don't.

It is just the same in public places, in agriculture, in buildings, in rivers and, to some extent, the sea. The human interest has to predominate, in our health and safety and thus in medicine, food safety, food production, personal and public hygiene and in transport. So what do we mean when we talk about 'upsetting the balance of nature'? – we're doing it all the time.

# Biodiversity in the garden

'Biodiversity' is one of those fashionable concepts (often called 'buzzwords') that receive general acceptance and, indeed, approval as a 'good thing', but little analytical thought. So, before considering how it applies to ordinary gardens, it is worth clarifying what it does – or could usefully mean.

Diversity, of course, simply means lots of variation and differences, so biodiversity has to mean many different organisms: it normally relates to species rather than individuals. In agriculture, in garden plants and in pets, we make enormous efforts to create more varieties or breeds (different forms within the same species), many of which produce near-monsters, including quite unnatural colours of plants and shapes of animals.

Farming, especially of grazing animals, has always depended on a wide range of breeds to fit different environments, for hills and lowlands, for example, and to satisfy different needs – in cattle some breeds have higher milk yields, while others develop extra muscle mass. Dogs have been represented by enormous diversity for a very long time.

When it comes to wild species, though – as opposed to humans and cultivated plants and animals – we really do not know much about individual variation: we cannot even tell one robin from another, never mind ants or woodlice. This is partly because natural selection means that animals with a certain set of traits will survive better than the 'oddities' that differ significantly from the norm.

So, being in favour of biodiversity really means being in favour of lots of different species; but then consider the following questions. Do we just want to retain the present species, not to lose any, or do we want to create more? If the latter, how? By genetic engineering, for example? If we only wish to retain species, do we wish to keep all of them? Even the pests, parasites and disease organisms (including the malarial parasite)? Bear in mind that in evolution some species 'split' into two or more forms over time, while others will go extinct.

The likelihood is that we really want to be selective: but can you have ladybirds without having aphids? The fact is that we cannot have any species without the habitat within which it can find the food, shelter, temperature, humidity and so on that it needs to survive, thrive and reproduce. A concrete garden will have no soil organisms and a garden without seeds or insects will have few birds, even as visitors.

Increased biodiversity can only occur with a range of habitats, each providing the needs of different groups of species. One way of combining what are otherwise conflicting requirements would be to encourage, within one garden, several different habitats, some of which are designed to produce particular results, such as relatively pest-free flower beds or vegetable plots.

It is clearly not possible to have one great mixture of plant species that would suit all garden animals simultaneously. What can be achieved in diversity of habitats will depend on the size of the garden but will also be constrained by climate. Soil type and rainfall can be modified by fertilisers and irrigation but temperature requires more elaborate control (as in glasshouses or cold frames).

Even the most carefully cultivated garden can host a richly diverse collection of plants – and the animals that live alongside them.

*A small town garden with a range of plants. To increase biodiversity, it's worth leaving a few 'wilder' areas even in a space like this.*

However, many people who are in favour of biodiversity in general terms do not want it in their own garden. But whatever sort of garden you have, it is possible to increase its interest by making it welcoming to a wider range of species. Simple things, like placing logs and stones where small creatures can hide under them, or leaving some plant residues for animals to eat and hide under, including some areas of rough grass, hedges, bushes and trees, can make a lot of difference.

The fact is that, in general, we want to preserve 'desirable' species, but this is a subjective judgement and varies with preferences and prejudices. This is well illustrated by the many people who want to feed tits and Robins in their gardens, but are far less keen to see Starlings or Woodpigeons on their bird tables.

Biologists are less affected by prejudice and are concerned about the decline in insects, slugs and snails – animals that may even be repulsive to many people. Housing developments have been adversely affected by finding quite unobtrusive but rare wild flowers or animals in their path.

*A welcome bird table visitor – the Long-tailed Tit.*

To preserve a species it is necessary to know why it is in decline. Is it a lack of adequate quantities of the right food? Or the presence of too many (uncontrolled) predators? Is it a result of human activity: disturbance, the destruction of habitat (newts, frogs and toads require ponds, for example), the use of herbicides or pesticides? Identification of the cause may suggest helpful action but the first necessity is to preserve the habitat.

Gardens can contribute little to the preservation of the habitat of large animals but this excludes surprisingly few species. Large gardens can support badgers, Foxes and some deer and it is astonishing how Foxes and Muntjacs, for example, which need sizeable ranges, make use of even quite small gardens as part of their range. For many species, a garden can provide a relatively protected environment, within which appropriate habitats can be developed. However, this is much affected by the presence of dogs and cats (see Chapter 17).

# Parasitism and symbiosis

Parasites are simply organisms that live at the expense of another plant or animal and contribute nothing to their host – but do not normally kill it as predators do as this would simply force them to find a new host. However, it can happen where, for one reason or another, parasite numbers are excessive or the host is weak. They may be plant or animal, though there are many more of the latter.

However, there are a whole group of organisms, called parasitoids, that do eventually cause the death of their host. So, for example, the Chalcid Wasp *Pteromalus puparum* lays its eggs in the caterpillars of the Small White butterfly and the larvae simply consume all but the skin before they emerge to pupate.

There are very few species, of plant or animal that are totally without parasites, nematodes (roundworms) alone occur in most. Nematodes occur as the intestinal worms of puppies, humans, rabbits and so on but others (called 'eelworms') parasitise potatoes and most other plants. They are deliberately cultivated to control slugs.

These are internal parasites but there are also external parasites, such as fleas, lice and mites (such as *Varroa destructor* in Honey-bees – see page 235). It is not always recognised that birds have fleas. Some are specially adapted to the bird's life cycle: for example, 15 fleas were recovered from a House Martin but 4,000 were bred from a single nest. Birds that re-use protected nests seem especially vulnerable.

Plant parasites are comparatively rare, and even the mistletoe is only a half-parasite, as it has green leaves that carry out photosynthesis. Fungal parasites are much more common.

Some parasites are only parasitic during one part of their life-cycle, many in the larval stage, and the adult simply exists to find a new host. A whole group of parasitic wasps are especially clever at locating their potential hosts deep within a tree trunk. They then drill down with their saw-like ovipositors to

A Large White Butterfly caterpillar that has been parasitised by the wasp Cotesia glomerata whose cocoons have formed underneath.

Mistletoe makes use of other plants but is not completely parasitic.

## Life-cycles of *Andricus kollari* and *Andricus quercuscalicis*

*Andricus kollari* is the gall-wasp that causes marble galls on oaks (one of some 70 different galls on oak alone). There are two alternating (sexual and asexual) generations. Sexual females lay eggs in May and June in the buds of oaks (*Quercus robur*, for example) causing the woody, spherical marble galls.

These mature in August, each producing a single female adult; these emerge and lay eggs between the embryonic leaves of the Turkey Oak. These eventually (in March and April) become thin-walled structures between the bud scales. Male and female wasps emerge from these in the spring and mate, the females going on to lay eggs on Turkey Oaks to repeat the asexual part of the cycle. However, it may sometimes be further complicated by the omission of the sexual generation.

Marble galls stay on the tree long after the wasp has emerged – the departure hole can be easily seen. Knopper galls, however, are quite different. A mosquito-sized wasp (*Andricus quercuscalicis*) lays its eggs in the fertilised flowers of oak and the galls form on the outside of the developing acorns. At this stage they are spiky and green but in the autumn they fall to the ground with the acorns, gradually turning brown and then almost black. The wasp emerges in the spring, having spent nine months in the gall. After emergence, it only lives for a few more weeks.

Parasitic wasps may drill through the gall, straight into the developing grub, laying an egg. They use their ovipositors both to drill (the tip is reinforced with zinc) and lay the egg.

Vestal Cuckoo Bee (*Psithyrus vestalis*)

place an egg on the host egg or larvae. Others parasitise insect nests – they follow their targets and enter their nest holes to lay their own eggs on those of the host, the emerging larvae feeding on the host's eggs. Cuckoo-bees and ruby-tailed wasps are examples.

Some of the most interesting parasites of plants are the gall-forming organisms. Galls are generally the result of a plant's reaction to the presence of an egg or a developing larva in its tissues, which proliferate to isolate the intruder, usually in a form that is almost external to the plant. So galls are abnormal growths on plants, rather like tumours, caused by the presence of another organism – known as the 'galler'! Gallers may be microbes, fungi, mites or, most commonly, insects. Most galls are caused by insects (see Table, left, and page 65), but in the UK about 50 different galls are caused by mites, while others are even due to eelworms. The greatest number of galls seem to occur on trees, especially oaks, sallows and willows – but not chestnuts. The bunches of twigs often seen on birches and called 'witches' brooms' are galls caused by mites, as are the 'nail galls' on lime leaves and 'big-bud' in blackcurrants. The easiest to see, as already discussed, are the most common galls of oak trees, since they are commonly found on quite young, easily accessible trees. The most spectacular are shown on pages 65 and 306–307.

There are, however, a great many less noticeable galls, like the little red galls on nettles, produced by a small midge, and the red galls on Ground Ivy leaves, caused by a gall wasp. Gall midges also cause the bunching of leaves on the ends of yew shoots, inside which will be found the orange larvae. Sawfly galls cause oval red bean galls on willow leaves. In addition to the gall-former, several other species, including parasites of the gall-former, also live within the gall. These uninvited guests are called inquilines and form quite distinct and self-contained communities.

Another spectacular gall caused by a tiny gall-wasp is the rose gall, also called the bedeguar or robin's pincushion. The gall may be over 2.5cm

The Robin's pincushion – a gall found on roses.

The lip of the Bee Orchid mimics the shape of a female solitary bee, encouraging males to try and 'mate' with the plant, so aiding pollination.

across and is quite a bright red (above). It is best seen on wild or cultivated rambler roses in mid- to late summer. It contains several cells, each with a single larva living on the tissue grown by the plant in response to the egg being laid by the gall-wasp. Gall-wasps' life-cycles may also be extremely complex (see page 65 and Box, opposite).

Symbiosis refers to relationships between organisms that are beneficial to both. Pollination is a good example (see pages 94–96). Some are actually essential to one of the species, such as that between orchids and mycorhizal fungi. The latter are saprophytes, living on the dead remains of plants and animals, and in this way they obtain nutrients that they are able to pass on to the orchid in the seedling stage when it has no green leaves. The orchid seed is infected at a very early stage and the association is needed because the seed is so small, with little reserve nutrients, and leaves may not be produced for years. In some species flowering may not occur for 13–15 years!

Other examples are lichens (see page 132), which are composed of a fungus and an alga in intimate interdependency. Legumes (such as clover, peas and beans characteristically have nodules on the roots – small swollen bits, often slightly pink (see page 112) – containing bacteria (of the genus *Rhizobium*) able to fix atmospheric nitrogen. This is released to the plant and makes it independent of nitrate absorption from the soil. The same thing occurs in alder trees.

There are other forms of associations of species. Association itself is a term used to describe the largest group of natural vegetation, usually dominated by one species but with another present in significant numbers. For animals, there are also mixtures of two species that are neither parasitic nor symbiotic. If two species simply live together, they are called commensals.

# 10 Animal reproduction and parental care

Young animals take many different forms. In the case of invertebrates, as well as fish and reptiles, many are self-sufficient miniature replicas of their parents, while the young of some insects, and also amphibians, look completely different but are still able to take care of themselves from birth. In the case of most mammals and birds, the young animals require some amount of parental care for the first few weeks or even months of their lives.

## Mammals

All British mammals produce live young that are suckled by the mother, so, by definition, they engage in parental care. However, this may take many different forms and last for varying lengths of time.

Some young are born blind, bald and helpless. This is so for the mole, for example. Its pink, hairless young are very small (weighing about 3.5g and measuring 3.5cm) but by three weeks are almost adult size and they may leave the nest after a month. By 17 days the body is covered with fur and by 22 days the eyes open. Many mammals are born with closed eyes because this has protected the eyes from damage by the amniotic fluid.

Foxes are born with fur but are blind and deaf: their eyes open after 11–14 days and they eat solid food (brought by the male to the edge of the den) from about four weeks. After weaning, at about 6+ weeks, both parents feed the cubs.

*A vixen is more likely to suckle her young cubs in the den than outside.*

*A female Mallard with her ducklings.*

*Young Hedgehog – though born helpless they develop swiftly.*

By contrast, deer give birth to alert miniatures of the adult (apart from coat colour), able to follow the mother virtually from birth. Their fawns (or calves, when referring to the larger species such as Red or Sika) are suckled for 6–12 weeks but may be given milk occasionally for even longer.

Mice, rats and voles tend to be born hairless and blind and, like most baby mammals, are cared for by the females only. Hedgehogs are born blind and naked but a coat of white spines appears soon after birth and a second coat of dark spines with white tips is visible after 36 hours. They can roll up into a ball at 11 days old. Pipistrelle bats are born blind but their eyes open in 3–5 days and they can fly and forage for themselves by 6 weeks.

## Birds

Birds, too, vary greatly in the condition of the young when hatched, but the eggs have to be incubated first and that may take many days (right). It has often puzzled ornithologists why some birds start sitting on eggs before the full clutch has been laid, leading to some eggs hatching before the rest. It seems this may be to protect the eggs from bacterial infection due to the greater humidity of exposed eggs. In the case of birds of prey, staggered hatching is the norm, meaning that if food is short the youngest chicks starve quickly and the parents can concentrate all their energies on the older, stronger chicks.

Those with well-constructed nests (such as thrushes, Blackbirds, finches and Robins) usually produce bald, blind hatchlings which require care from both parents (opposite, top). Some ground-nesting birds, like the Pheasant, produce young that hatch fully covered with down and able to run about and feed themselves almost immediately (opposite, below). This is clearly advantageous for ground-nesting birds for, although the female bird can sit motionless on the eggs and is well camouflaged, the numerous offspring would be more difficult to hide.

Ducks, Coots and Moorhens, like most birds that live on the water, may make well constructed nests but their chicks can take to the water in a very short time (and swim remarkably fast).

Birds with helpless nestlings have to keep them warm and feed them for some weeks: in most cases this is done by both parents. In birds with active chicks, often one parent (usually the male) has very little to do with the chicks once they are hatched. In fact, a male Pheasant's rather gaudy presence would be more likely to endanger the chicks as far as most predators are concerned. A female Pheasant can be surprisingly aggressive when the young are present but, like a domestic hen, she does not actually feed the chicks – simply drawing attention to useful foods.

## Numbers of eggs/young

| Birds | Clutch size (No. of eggs) |
| --- | --- |
| Blackbird | 4–5 |
| Blue Tit | 7–12 |
| Chaffinch | 4–5 |
| Great Tit | 8–13 |
| Green Woodpecker | 5–7 |
| House Martin | 4–5 |
| House Sparrow | 3–5 |
| Mallard | 7–12 |
| Moorhen | 5–11 |
| Robin | 5–6 |
| Song Thrush | 4–6 |
| Starling | 5–7 |
| Woodpigeon | 2 |

| Mammals | Typical size of litter |
| --- | --- |
| Badger | 2 |
| Bat (Pipistrelle) | 1 |
| Deer | usually 1 |
| Wood Mouse | 2–9 |
| Fox | 5 |
| Hedgehog | 3–7 |
| House Mouse | 3–5 |
| Mole | 3–4 |
| Rabbit | 3–5 |
| Rat | 7–8 |
| Shrew | 6–7 |
| Squirrel | 3–4 |
| Vole | 5 |
| Weasel | 4–6 |

Blackbird chicks (top) are born featherless, sightless and helpless, while young Pheasants run and feed almost as soon as they are born.

A female Adder (right of image) with a clutch of much smaller, but otherwise identical, young.

## Other animals

British birds all incubate their eggs (not a completely universal trait) but this is not so for amphibians and reptiles. Frogs and toads, once they have spawned, simply leave their eggs (and, indeed, the water) where they are deposited. They may take some care about exactly where this is: toads wind their two-stranded spawn round water weeds (to anchor them?) and frogs appear to be able to judge an appropriate depth of water, so that the spawn is not in danger of drying out.

Reptiles, too, simply leave their leathery eggs in an appropriate place: the Grass Snake favours compost or heaps of grass, so that the eggs are, in fact, incubated by the heat generated. The Adder is an exception, being viviparous. It gives birth to live young which can lead independent lives immediately.

Some fish exhibit parental care, the most notable of those that might occur in a garden being the Three-spined Stickleback (below). Here all the work is done by the male, which develops a bright red 'chest' in the breeding season. He builds a barrel-shaped nest on the floor of the stream (the most common habitat), made of plant fragments, and persuades the female to lay her eggs in it. He then guards it and, by fanning his tail, maintains a stream of fresh (oxygenated) water to flow over the eggs.

Male (top) and female Three-spined Stickleback in their nest.

Even less does one expect parental care in the case of invertebrates, with the well-known exceptions of the bees, wasps and ants. Many bees and wasps and all ants all live in highly organised societies, in which care and protection of eggs, larvae and pupae is paramount. They live within a nest of wax (Honey-bees), paper (wasps and hornets), or underground (ants).

Butterflies and moths lay or drop their eggs on plants suitable for the feeding caterpillars and all insects place their eggs in relatively protected positions, in cracks and crevices in bark or on the undersides of leaves, or in the soil.

Less well-known are the reproductive habits of slugs, some of which carry their eggs in a liquid-filled brood pouch for a month, woodlice, whose females carry their eggs on the underside of their bodies for a month until they hatch, and harvestmen, where the females carry their eggs in their jaws – and thus cannot feed until they hatch!

Many kinds of invertebrates go even further and look after their young even after they hatch. Earwigs lay their eggs in a cavity they make in the soil and even lick them to prevent fungal growth. Centipede females coil round their eggs (and also lick them) for several weeks. Millipedes mostly make nests for their eggs and young. One species of shieldbug, known (appropriately) as the Parent Bug (bottom, right), lays up to 30 eggs on the underside of a birch leaf and remains covering them even after they hatch.

Many spiders, such as wolf spiders carry their eggs on their backs or tow the egg sac behind them until they hatch. Others, the funnel web spiders, construct a silken tent within which a cluster of eggs is protected until they hatch, and the baby spiders remain inside for some time. However, many spiders, such as the orb spiders use their webs just to catch their prey.

A wasp nest built in a hedge.

The Parent Bug (Elasmucha grisea) adult with its young.

Top left: Wolf spider with egg sac; below left: Orb web spider; right: Funnel web spider.

## Breeding frequency

| Mammals | No. of litters per year |
|---|---|
| Badger | 1 |
| Bat (Pipistrelle) | 1 |
| Deer | 1 |
| Field mouse | 6 |
| Fox | 1 |
| Hedgehog | 2 |
| House mouse | 10 |
| Mole | 1 |
| Rabbit | 2 |
| Rat | 5 |
| Shrew | 2 |
| Squirrel | 1–2 |
| Vole | 3–6 |
| Weasel | 2 |

# Reproductive strategies

The aim of reproduction is for the parent animals to pass on their genes to as many new individual animals as possible, and the result of successful reproductive behaviour is a stable population of the species as a whole. The first and most obvious way to achieve this is to produce large numbers of eggs or young at birth, enough to offset the inevitable losses due to predators, disease, damage or destruction by environmental impact, such as desiccation, drowning, overheating or freezing.

The numbers of offspring thus vary with the extent to which the parents are able to protect them. So larger animals tend to have fewer offspring. The second strategy, therefore, is to concentrate resources on protecting a limited number of young. This is easier if the babies are active soon after birth or hidden in dens. The Rabbit takes the latter to an extreme, hiding the young in an underground burrow which is sealed off at the entrance except for one visit a day by the doe to suckle them. The range of numbers of eggs or young produced by different species and groups of animals is illustrated on page 167.

A third strategy is to breed more frequently (see left), relatively easy for smaller animals (see below) but difficult for larger mammals with long gestation periods (opposite) and for smaller animals that exhibit parental care. Invertebrates may be limited by temperature, since they are cold blooded, but all animal reproduction has to be phased in relation to the availability of food supplies.

### Examples of reproduction in small animals

#### Invertebrates

**Aphids**
One aphid can produce several daughters daily: these start reproducing 8–10 days later. Thus one Black Bean Aphid can give rise to 1,300 individuals after 14 days. Some think that this a gross underestimate and that, if all survived, after 300 days, one aphid would produce $210^{15}$ individuals.

**Houseflies** lay five batches of 150 eggs which hatch in a few hours: the maggots grow for 4–5 days, pupate for 2–3 days and emerge as breeding adults.

**Bluebottles** lay 600 eggs: new adults emerge after 1–2 weeks.

**Leaf-hoppers**, with six generations and each laying c.50 eggs, would produce 500 millon in a year (if all survived).

#### Amphibians

**Frogs**
Counts vary from 1,555 eggs to 4,005 from one frog. It has been estimated that about 10,000 die for each pair that breeds.

**Toads**
Counts vary from 3,132 to 6,840 eggs per females.

#### Birds

Female Starlings produce about 16 eggs in their life-time, resulting in about two breeding adults.

The number of offspring needed to maintain a population also depends on the average longevity and this tends to be greater in larger animals (see page 156). This was also dealt with in Chapter 9.

One interesting device employed by some mammals to ensure the best timing for the young to be born is delayed implantation. This involves a delay between fertilisation of the egg and its implantation in the wall of the uterus. During the interval the fertilised egg develops for a while and then floats freely in the uterus. In the case of the Roe Deer (the only deer to exhibit it), this delay is about 150 days, from mating in July to August to implantation in December. Delayed implantation also occurs in the Stoat.

A similar effect is obtained by storage of sperm after mating, before ovulation and fertilisation. Pipistrelle bats, for example, mate in the period between late August to late November but the sperm is stored in the uterus until ovulation in April – a better time to give birth.

## Gestation periods of mammals

| Species | Length of gestation (days) |
|---|---|
| Fallow Deer | 230 |
| Roe Deer | 144 (post-implantation) |
| Badger | 49 (post-implantation) |
| Fox | 52–53 |
| Rabbit | 28–33 |
| Hedgehog | 31–35 |
| Short-tailed Field Vole | 18–20 |
| Wood Mouse | 19–20 |
| Common Shrew | 20 |
| Common Pipistrelle Bat | 44–80 |

Young Roe Deer – a rare example of delayed implantation of the fertilised egg.

# 11 Animals that occur all over the garden

In this chapter we take a look at garden animals of all kinds that can be found easily in most gardens, beginning with insects and other invertebrates.

## Ants, aphids and ladybirds

There are three species of ants commonly found in gardens. The most noticeable is the Black Garden Ant which lives underground, in long grass or under brick paths. However, it is most prominent for the short period in the summer when it produces the larger, winged males and females – those most commonly seen are wingless workers that do not breed – and in association with aphids. Wherever aphids occur, black ants will be found feeding on their sugary secretions. Interestingly this 'honeydew' turns out to be a far better fuel for flies than nectar. A researcher in Canada found that 1 microlitre of nectar enabled a blackfly to fly 44 metres, whereas a microlitre of honeydew was good for 243 metres!

Ants are often described as 'milking' them but, in fact, aphids have to excrete the excess sugar they take in when they suck enough sap to meet their protein needs. Nevertheless, the aphids do benefit from the protection afforded by the ants, which attack other predators on the aphids (larvae of ladybirds, lacewings and hoverflies). The adult ladybirds are a tougher proposition and secrete a noxious fluid themselves, from their leg joints.

Ladybird feeding on aphid.

An ant protecting its supply of aphids.

The snail – scourge of many gardeners but a useful source of food to birds and other garden animals.

Red Ants with their grubs and eggs – found under a dustbin lid.

Most ladybirds feed on aphids (page 173), including the common Two-spot, Seven-spot and 14-spot. There is quite a lot of colour variation. The situation is complicated by the range and variety of aphid species, some of which live underground (on roots), inaccessible to ladybirds, and some of which store plant toxins in their bodies. There may be up to 40 species of aphids in British gardens!

Ladybirds are now considered to be under threat from competition from the Harlequin Ladybird, first spotted in the UK in 2004. It is larger than the species mentioned above, at 7–8mm) and may be black with variable numbers of red spots, or vice versa. It has mostly brown legs.

Root aphids are treated in the same way by the Yellow Meadow Ants that nest and live underground in lawns but build earth mounds (see page 114) up to 40cm high and twice as long (usually oriented east to west with the highest point at the east end), in long grass.

The third common ant species is the Red Ant. This also nests underground but in much smaller colonies than the black ant. All three ant species breed continuously during the warmer parts of the year (virtually all except winter) but, in each case, the much larger queen is the only egg-producer: the eggs, grubs and pupae (top left) are looked after by the large number of workers. Aphids are also prolific breeders but give birth to live young, which themselves start reproducing after a few days.

Ladybirds lay small, yellow eggs, usually on the underside of the leaves of plants harbouring aphids. The larvae that emerge are slate-blue, spiny and look nothing like the adults, but feed just as voraciously. After about three weeks the larvae pupate still with the old larval skin covering them. Ladybirds ('the beetles of Our Lady') are protected by their 'warning' coloration – and for good reason. When attacked, they exude distasteful or toxic alkaloids, pyrazines and glucosides, through pores in their legs.

Ants are remarkable creatures, able to lift and carry more than 50 times their own weight. They are sometimes pests in or near buildings: it is said that ants will not cross a chalk line (or white vinegar, or Campbells' tomato soup – stand table legs in empty tins!).

# Spiders and harvestmen

Harvestmen look like very long-legged spiders but are in fact not true spiders, though both belong to the class Arachnida.

## Spiders

Spiders are wholly useful, consuming enormous numbers of pests and insects that annoy us, and British spiders are completely harmless to human beings. Although they kill their prey by injecting a poison, their jaws are generally too weak to penetrate our skin and even the largest do not produce an effect much worse than a nettle sting. Yet they are disliked by most people (nearly 80 per cent of young British adults are arachnophobic).

Male and female spiders fighting over prey – the female (below) is larger.

Though most of these arachnophobes wouldn't go out of their way to kill a spider, they would rather avoid them at all costs. Yet spiders are extraordinarily interesting. One of their most remarkable characteristics is their ability to produce silk that is, weight for weight, when stretched, stronger than steel. The Box, right, describes in more detail the remarkable properties and production mechanism of spider silk.

There are some 600 species of spiders in Britain. Some of these are very numerous in gardens (and houses) but only the orb spiders, with their prominent webs, are really noticeable, most other species have more discreet habits. All spiders have eight legs, six or eight eyes, a characteristic shape (generally, a combined head and thorax and a largish abdomen) and no antennae but two short 'pedipalps' on the head. They come in various sizes, the largest being the house spiders, with a body length of less than 2cm, although the legs can be quite long. The males are generally smaller than the females.

Spiders live in all garden environments, including the pond (see Chapter 14) and not all construct webs. Some, the jumping spiders (see Chapter 18), simply run and leap on their prey: others only use silk to protect their eggs and young.

One of the most prominent of the 'orb' spinners is the Garden Spider (below), sometimes called the 'cross spider' called because of the white cross on its back. During the day it sits in the centre of its large web (often more than 30cm across), head down, waiting for an insect to fly into it. In the autumn, the female lays a clutch of up to 100 eggs in a silky web: these do not hatch until the spring, when you can see the baby spiders running in all directions and then bunching together if disturbed. Few adults over-winter: most die off.

Spiders are very good climbers and the jumping spiders can cling to a ceiling by their extraordinary hairy feet: in this position it is said that they can carry 170 times their own weight! There may be 20,000 hairs on each foot and each hair subdivides with cups at the ends.

## Spiders' silk

Spiders' silk is quite extraordinary. The silk thread is extruded through spinnerets as a liquid that solidifies on exposure to air. The silk gland itself is a microscopic structure – no wider than a human hair – which sucks the water out of the liquid as it is extruded, to produce a complex fibre insoluble in water. It is the water that prevents the silk from solidifying before extrusion.

A spider may produce seven different types of silk, varying in strengths and stickiness, from different silk glands. The silk consists of a number of amino acids but it has not yet been possible to produce the equivalent artificially.

Each fibre can stretch by 40 per cent of its length (in some cases much more) and absorb a hundred times as much energy as steel without breaking: furthermore, it maintains its strength even at extreme temperatures – in one study, over a temperature range of $-60°C$ to $150°C$, above which the threads got weaker but did not break down until they reached $370°C$. This suggests that they could be heat-sterilised before being used in surgery. It is said that one spider can contain enough silk for 400 metres!

Orb web spiders can produce 30–50cm of silk in one hour and the web may contain 1,500 connections. Insects can't see it and get caught on the gluey droplets, which contain coiled silk thread to absorb the shock of prey landing. Spiders' feet are oily to resist the glue. The prey is wrapped in a different sort of silk sheet.

Webs are usually made by floating a line and then reinforcing it with extra strong spokes. The first spirals are often temporary and then get eaten: the final spirals are done from the outside - all in about an hour.

Some other invertebrates produce silk. For example, lacewings lay each of their 300 or so eggs (twice their body weight) on silk stalks. Pulling the silk out changes it from liquid to solid. Commercially, silk is produced by silk worms (the larvae of the Silk Moth).

A garden 'cross' spider – a typical 'orb web' spinner.

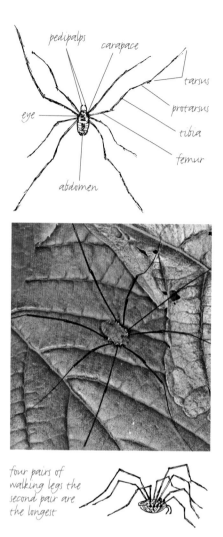

pedipalps
carapace
tarsus
protarsus
eye
tibia
femur
abdomen

four pairs of walking legs the second pair are the longest

*A harvestman – notice how the body is literally suspended between the legs.*

Wolf spiders (page 169) are very common in gardens but are most noticeable when the females are carrying their egg sacs. Normally, they do not spin webs but have a silk 'drag line'. The female lays her eggs (several dozen) in a drop of liquid which she covers with silk, then a tougher silk layer which she cuts free. She then adds a waterproof layer and carries the sac around for several weeks. When the eggs hatch, the young climb on to the female's back, secured by their silk. Then, in the autumn, each young spider produces a silk line for wind dispersal – sometimes for hundreds of miles. Other spiders spin silk tents to protect their eggs and young.

## Harvestmen

These small-bodied, spindly-legged arachnids have undivided globular bodies, suspended in the centre of their eight legs (see left), with two eyes on a little turret on the top. They do not spin silk and have no venom. They are mainly nocturnal, partly because their skins are not waterproof and can lose water by evaporation. They are completely harmless and, like spiders, carnivorous, eating caterpillars, millipedes, centipedes, mites and woodlice, as well as a range of small insects. Some of them eat slugs and snails and some eat fungi.

Harvestmen can lose several legs without much problem, so if you come across what you think is a three-legged spider – it's a harvestman! However, unlike spiders, they cannot regenerate them. Spiders are repelled by their unpleasant secretions and will actually release them if caught in their web. Harvestman eggs are tiny (like full stops) and are placed in crevices in soil or bark. Several different species may be found in the garden.

# Butterflies, moths and their caterpillars

Everyone is familiar with butterflies and moths and most people will see many more of the former than the latter (see Table right), so it may come as a surprise that the UK has 2,450 species of moths (of which several hundreds visit even small gardens) but only 57 species of butterflies (plus several migrants), of which about 25 regularly visit gardens.

This is because butterflies are diurnal and most, but not all, moths are nocturnal. In fact, there are more day-flying moths than there are butterflies!

Both feed by sucking up liquids, mostly nectar but butterflies will derive minerals from muddy puddles and even animal droppings, through their long proboscis or 'tongue'. Red Admirals apparently have a craving for fermenting fruits. The tongue may be as long as the insect's body but is coiled up under the head (see page 64) when not in use. It consists of two halves that together form a flexible tube. The Peacock Butterfly tongue is about 14mm long. However, some moth species lack feeding apparatus and survive on fat stores through their short adult lives.

Butterflies and moths have two pairs of wings, which in moths generally have an arrangement for linking forewings and hind-wings (see page 62) – butterflies, however, lack these. There are other structural differences. For example, both have antennae (or 'feelers') but those of most butterflies end in a 'club', whereas most moths have fine-tipped or feathery antennae (below). Among moths, some of the burnet moths have clubs: both may detect wind pressure.

Most butterflies have no ears and are only sensitive to loud, low frequency noises: they depend more on sight. They can see each other's colours in ultraviolet (their predators, however, tend to see what we see).

Many moths, on the other hand, possess ears on the sides of their bodies. These detect the high-pitched sounds of hunting bats, enabling the moths to take evasive action. Being nocturnal, moths depend less on sight and more on the detection of scent, to which their antennae are sensitive. Both butterflies and moths appear to be able to taste through organs on their feet. Being cold-blooded, like all insects, they need to warm up before they can fly. Butterflies can raise their temperature as high as 30°C by sunbathing but moths depend upon 'shivering'. Most butterflies and moths only live for a few weeks and for much of this time the weather may be too cold, wet or windy for them to operate.

Most butterflies rest with their wings perpendicular to their backs (except some of the moth-like skippers): very few moths do this, they normally rest with wings outspread. The wings are covered with tiny scales (right), which can easily brush off and which give butterflies and moths their colours and iridescence. Hence the name of their order, Lepidoptera, from the Greek 'lepidos' (a scale) and 'pteron' (a wing).

*Butterfly wing scales.*

## Butterflies and moths commonly seen in gardens

### Butterflies

Small White

Large White

Gatekeeper

Meadow Brown

Common Blue

Peacock

Green-veined White

Red Admiral

Small Tortoiseshell

Ringlet

### Moths

Six-spot Burnet

Silver-Y

Hummingbird Hawkmoth

*Feathery moth antennae compared to club-ended butterfly antennae.*

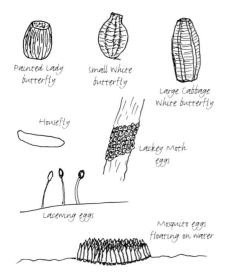

Painted Lady butterfly

Small White butterfly

Large Cabbage White butterfly

Housefly

Lackey Moth eggs

Lacewing eggs

Mosquito eggs floating on water

*Varieties of insect eggs.*

*The vibrantly-coloured caterpillar of the swallowtail butterfly – it is rare in the UK so you are unlikely see one in your garden.*

*Honey bees at the entrance to their hive.*

Eggs have characteristic shapes (top left) and are laid on the caterpillars' food plants. The caterpillars, which are often spectacular (centre left), grow at a tremendous rate, increasing their initial weight many hundred-fold before pupation. This may take place on the plant but, more usually, in a protected place, including sheds and underground, depending on the species.

It has been assumed for hundreds of years that caterpillars, like all insects, take in air passively through a row of holes (spiracles) along their sides. This then permeates through a network of tubes (tracheae and tracheoles). However, it has recently been found that a larger pair of spiracles at the rear end lead into a primitive pair of 'lungs' attached to the heart muscles.

# Bees and wasps

These insects, along with the ants and sawflies, are members of the order Hymenoptera (hymen, a membrane; pteron, a wing) with two pairs of wings, the hind ones being linked (for example by hooks, see page 62) to the forewings so that they move as one. They belong to a major division of the order that possess a waist between the thorax and the abdomen and they possess a sting at the rear end.

Most bees are 'furry' but wasps have much less hair on their bodies. Bees feed on nectar and pollen but wasps are carnivorous as grubs whilst the adults feed on liquids, including nectar, ripe fruit juice and jam! The best known bees and wasps are the social species but many more are solitary.

## Social bees and wasps

Honey-bees and Common Wasps form large colonies (Honey-bees can number in excess of 50,000 workers but wasp nests usually have nearer 15,000) but whereas the bees may overwinter in a hive or well-protected wild site, wasps die off at the beginning of winter and only the queens hibernate, often in your loft or a hollow tree. Only about 1 per cent of overwintering queens manage to establish new nests, mainly because of a shortage of suitable sites.

When a bee-hive produces new queens they take off with a swarm of workers to found a new colony. Wasps do not do this. Bees make their nests of hexagonal wax cells, of a similar shape to those that wasps make of 'paper' – wood scraped off dead trees and chewed up with saliva (see below opposite). Up to half of a bee colony (some 20,000 workers) will 'swarm' and send out scouts to reconnoitre new nest sites. This is a complex process, involving many bees in actually making the decision on the new location.

Bees store honey for winter use but social wasps store nothing. In both social bees and wasps, all the egg-laying is done by the queens, the female workers do not produce eggs and the male 'drones' only serve to mate with the new queens. It is claimed that a queen bee can lay 2,000 eggs in a day!

Besides Honey-bees, the larger bumblebees are also social. They are easy to recognise by their rotund furry bodies, generally coloured with black, orange, red or silver bands of hair. Bumblebee colonies are much smaller (a few hundred at most) and their nests, made mainly of moss, are mostly underground, often in old mouse holes.

One or two bumblebee species, the carder bees, build their nests above ground in long grass. There are probably about six species of bumblebee to be seen in British gardens, depending on the species of plant grown (see Chapters 1 and 13).

In general, bumblebee species seem to be in decline, intensive agriculture and 'tidy-minded' local authorities are blamed, but gardeners are also held to be partly responsible by using modern varieties of plants that have little nectar. Bumblebees seem to prefer yarrow, Michaelmas daisy, knapweeds, sweet William, lavender, tobacco plant, Foxglove, myrtle, geranium, rosemary, lilac, thyme, vetch and primrose.

There are several species of social wasps besides the Common Wasp, all with bright black and yellow 'warning' colours. Wasps often build their nests in lofts, especially where access is easy, for example, in old houses with ill-fitting tiles. Otherwise, most wasp nests are underground, often using old mouse holes greatly enlarged. Whilst this excavation is going on, wasps can be seen flying out with particles of soil, which they drop some distance away. This behaviour, like the removal of nestlings' droppings from the nest, avoids giving away the location of the nest. In fact, the behaviour of incoming wasps is also interesting. In long grass, for example, some wasps will break off to bite through grass that is interfering with their flight path.

A Buff-tailed Bumblebee collecting nectar from lavender flowers.

There are five species of social wasps in Britain but they are all very similar to each other and only two species are at all common in our gardens, the Common Wasp and the German Wasp. The others are the Red, Tree and Norwegian Wasps: the last two usually nest in trees or bushes. Wasps are more aggressive than bees but not as much as hornets, especially near their nests.

A vast wasps' nest removed from a roof space at my cottage.

A hornet feasting on a pear – note the brown stripes that distinguish it from a wasp.

Hornets are much larger than wasps, their stings are much more severe and their attacks are more direct. I have had Hornets nest in the walls of my cottage, within 20cm of my front door, so I have had to deal with them. If you have the same problem, wear full protective clothing!

Hornets mostly nest in hollow trees and are more common in the south. They also have warning coloration but have brown, not black, bands and their yellow parts are a deeper shade (top left). Recently swarms of the Asian Giant Hornet have appeared in France: they destroy Honey-bees and have devastated honey production and appear to be spreading north. They have not yet been seen in Britain.

## Solitary bees

There are a great many species of solitary bees, with different habits, and some are very small, mainly black and often hairless. Some species emerge very early in the year and play a major role in pollinating plum and pear trees. Amongst the most noticeable species in the garden are mining bees (about 7–9mm in length), the leaf-cutter bees and the mason bees.

The Tawny Mining Bee generally digs out a burrow in the lawn or in hard-packed earth, in which to lay its eggs on provisions of pollen and honey. There are several related species and they look rather alike, up to 1cm in length and covered in orangey-brown hairs. Their burrows may be 20cm in depth, with branches off the main channel. Although each female is solitary, they will often group their burrows together and bees return to them each year. Of course, these are not the same individuals, since they live for only a few weeks, but the next generation.

Hanging about near the burrow entrances are often small wasp-like cuckoo-bees (of the genus Nomada) that parasitise the larvae of the mining bees, laying their eggs in the burrows.

The smaller (c.8mm) leaf-cutter bees, as their name implies, make their cells of leaf segments cut out of the edges of rose leaves, though some species use other plants, in June and July. These are used to make cells, formed into a tube packed into a hole found or drilled in wood. If you ever wonder whether everything insects do is by instinct, consider the way in which the bee cuts about a dozen pieces of leaf for each cell, with circular pieces for the ends, all to make a tube that fits the hole! An egg is laid in each, on the food supply of pollen and honey.

The Red Mason Bee does a similar thing but makes its tubes of mud/soil mixed with saliva to form a cement, which sets quite hard and survives for a whole year – from egg-laying in one year to the emergence of adults in the next. It frequently nests in cracks and crevices in the walls of old houses (see Chapter 18) but can readily be persuaded to use nest boxes filled with tubes (see Chapter 13).

## Solitary wasps

There are many species of solitary wasps and, like the solitary bees, they nest in holes, in the ground (the digger wasps), in walls (the mason wasps),

A Leaf-cutter Bee with a portion of a leaf.

in old beetle holes in dead trees or even in hollow stems, such as bramble. Similarly, they all have parasites, waiting to lay their eggs on those of their hosts. Some are themselves parasitic, such as the spectacular ruby-tailed wasps (see Chapter 18).

Some wasps are tiny and black, others are 5–10mm in length, with black and yellow bands, rather like the social species. They sting their prey but are neither aggressive nor harmful to humans, though if handled they do sting! Those that burrow, usually in sandy soil, generally dig side tunnels off the main shaft, which may be 5–10cm deep. They push the excavated soil up backwards to the surface, where it forms a miniature volcano and when the female leaves the burrow it often blocks the hole with soil particles or a small stone.

Each wasp species provisions its nest with a given kind of invertebrate, spiders, weevils, caterpillars, aphids, flies, froghoppers or solitary bees, so they can be identified by the sort of prey they are carrying in to their nests. The prey is usually stung, although aphids are often bitten behind the head; this paralyses but does not kill them, so the developing grubs have fresh food to feed on.

Some of the wasps that nest in holes in wood plug the entrance, when they have finished, with resin, perhaps from pines. The digger wasps, especially, like their bee equivalents, form colonies where hundreds of holes may occur in a quite limited area (see Chapter 18) and be used year after year. This makes them very easy to observe (on dry sunny days), since they are quite unperturbed by the presence of people, even quite close to the entrance holes.

Three curious kinds of behaviour may seem puzzling. First, a returning wasp often seems unable to identify its own hole and flies from one to another, sometimes entering the wrong one and being ejected by the owner. Secondly, some wasps appear to fly about attacking those busy with their nests. These are probably males trying to mate with females, which may already be mated. Thirdly, a returning female may deposit her prey by the entrance hole, in order to unblock it, and then fly off having forgotten about the prey, which being still alive may struggle about for a while. Meanwhile, the female goes off to hunt another one.

A digger wasp carrying a grasshopper that it has paralysed off to its burrow.

A banded snail.

# Slugs, snails, beetles and woodlice

The reason for grouping these together is that they tend to be found in the same, or similar, places, especially under rotting logs. Of course, so are many other creatures, including young newts and, notably, centipedes and millipedes. In fact, so common are the latter that I have devoted a small section to them, too.

## Molluscs

This is the group that contains both snails and slugs, which are basically similar. In fact, slugs are really snails that have, during evolution, lost their shells, although some retain remnants, usually at their rear ends.

Both snails and slugs travel on a 'foot', using a trail of mucus (see Box, left), which lubricates their path but can be used to retrace their route, during which much of it may be reabsorbed. A slug's trail is continuous, apparently, but a snail's trail has breaks in it (page 88). This has been so for all the species I have tested but they do not lay mucus trails on very wet surfaces.

Both slugs and snails have tentacles, usually four but in one species only two, with eyes placed at the tips of the larger pair. These are sensitive to light but probably cannot 'see' shapes, and the tentacles are also sensitive to smell and touch. On the upper side of the body is a thicker 'mantle' with a gap in the side leading to a cavity which functions as a 'lung'. The main difference between slugs and snails is the latter's large, spirally coiled shell, filled with the visceral hump containing most of the internal organs.

The commonest snails are the quite large, dark brown Garden Snail and the two kinds of banded snail (left), the Brown-lipped and the White-lipped. Both of these have a variable pattern of brown and yellow spiral bands round their shells and both normally eat grass and weeds.

Garden snails, like most slugs, prefer decaying vegetation but all of the common snails may attack lettuces, strawberries and seedlings generally. In spite of their similarities, most people dislike slugs more than they do snails and, probably, more than any other invertebrate.

There are three main sorts of slug: shelled, keeled and round-backed. Probably a dozen different species occur in gardens. Most of the shelled slugs live underground and are carnivorous, feeding mainly on earthworms. The keeled slugs have a ridge on the hind part of the body. The largest is the Great Grey or Leopard Slug, common in gardens. The Yellow Slug feeds on fungi and decaying matter: it is also grey but has a yellow sole. The grey field slug is a small fawn and white slug and is one of the most damaging but unfortunately the most common amongst lettuces and cabbages, for example.

The round-back slugs include the Large Black Slug which feeds on a wide variety of vegetable matter but is not reckoned to do much damage in the garden. Perhaps the most destructive is the Garden Slug, smallish, brownish grey or black: it is the one most likely to damage potatoes. All in all, however unattractive you may find them, most slugs, like snails, do little damage, but the few really destructive species are common and can be numerous.

The eggs of slugs are spherical, creamy white, about 1.5mm across and are laid in groups of up to 20, commonly under rotting logs but also in crevices in the soil. The eggs of snails may be a bit larger (depending on the species, of course), tend to be grey but more commonly found buried in the soil. Eggs usually hatch within a month or so but some slug eggs remain for months and overwinter. Most slugs and snails are hermaphrodite but usually cross-mate and they breed throughout the spring, summer and early autumn.

The Great Grey or Leopard Slug.

## Beetles

Apart from those that live in ponds (see Chapter 14) there are several kinds of beetle that may come to the notice of the gardener. The ground beetles live under logs and other such protected places but may also be seen running rapidly over the ground (or the lawn). There are many species, varying greatly in size and colour (though most are dark brown, black, green or violet-tinged), many are diurnal but some are nocturnal, and most are carnivorous, many living on slugs. Some are omnivorous as adults but the larvae are generally carnivorous. Some digest their food internally, others do it externally and can only ingest liquids. It is the adults that over-winter, so they can be found at any time of the year, but the larvae do not really resemble the adults.

One other ground-dwelling beetle is worth mentioning, it is the black Devil's Coach-horse, which adopts a threatening attitude if disturbed – earwigs do much the same. It is not actually a ground beetle but a rove beetle, easily distinguished because the wing cases only cover about half the wings.

The most familiar beetles are, of course, ladybirds, but there are two much more spectacular beetles that may often be encountered, although only at certain times of the year: these are the Stag Beetle (seen between May and August but mostly in July – see chapter 7) and the Cockchafer or 'may bug' (seen, or heard, in May or early June).

The Devil's Coach-horse.

The substantial Cockchafer can be 25–30mm in length when mature.

The Cockchafer is also large (above) but reddish brown and flies about among the tops of oak trees, mainly at night, feeding on leaves. The larvae, however, are root-feeders (on grass and other crops) and spend two or three years underground. The adults are quite harmless but very clumsy and may blunder into you or in through lighted windows, making a loud buzzing (or humming) sound.

Weevils may also be found in the garden. They are distinguished by their long snouts (top left). Generally fairly small, black, brown or green, they eat carrot or other leaves, or seeds (depending on the species).

You'll need to look closely to see a weevil as they are rarely more than 6mm in length.

## Woodlice

Although there are 46 species of woodlice in Britain, only two kinds are really likely to be distinguished, although about eight species occur in our gardens. They are mainly decomposers, eating decaying plant matter, wood and fungi, and recycling their own droppings, just like rabbits. Females carry their eggs on their undersides and the young, like all arthropods, can only grow by moulting their hard exoskeletons (but they do this usually by halves!).

The most common species, the Common Woodlouse (below left), has pale edges to its 'shell'). It is nocturnal and very susceptible to drying out (like centipedes), so it hides away, under logs and stones, where it is damp. However, it can walk great distances (up to 100m in a night!), with its seven pairs of legs.

The Pill Woodlouse or 'pill bug', on the other hand, can tolerate dry conditions, because of its much harder carapace. It is well-known for its habit of rolling up into a ball when it is alarmed, for greater protection. This resemblance to a pill gave rise to the name and it is said that, hundreds of years ago, it was sometimes fed to cattle to cure various ailments – not a healthy outcome for the woodlouse!

Common Woodlice – note the light-coloured rim to the 'shell'.

# Reptiles and amphibians

This is one group where it is quite easy to know all the British species, as they are very few in number, though not all are common in gardens.

## Reptiles

We have three native snakes and three lizards, all legally protected, and all feed on small vertebrates but Adders and Smooth Snakes concentrate on reptiles and small mammals, whereas Grass Snakes prefer amphibians.

The Grass Snake is the most common. It is usually olive brown (rarely white – see left) with black bars down the sides and a yellow collar. As with the Adder, the female is larger than the male, usually 70–100cm, and lays leathery eggs, commonly in compost heaps or cut grass, which generate heat. Fond of wet land it can be found swimming in ponds.

The Adder (or 'viper') is our only venomous snake (page 168). It is not as long as the Grass Snake (about 55cm), grey-brown with a dark zigzag pattern on the back and no yellow collar. It prefers drier areas and is viviparous (bears live young). Adders are shy and not aggressive but have a venomous bite, said to be not much worse than a wasp sting, but people vary in their reactions to such things, so it is wise to take no chances (there have been 12 deaths in the last 100 years). The rare Smooth Snake is found only on the heathlands of southern England. It is usually about 55cm in length, and is grey-brown with rows of dark blotches along the back.

The Common Lizard is also viviparous. It spends much time basking in the sunlight on stone walls or banks. It is generally brown, finely marked with spots and stripes, and is about 14cm long, including the (detachable) tail. The Sand Lizard is rare, only found on heathland in southern England. It grows to 20cm: males have vivid green sides but otherwise both sexes are grey-brown. It lays eggs on open sand patches warmed by the sun. The Slow Worm is a grey-brown legless lizard that looks rather like a snake, and reaches c.35cm in length. It can be common in urban areas. It is viviparous.

*Grass snakes including a rare white one, discovered beneath dustbin lids in my garden.*

*A female Common Lizard subathing on a log.*

Common Toad.

Natterjack Toad.

All three lizards eat insects and other invertebrates but Slow-worms prefer slugs. However, when young, all reptiles eat smaller prey (and adders are venomous from birth).

## Amphibians

These animals spend part of their life-cycle in water, although the adults all spend most of their lives on land, coming to the water only to breed. We have seven native amphibian species in Britain – two toads, two frogs and three newts.

## Frogs and toads

The Common Toad is a warty, dry-skinned animal with a poison gland behind each eye which discourage predators by the irritating and distasteful liquid they secrete. The females, up to 10cm long, are larger than the males and both eat snails, slugs, beetles, woodlice and ants (a favourite, apparently).

All amphibians have to hibernate through the winter. In the case of toads, this may be in the same sheltered spot that they inhabit for the whole year. I had a toad that lived permanently in a hollow branch for several years, emerging further out at night where it could be observed by torchlight, just sitting and thinking!

The Natterjack Toad is much smaller (c.8cm) with a distinctive yellow stripe down the back, and is the rarest of our amphibians. It has shorter hind legs and runs rather than crawls (as the Common Toad does).

There are only two frog species indigenous to Britain – the Common Frog and the rare Pool Frog. Several others have been artificially introduced, most notably the Marsh Frog which is now well established in the south-eastern corner of England.

The Common Frog is well-known and is more readily seen that the Common Toad, partly because of its spectacular jumps when disturbed. Both frogs and toads only spend a few days in the water to deposit their spawn in the spring, but frogs are occasionally seen in ponds at other times, swimming powerfully with their long hind legs. Some frogs hibernate in the mud at the bottom of ponds or ditches.

Frogs show less liking for ants than toads do, and more liking for slugs and caterpillars, but both eat beetles, woodlice and many other invertebrates. Toads tend to be longer-lived, with exceptional cases recorded of 40 years, but, of course, the average is much less.

Both frogs and toads appear to synchronise their breeding and will migrate en masse, often across busy roads, to reach their chosen ponds. As explained in the previous chapter, the male grasps the female from behind, in a tight embrace (called amplexus), until the eggs are released. This is so that he can release his sperm immediately the eggs are produced, allowing fertilisation before the jelly absorbs water (99.7 per cent) to form an impenetrable barrier.

Frogs produce the well-known masses of floating spawn, whereas in toads, the eggs are laid in a double string wound round pond plants (opposite below). Toad spawn has been found to contain more than 6,000 eggs, frog spawn somewhat less, but this must be very variable. The individual eggs are small (1–2mm in diameter) and black: they hatch in 10–12 days and the tadpoles emerge to feed on algae (or each other if crowded and food is short!). The colour of the eggs is significant as they warm up in sunshine and the jelly is insulating: the egg mass is often 0.6°C higher than the water.

Eventually, the tiny frogs and toads scatter and find hiding places, showing themselves mostly after rain. They do not reach sexual maturity until about four years old.

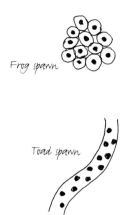

Frog spawn

Toad spawn

Comparison of frog and toad spawn.

## Newts

The most common species is the Smooth Newt, which is also the only newt present in Ireland, the largest is the Great Crested Newt (now much less common) and the smallest is the Palmate Newt. In most gardens it is the Smooth Newt that will be found, usually only in the pond during the spring breeding season, when the crested males display their bright orange undersides to the rather less colourful females.

The adults are present in the garden for the whole year but remain hidden in damp places, including under logs and rocks. The eggs are laid in bent-over leaves of aquatic plants (right) and the 'newtpoles' leave the water in the autumn, returning some two years later as breeding adults.

Newt egg folded into a starwort leaf.

# Birds

Since birds can fly into any garden, a great many different species may be seen, so we will concentrate here on those likely to nest or, at least, visit regularly for some part of the year. Much depends, of course, on the size of the garden and whether it has trees, bushes and hedges, which provide nest sites: indeed without them, few nests will be found. Those that nest in trees and hedges are described in Chapter 7, those whose nests are associated with buildings are dealt with in Chapter 18.

In urban gardens, House Sparrows, Starlings, Blue and Great Tits, Blackbirds, Song Thrushes, Robins, Dunnocks, Wrens and Chaffinches are among the most common, although some species, such as the Song Thrush, have become rarer in recent years. All of these will nest in gardens, provided that they can find suitable nest sites, and many more in some gardens, including Greenfinches, Goldfinches and Coal Tits. Many can be seen collecting nesting material even when they nest elsewhere.

Birds come to the garden for food and water all year round and this can be provided by putting it out on bird tables (see Chapter 13) or by growing plants that carry seeds, fruits and berries or upon which insects and other invertebrates may be found. Birds can also be attracted to gardens by nesting sites and nest material (see Chapter 13) but all this can be counteracted by cats and dogs (See Chapter 17).

Male Greenfinch.

A totally pest-free garden would also lack predators and thus insectivorous birds. Snails, a favourite food of Song Thrushes, are unpopular with most gardeners but Song Thrushes are welcome! Why would they come, though, if there are no snails?

All birds lay eggs and most construct nests, the bigger birds (like Rooks, crows, Woodpigeons, Jays and Magpies) using twigs and the smaller birds (Robins, finches, Blackbirds and thrushes) weaving elaborate nests of moss, hair and dried grass. A few use mud (Nuthatch, Song Thrush, Blackbird and House Martin), as the main structure or as a lining. The Nuthatch is the only one to use mud to constrict the entrance hole in a tree.

Most garden birds lay a clutch of eggs (see Table, page 167) and many do this more than once a year, especially if they lose the first clutch. Eggs are vulnerable to egg-thieves such as squirrels and Magpies, as are nestlings, but the latter may be defended by the sitting bird. On balance, however, a female will save herself rather than eggs or nestlings, since she can at least have another go and does not want to risk injury.

Eggs vary greatly in size, shape and colour (see page 150). Most are 'egg-shaped' but some (like those of owls) are near-spherical. It is surprising that a few are so brightly coloured, for example the blue eggs of the Song Thrush, since this makes them stand out when the bird is not sitting, but most are well-camouflaged and many are speckled. Colours are characteristic, as are nests, and species can be identified from both.

Female Blackbird feeding nestlings.

Feeding the nestlings requires tremendous activity on the part of (usually) both parents, except in those independent from hatching, and the number of food-laden journeys is very large. That is why the easiest way to locate nests is to observe the journeys of birds with bills full of food. Mind you, if they think they are being observed, they are quite clever at taking an indirect and confusing route!

Some nestlings that are being fed have a bright yellow 'gape' – a protruding flange surrounding the mouth. This is typical of song birds (e.g. thrushes) and is opened wide when the parent approaches, acting as a stimulus to feeding (see page 29).

# Mammals

The most numerous mammals in the garden are not necessarily those most often seen or the most obvious: in any case, what is seen depends greatly on the size and location of the garden.

## Foxes

*The Fox – as common in city gardens as in the countryside.*

These are now common in urban gardens, where they are probably more readily seen than in country gardens, albeit mainly at night. Foxes will eat almost anything that is edible but, unless fed, a major part of their diet is earthworms.

Cubs are born underground in March and remain in the 'earth' for about a month. In late summer adult Foxes moult and may look rather scruffy at this time: they may also suffer from mange. In fact, Foxes, especially in cities, appear to be very susceptible to diseases and the average life of the urban Fox is only about 15 months.

*The omnivorous Badger – increasingly common in suburban gardens.*

## Badgers

These unmistakable animals are less common in gardens than Foxes, depending on the garden size and its proximity to woodland, but they are numerous in many parts of the countryside. Like Foxes, they consume vast quantities of earthworms – estimated at c.200 per Badger per night.

Badger protection was put in place in the UK in 1973, largely as a reaction to the so-called 'sport' of Badger-baiting. Since then tuberculosis has again become a major problem in both cattle and Badgers.

As already noted (Chapter 4), the Badger has an acute sense of smell (some 800 times as sensitive as ours), so it can usually only be observed with great care. Badgers will dig up and eat bumblebee nests and will eat Grass Snakes, slow-worms, frogs, eggs of ground-nesting birds and Hedgehogs.

## Moles

Moles can accomplish almost 100 metres of tunnelling in a day, which results in large numbers of molehills to dispose of the soil. All this is largely in search of earthworms, though they have been known to eat mice and even other Moles! There are estimated to be about 31 million moles in the UK.

They are not scared away by ultrasonic deterrents or by the wind blowing over the top of a bottle sunk in one of their tunnels! Moles are almost blind and hard of hearing but they pick up vibrations through hairs on their noses and on the ends of their paws. Their runs may cover up to a quarter of a hectare, and a Mole will explore all of this in 24 hours.

## Hedgehogs

Like the previous three, Hedgehogs are earthworm-eaters, and also enjoy beetles, caterpillars, centipedes, spiders and occasional birds' eggs, but their favourite food is slugs. They hibernate from November to March and need to weigh at least 500g to see them through the winter. They will readily take food put out for them, preferably dog and cat food (not cow's milk although they quite like it). They currently appear to be in decline.

Hedgehogs are well known for harbouring lots of fleas: each animal may have up to 500 fleas but, happily, these only live on hedgehogs. If you wonder why they have so many, just consider the problem of scratching spines and the protection these afford to the fleas!

## Voles

There are four species in Britain but only two are common. The Orkney Vole is only found there and the Water Vole is now rather rare. The two likely to be found in gardens are the Short-tailed Field Vole and the Bank Vole. Their numbers fluctuate spectacularly since they breed from March (litters of four to nine), every four weeks or so until the end of the summer. However, a wide range of predators feed on them, from Weasels and Foxes to Adders, owls and Kestrels. Magpies, crows and Badgers will also take them and, of course, domestic cats.

In a normal year, about 677 million Short-tailed Field Voles will be born, but the breeding population the following spring will be down to about 75 million. The Bank Vole, which is slightly larger and more mouse-like in appearance, is less numerous, with a breeding population of about 23 million.

## Shrews

Our tiniest ground mammals, these are most often seen dead, left by cats because they have an unpleasant taste: owls, however, do not seem to mind. Shrews have long noses and feed largely on invertebrates such as worms, slugs and snails, beetles, woodlice and spiders, often digging for prey. They have such a high metabolic rate that they have to feed almost continuously, with only short periods of rest about 10 times a day. Mainland Britain has three species of shrews, of which the Common and Pygmy are the species most likely to visit gardens.

The young are born hairless (until nine days old) and blind (until 16 days old) and feed independently at about 21 days. Adults are largely solitary and aggressive. They depend more upon smell, touch and hearing than on sight. In the winter, shrews spend about 80 per cent of their time underground.

A Common shrew.

## Wood Mice

The Wood Mouse is also called the 'long-tailed field mouse': it has large ears and eyes and lacks the characteristic smell of the House Mouse. It is largely nocturnal and feeds on both invertebrates and vegetable foods (seeds, seedlings, fruit, nuts, buds, fungi and galls).

In woodland, its range is about 600m² It has up to four litters of five blind, naked young a year, which are independent by three weeks of age. Adult Wood Mice are very agile and can jump well, but nevertheless are prey to a wide range of predators – owls, Kestrels, Weasels, Stoats, Badgers, Foxes and, of course, cats.

## Rats

Rats are regarded as thoroughly undesirable, partly because of their capacity for spreading disease (leptospirosis and, sometimes, salmonella and toxoplasmosis), but it is reckoned that none of us are far from one (or more) wherever we live and numbers are increasing. In Britain, the introduced Brown Rat is the ubiquitous species.

Brown Rats are largely nocturnal, omnivorous, attracted by rubbish, but they also eat slugs and snails, frogs, birds' eggs and the young of smaller mammals. They, in turn, are eaten by Foxes, cats, Tawny Owls, Weasels, Stoats and, occasionally, Badgers. They often live underground, in extensive tunnels, but may travel 3–≥4km per night. Rats swim well and are very good jumpers. They produce an average of five litters per year, each comprising seven to nine babies.

*The ubiquitous and adaptable Brown Rat.*

## Stoats and Weasels

Neither of these animals are likely to occur in small gardens. Both are similar in shape (in fact, the scientific name of their genus – *Mustela* – is the Latin word for weasel) but the Stoat is much larger. Both are ferocious

*You can see how small the Weasel is by comparing it to the size of the leaves that surround it.*

predators, tackling prey up to their own size or even larger, killing by a bite to the neck. Weasels (below left) eat smaller prey, such as voles, compared to that of Stoats, which favour Rabbits. In northern regions, the Stoat turns white in winter. White Stoats are sometimes known as 'ermines'.

Stoats breed once a year (litter size five to 12); weasels may breed a second time (litter size four to six). Both are active, periodically, by both day and night.

## Deer

In Britain. there are several species of deer but, in most gardens, the most common are the Roe Deer and the Muntjac (also known as 'barking deer'). In both species, only males grow antlers, which are shed and regrown every year. The Muntjac, when alarmed, erects its tail, but the Roe Deer appears not to have one. Both are generally crepuscular (active at dusk and dawn) but may also be seen during the day.

Both breed once a year but the Muntjac has only one fawn, whereas the Roe Deer has mostly twins, or even triplets. Deer often leave their fawns hidden in dense vegetation whilst foraging: if found, they should be left where they are – they have not been abandoned.

## Rabbits

Everyone is familiar with Rabbits and they are rarely popular with gardeners, since they will eat almost any plants. I have seen them eating Ground Elder and if they confined themselves to this many people would welcome them.

They reproduce famously quickly, all the year round, but they are vulnerable to Foxes and raptors, especially when young, which is perhaps why they are confined to a blocked burrow for the first four weeks. Females may produce three to seven litters of five young per year. The young are born naked and blind, fed only once a day and are weaned at about 28 days.

Rabbits and hares form the order Lagomorpha, which have double front incisors (i.e. behind the two upper front teeth are two more) and their teeth have no roots. Another feature is that they engage in refection, producing special soft faeces that are eaten to achieve two goes at digestion. This is called coprophagy and, if prevented from doing this, Rabbits die within three weeks.

Their burrows are sited on a slope to guarantee drainage and are often grouped in warrens. Rabbits range over areas up to 2ha – males going further than females: males' territories may include those of several breeding females. Urine and faeces are used to mark territories. They thump their feet when alarmed and their field of vision, because of their prominent eyes, is 360°.

## Squirrels

In Britain there are two species of squirrel – the native Red and introduced Grey, are broadly similar but differ in important respects (see Table, page 192). Today, Grey Squirrels are found mainly in deciduous woodland while Reds are more often found in coniferous forests.

Young Muntjac deer.

## Squirrels

| | Grey Squirrel | Red Squirrel |
| --- | --- | --- |
| Eartufts | Small | Prominent in winter |
| Size | Larger (450–650g) | Smaller (250–350g) |
| Habitat | Deciduous woodlands | Coniferous forests |
| Behaviour | Diurnal | Diurnal |
| Food | Acorns Beechmast Tree shoots and sappy tissue under bark Nuts Fruits Roots Seeds | Conifer seeds Acorns (to a limited extent) Beechmast Buds and shoots Bark and sap tissue Fungus Nuts Fruits Berries |
| Range | 2–10ha | 2–10ha |
| Litter size | 1–8 (average 3) | 1–8 (average 3) |
| Life span | 1–2 years | 1–2 years |
| Distribution | Widespread | Now confined to Scotland, Cumbria, Introduced Northumberland, Lancashire, Isle of Wight, some islands in Poole Harbour and parts of Wales |

There is probably no greater wildlife controversy, as far as garden animals are concerned, than Grey vs Red. Grey Squirrels do damage young trees, by bark stripping, though I have found none of significance in 38 years of living with Grey Squirrels in my 1.25ha of woodland. They are also believed to take birds' eggs but that does not seem to have happened to any great extent either. (Isn't it strange that everyone loves the Cuckoo – the greatest specialist in turfing out the eggs of its 'hosts'?)

However, there are those whose antipathy to Greys is so strong that they believe they should all be exterminated. Certainly the Greys are numerous: it is estimated that there are about 2.5m Greys in the UK but less than 150,000 Reds. It is generally the case that a higher value is placed on rare animals (even snails) but many people also regard the Red as more attractive.

There are four main charges brought against Greys.

1. They are aliens. So, of course, are many other animals (and people) and it is an odd argument for gardeners to use, since gardens have always benefited from plants brought back by famous plant hunters from all over the world.

2. Greys damage trees. Reds also bark trees but there are fewer of them!

3. Greys kill Reds. This is often said but evidence is scarce – I have seen none. However, greys are thought to carry parapoxivirus, which produces a deadly disease in Reds while having no apparent effect on Greys.

4. Greys are said to 'drive out' reds but there is little evidence of direct physical attack. However, it cannot be denied that the range of the Red Squirrel has retreated as that of the Grey has expanded northwards. Red squirrels are a protected species by law.

Grey (left) and Red squirrels – the Grey is significantly larger than the Red.

## Bats

Nearly a quarter of all mammalian species are bats (951 species) but only a few are likely to be found in our gardens – especially the Common Pipistrelle, the Soprano Pipistrelle and the Brown Long-eared Bat (see page 57). (All species, and their roosts, are protected in the EU.) Of these, the most common is the Common Pipistrelle. Its genus name (*Pipistrellus*) comes from 'pipio' (a squeak) and therefore means 'little squeaking beast'. This is slightly odd, in that most of the time we are unable to hear its squeaks.

Bats are our only flying mammals and have leathery wings (see page 69): they often live in large colonies, in old buildings or hollow trees. They breed rather slowly, producing just one baby every two years, but they can live for up to 25 years (an average of four years, however). They mate in the autumn or winter but the female stores the sperm alive in her body until the following spring, when she becomes pregnant.

They feed on the wing, consuming large numbers of flying insects (some 3,000 each night), including mosquitoes and midges, finding them by echolocation. A dead bat is best left untouched, since some carry antibodies to bat rabies, though none tested have been positive for the active virus itself. A very few have been found to have bat lyasavirus, which can infect humans.

# 12 Residents and visitors

Some garden animals – principally the smaller and slower-moving ones – are permanent residents, and could not travel far even if they wanted to. However, larger and more mobile animals may fall into the category of regular or casual garden visitors, including your garden as part of a much wider home range. Others may only visit at certain times of the year. This chapter looks at animal movements.

## Mammals

The main mammal residents are described in detail in Chapter 11, and these include the possible visitors as well. This is because the distinction largely depends on the size of the garden. A small garden can only provide a permanent home for very small creatures, whereas a very large garden can accommodate even the larger species of deer.

Some species of bats, however, are unlikely to confine themselves even to large gardens and may travel long distances from their roosts to their feeding grounds. This is to a large extent because suitable roosting sites are scarce and may not coincide with their feeding ranges. The likelihood of a species residing in a garden is therefore greatly influenced by its normal range. This is illustrated for the commoner species in the Table right.

Whether smaller gardens receive far-ranging animals as visitors depends on how accessible and attractive the gardens are. Continuous high walls are the most effective barriers: fences are usually jumped over, wriggled through or burrowed under. Some hedges are impenetrable but most have gaps near the base.

Whether gardens are attractive or not depends on the vegetative cover, availability of food (including prey) and water sources, the presence of cats, dogs and children. However, many mammalian visitors are nocturnal and rarely seen: droppings and prey residues may be the only signs left behind but, at least, they can tell you what's been happening and who was there!

*The Roe Deer – a shy but quite frequent visitor to country gardens.*

### Ranges of common mammals

(sometimes best expressed as area of territory

| Species | Range |
|---|---|
| Roe Deer | Up to 100ha |
| Badger | Territory of 30–50ha |
| Fox | 20–40ha in cities 200–600ha in agricultural land |
| Rabbit | 0.4–2ha (may travel up to 400m) |
| Mole | 200–2,000m$^2$ |
| Hedgehog | Territory 15–40ha |
| Grey Squirrel | 2–10ha |
| Vole | 100–1,000m$^2$ |
| Shrew | 370–630m$^2$ |
| Pipistrelle bat | 16 sq km |

# Birds

As birds are capable of sustained flight they are the most mobile of all our animals. The 'loss' of their forelegs has led to the development of a great variety of bill shapes, to carry out some of the functions that front legs and feet serve in mammals, for example.

Bills are extremely varied between species but remarkably alike within most species. (This may be simply that we cannot detect the differences that exist and may be perfectly plain to other birds!) Page 58 illustrates the variation and indicates the main function of each type of bill. It is this function that will often tell us about the diet of the bill's owner.

However, bills are also used for other purposes, especially in making nests, including carrying and manipulating mud. Woodpeckers use their chisel-like bills for drumming – as an aid to establishing territory and attracting a mate, and also for excavating holes in tree trunks. The Green Woodpecker also digs holes in the lawn to find ants.

Flight is not the only way that birds can get around – they also travel on foot, whether walking, hopping, running, swimming or climbing. Page 59 illustrates the ways in which the foot is modified for these purposes.

The most common bird residents are described in Chapter 11. Many more, however, are visitors only, especially in small gardens, and few species spend their whole time in one garden. Some visit for food, water, nesting materials or nesting sites.

Large predators usually make only fleeting visits. The likeliest to be seen in gardens are Sparrowhawks, Tawny Owls and (if ponds contain fish) Grey Herons. However, some visitors are migrants (see table, left) generally spending only a part of the year here, some in the winter (such as Fieldfares) and some in the summer (like Swallows and House Martins).

# Butterflies and moths

Many of our butterflies are only found in a specific habitat (sandy heath, for example), so distribution is very patchy. Several of our butterflies are limited to chalk downs and limestone hills (including, rather obviously, the Chalkhill Blue). Some are limited by their food plant. The Brimstone, for example, so common in many gardens, does not occur in Scotland and is only found where buckthorns grow. Many are woodland species (for example, many of the fritillaries) but the Comma, also a woodland species but with less exacting habitat requirements, is commonly found in gardens throughout southern England and Wales.

All this is expected to change with 'global warming' (see Chapter 21) but, like the mammals, butterflies are attracted by food, nectar for the adults and the presence of food plants for the caterpillars.

A Comma butterfly feeding on spring blossom.

About 35 species hibernate as larvae and a few as eggs: very few hibernate as adults, but these include some of the more spectacular, such as the Peacock, the Small Tortoiseshell, the Brimstone and the Comma (above). The best known migrants are the Red Admiral and the Painted Lady.

The number of butterfly and moth species migrating to Britain in summer has increased four-fold in the past 25 years, apparently, and 'global warming' is likely to increase this still further. It has been estimated that, with each degree of temperature rise, a further 14 species can be expected to cross the Channel!

Although there are vastly more moth species in this country than butterflies (see Chapter 11), they are seen less often. This is partly because so many are nocturnal but also because many are quite small and not very noticeable. Their caterpillars may be more noticeable, and of course don't wander very far, but they too may be well hidden. For example, the caterpillars of the leaf-mining moths tunnel into leaves and most people, if they noticed the tunnels at all, would see no reason to associate them with moths. Tunnels show up as pale, winding tracks on the leaf, because the green material between the upper and lower surfaces is eaten away (see page 229). They may be seen on the leaves of poplar, bramble, elm, hawthorn, roses, willow, beech and sow-thistle. The larvae make progressively larger tunnels as they grow bigger and can be found if the wider end of the tunnel is opened.

Some moths are serious pests, such as the Codling Moth on apples and quinces, whose caterpillars live and feed in the fruit, and the Magpie Moth caterpillars on currant bushes. One small moth, the Foxglove Pug, lays its eggs on the Foxglove flowers and the green caterpillars feed on the stamens and developing seeds, so they are not obvious to the casual observer.

## Migrating moths and butterflies

(not all occur every year or in all parts of the country)

| Moths | Butterflies |
|---|---|
| | (other species occur occasionally) |
| Hummingbird Hawkmoth | Clouded Yellow |
| Hoary Footman | Red Admiral* |
| Small Thistle | Painted Lady* |
| Gypsy Moth | Large White |
| Convolvulus Hawkmoth | Small White |
| Dark Sword-grass | |
| Pearly Underwing | |
| Silver Y | |

*These are examples of species that depend on immigration to maintain their presence here.

Some moths are large and spectacular, like the Emperor Moth whose caterpillars feed on heather, and the Six-spot Burnet (all the burnets are poisonous) with larvae feeding on legumes (cloverss, trefoils and vetches). Burnets are among several brightly coloured moths that fly in the day-time (see left) and are poisonous – so the colours are a 'warning' to predators. By contrast, many rest by day and their caterpillars are hidden in the leaves.

# Wings and flight

The capacity to visit gardens is greatly increased by the ability to fly, but wings also confer speed, manoeuvrability and acess to more space (vertical as well as horizontal). In terms of vegetation, squirrels and some invertebrates can climb to the treetops, but flight also allows exploitation of the air way above the tallest trees.

Wings are characteristic of all birds (and all birds in the UK can fly) and many insects, but only one group of mammals – the bats. The structure of the wings is quite different in these groups.

Bats' wings (see page 69) are skin-like membranes, stretched over all four legs, modified for the purpose, with only the hind legs retaining 'feet' (from which the bats suspend themselves upside-down). Birds' wings only incorporate the front limbs and insect wings do not use any of their six legs.

The possession of wings is clearly a prerequisite for flight but so is light weight. The heaviest British bird is the Mute Swan, at around 15kg and the limit on weight effectively limits size. As an animal gets bigger, its volume and weight increase as the cube of its length. Just as, if you take a cube (like a dice) and double the length of one side, the volume and weight will rise by a factor of eight. In addition, the greater the weight the greater the strength needed in the bones that have to support it. That is why most birds have hollow bones – to keep the weight down. The loss of teeth is another weight-saving adaptation.

Insects, on the other hand, have a quite different problem. Their body support is external – an exoskeleton of hard chitin – and this is proportional to the surface area. Such exoskeletons are relatively heavy and inflexible (as with knights of old!). This means, incidentally, that insects (like crustaceans) can only grow by moulting: so flight only occurs in the fully grown adults.

Birds and insects have quite different wing structures. In birds the bones provide the framework, with small muscles attached. This is covered by a membrane of skin, into which the feathers are inserted. Feathers have an extraordinary structure, and are very numerous (1,000 even on a small songbird; 25,000 on a swan!), but the flight feathers are relatively few – in most birds there are between nine and 11 primary feathers, and between six and 40 secondaries. The long tail feathers also assist with flight – mainly for braking and steering rather than supplying lift.

Each feather has a (usually) hollow shaft made of keratin (like our fingernails) with branches (barbs) that further branch and have smaller barbules. These hook together in an ingenious way, such that, if disturbed, they easily rejoin to present a plane surface. Most feathers, even the large flight feathers, have soft down at their bases for insulation. Many small birds use feathers in the construction of their nests, for warmth and softness. The Long-tailed Tit, for example, may use as many as 2,000 tiny feathers in addition to lichens, cobwebs, hair and moss. Feathers are amazingly light, considering how rigid a wing they form. The flight feathers are replaced by moulting, a very vulnerable period.

It is not always realised that birds' wings are also liberally supplied with blood vessels and nerves, as well as the smaller muscles – the large breast muscles, attached to the breastbone, are the main source of power for flight.

The detailed manoeuvres of flight in different species are fascinating, especially take-off and landing, even in high winds and on slender, moving branches, with only rare mistakes. Some flight forms are characteristic of the species: such as the dipping flight of woodpeckers, the hovering of Kestrels and the short spells of rapid wing beats in Starlings.

Speed of flight also varies. Pigeons are estimated to achieve 90km per hour, the Magpie c.45kph, sparrows 50kph and the starling 80kph: however, some raptors can fly much faster than any of these.

Differing flight styles in the Raven (above) and Kestrel.

Green Hawker dragonfly in flight.

Insects generally fly at much lower speeds and their wings are quite different and more variable in structure. Speeds are typically about 11km per hour (and about 24kph for a cruising bee, with a wingbeat frequency of about 150 per second) but some insects can fly much faster, e.g. dragonflies at 3–11m per second or 36 kph (depending on the species) with wingbeats at 16–50 per second! They can also hover, fly upside down and backwards, and take off and land vertically.

Classification of insects makes great use of the number and characteristics of wings. Indeed, more detailed identification of species often depends upon the precise patterns of the wing veins. This is rather more detailed than most gardeners would want to bother with. But there are some wing details that are both interesting and helpful in sorting out one group from another.

Dragonflies are, in evolutionary terms, a very ancient group and have two pairs of wings with the forewings separated from the hind-wings. In many insects, the situation is quite different and the forewings and hindwings on each side are joined together (in a great variety of different ways, depending on the type of insect) so that they move in unison.

In butterflies, for example, the hind-wings simply overlap the forewings and thus move with them. In moths, however, there is generally some locking mechanism (see page 62) usually consisting of bristles, hooks and hairs: bees, bumblebees and wasps have a row of hooks on the leading edge of the hind-wings that latch on to a ridge on the trailing edge of the forewings. Most groups of insects have two pairs of wings but the true flies (Diptera) have only a pair of forewings, the hindwings being replaced by stalked knobs (halteres – best seen in crane flies – see page 71), thought to play a role as gyroscopic stabilisers. In beetles, the forewings are modified into hard wing cases or elytra, which protect the hindwings when they are not in use.

A major difference from the wings of birds is that insect wings contain no muscles – these are all in the thorax. In spite of this, their wings are capable of remarkable manoeuvres, flapping, twisting and rotating in flight. Even the fluttering of a butterfly may be deliberately used to take advantage of wind eddies.

Wing structure showing folded wing

expanded wing

wing viewed from underside

elytra

Wing structures on a female Stag Beetle.

In birds, the rate of wingbeats in flapping flight varies from 1 to 50 a second (hummingbirds). In insects it may be 20 a second in large insects and up to 200 a second in small ones (such as midges in the still evenings).

Insect wing shapes vary from the feathery wings of some small moths, the folded fan-like wings of earwigs and ladybirds, the stiff membranes of dragonflies to the large scale-covered wings of most butterflies and moths. In spite of this variation, they are formed in the same basic fashion. When the adult emerges from its pupa or nymphal casing, its wings are soft and crumpled. They are sac-like with two membranes that are then pumped up with fluid: this expands the wings to the normal shape, with all the hollow wing veins in place. These veins are filled with a special secretion, which sets so that they form solid rods fused to the membranes. The liquid between them is then reabsorbed and the two membranes fuse together to form a single sheet. All this can be observed when dragonflies emerge from the pond (see Chapter 14).

Remarkably, the hindwings of beetles like the ladybirds and the Stag Beetle (left, below) that have to fold them beneath the hard wing cases, are then able to fold, automatically, in quite complex ways — without any muscles, nerves etc. in the wings themselves! This has to be done quickly and precisely the same way every time. It is really quite extraordinary: you can easily see this in ladybirds, for example, when they take off. The ladybird looks quite different when flying. The wing cases stick out at an angle of 45° (to the horizontal) and the membranous wings expand and beat rapidly.

This ability to fold wings in such complicated ways is more remarkable when you consider the role of the wing veins in providing a rigid framework on which the membrane is stretched. The development of the wing is easily seen in newly emerged dragonflies and damselflies. These insects emerge in full view when the nymphs climb out of the water and up a near-vertical surface — water irises, rushes and reeds are excellent for this purpose but even flat lily leaves will be used if there is nothing else. How the nymph knows that the weather up there will be suitable for an emerging adult to dry out, I have no idea. (They must be excellent weather forecasters!)

The nymph case splits down the back and the adult emerges with very crumpled wings. These are then suffused with 'blood' (the body fluid) pumped into them which inflates the wings between the upper and lower membranes. When fully stretched out they are allowed to dry: all this may take an hour or two, during which time the insect is very vulnerable, especially to bird attack.

In some insects air spaces remain between the upper and lower membranes but in others these fuse together. So how does the ladybird fold its wings? I said that this can be seen easily but in the living insect it all happens very quickly. Occasionally when stationary, the ends of the membranous wings stick out at the back, showing that they are longer than the wing cases. However, the wing cases of a dead ladybird (these often occur on windowsills during the winter) can easily be separated and the membranous wings unfolded to see how it's done. (Only freshly dead beetles are suitable – otherwise everything becomes very brittle.) Of course, by far the most easily seen are the wings of large beetles, but these are not found so often.

Top: Damselfly nymph ready to moult. Bottom: Adult damselfy emerging. Note how the wings are folded.

Ladybird in flight showing how the wings unfold.

*A female Common Earwig showing rear pincers used to help when the wings are folded.*

The veins form a major hinge at the point where the hind part of the wing folds under the forepart. But since there are no muscles within the wing, how on earth does the insect initiate and power the folding process? And how does it operate the unfolding process? If there was any spring-loading it would only operate in one direction, yet it is all accomplished faster than you can see it and in exactly the same way every time.

This is a good example of a fascinating problem that anyone can think about and explore, even though, in fact, the detail has been worked out for many years and published. But it is never all known for all species and, in any case, discovering things for yourself is both more fun and more easily remembered. In fact, the best approach to education is first to generate a need or desire to know more and then to read the relevant publications. Reading is then a real search for what you want to know.

So now is the time to reveal that, apparently, the way wings are folded is so ingenious that they automatically open and close when they are used. However, some of the earwigs, which also fold their wings (though most species rarely fly) actually use their rear 'pincers' to help in the folding process: they and the beetles have been called the insect exponents of 'origami' – the Japanese art of paper-folding.

Many insects, such as dragonflies and butterflies, can fly for immense distances during their migrations, but they may spend up to 80 per cent of their time gliding. Not all can do this, however, and it has been estimated that the Large White and the Peacock butterflies only glide for short spells, for about 1 metre. Dragonflies also can glide. Detailed knowledge about wing movements can now be obtained by using high-speed cameras (at 6,000 frames per second) and the film can be slowed down.

Insect flight is not particularly efficient in the use of energy (c.6 per cent and the result is that considerable heat is generated. If this becomes too much, a bee will slow down its wing-beat frequency to compensate.

Bats' wings are built on a basic design, of upper and lower skin membranes stretched over modified legs and reaching to the 'fingers' and 'toes' (page 68). They vary in wing spread according to the species. The space between these flexible, elastic membranes contains connective tissue, small muscles, blood vessels and nerves, as well as the extended, slender bones. As the wings are folded, the skin membranes are 'puckered' by the action of small muscles.

All British bats are insectivorous and will choose flight paths to where flying insects are likely to be found; sometimes this leads to skimming over vegetation or water. Their flight is extremely manoeuvrable, especially when catching insects (sometimes two or three are captured per second). Insects are located by echolocation, using ultrasound, at frequencies of around 100 kHz or more (the limit of young human hearing, pre-rock concert-going days, is 20 kHz). Most bat species are nocturnal, so echolocation is a great advantage, but not all bats are blind – some see quite well.

Speed of flight has to take account of the effectiveness of the echolocation system, which is increased in some species by the possession of specially

Common Pipistrelle bat, in flight.

modified lips and ears. Speeds vary with species and bats can go from 0m/s (when hovering) to 12m/s for the larger species. Echolocation is also used to avoid objects as well as in hunting.

Bats pick insects off in flight but have greater problems in 'cluttered' environments and especially if the prey is actually on the background (for example resting on a leaf or the ground).

Most bats are difficult to identify when flying but there are now readily-available miniature bat detectors which allow identification from their calls (frequency range, continuous or not, nature of clicks etc.).

Here are some interesting questions about flight.

Why do some birds fly in short bursts? For smallish birds (passerines) this seems to be an energy-saving mechanism, alternating flapping with periods where wings are tightly held against the body. The savings in drag by not having the wings out there more than compensates for the extra energy required to pack all the lift and propulsion into the flapping part. This is worth it when wing drag costs are comparatively high, as is the case for small birds. Slightly larger birds, like the woodpeckers, use gliding periods with their wings outstretched. It is less clear why this happens, though similar arguments can be made as for the 'bounding flight' above. This variant, 'flap-gliding' may also represent an energy minimum because a gliding wing generates less drag (and plenty of lift) than a flapping one.

Why do some birds fly in a dipping flight? Perhaps this is an inevitable consequence of the above, or perhaps it is used for signalling mates. It certainly is very characteristic from species to species and is most noticeable in woodpeckers.

What is the relative energy cost of flight? Flight is very expensive in terms of energy/time. However, it is significantly lower than for running. It is also very much faster to get from A to B. In order to maintain flight, an animal needs a high energy food source, or lots of it. Migrating birds store their fuel as fat and metabolised fat has roughly the same energy content as combustion of fossil fuel.

High-flying swifts which are believed to sleep on the wing.

Why do some birds hop or run rather than taking flight? The most expensive part of flight is slow flight – like landing and taking off. It is most likely much cheaper to run or hop if your food source, or mate, is on the ground and only a few hops away.

What is the key to hovering in birds and insects? Small size. As mentioned earlier, the surface/volume scaling laws make flight easier as you get smaller. Most insects can hover (but I doubt that Stag Beetles can), but among birds there are few accomplished hoverers, Hummingbirds are the obvious exception, while warblers, flycatchers and other passerines can do so for short periods. Birds of prey like Kestrels and Barn Owls can also hover, though they require wind assistance to do it.

Why do birds, bats and flying insects not look like planes? Animal wings must combine thrust and lift production, while our aeroplanes have wings for lift only, and separate engines for thrust. Having evolved solutions in flapping flight, it is likely that these are about the same efficiency as propellers. So they don't need to look like planes.

If long wings are more efficient than short ones, why don't all birds have long wings like albatrosses? Bird and bat wings do more than just act as lift providers, and length is limited by requirements to fold them up on the ground, navigate through cluttered environments, and land and take-off. Very long flapping wings may not be very efficient and albatrosses are mostly gliders, flapping very little, and live in a relatively uncluttered environment.

Are birds more efficient than planes? Probably not, but it seems like they are quite comparable. However, we humans may learn something about system integration and control from studying natural flight systems.

Can birds sleep in flight? Swifts are thought never to land, except for nesting. Therefore, they must sleep on the wing. So must birds on long migrations and this raises interesting questions about the function of sleep, and how and when it is required. (One function for us is to keep quiet and out of trouble when our vision doesn't work as well as for nocturnal predators.)

# Plants

Most garden plants, whatever their origins, are residents and none can be regarded as visitors, in the sense that they come and go. However, seeds do arrive from elsewhere, on the wind and on the feet of birds, and are often excreted by fruit-eaters. In the same sense, many insects and other animals may come from outside the garden and take up residence there. Equally, of course, seeds and animals may leave the garden to live elsewhere.

Some people interpret 'residents' much more strictly, as native or indigenous, at least to the country, and object strongly to 'interlopers' such as rhododendrons. On the other hand, there is a very strong tradition of 'plant-hunting' all over the world and many of our most popular garden plants have their origins in other countries.

This debate becomes even less relevant, or rather, is being overtaken by the need to consider what plants will suit the results of climate change (see Chapter 21). A rather separate issue, but one which will also be affected by climate change, is that of 'invasive' species, which may be plants or animals. This is already a big problem and a threat to native wildlife which is extremely costly to control.

Well known examples of voracious weeds that swamp others are Japanese Knotweed (*Fallopia japonica*) – deliberately introduced as an ornamental plant in the 1800s – and New Zealand Pigmyweed (*Crassula helmsii*), which occurs in aquatic environments. More than a dozen plant species are problems in terrestrial environments, including Himalayan Balsam (*Impatiens glandulifera*) and Giant Hogweed (*Heracleum montegazzianum*). Other aquatic invasive plants (more than ten of which are listed as the most damaging) include Parrot's Feather (*Myriophyllum aquaticum*), Floating Pennywort (*Hydrocotyle ranunculoides*) and Water Fern (*Azolla filiculoides*).

Many of these species are defined as 'controlled waste' and must be disposed of properly at registered sites. Prevention of seeding is obviously vital but many species can be spread by quite small plant fragments.

In the sense that they are not deliberately planted, many weeds could be regarded as 'non-resident' to a particular but, whatever their origin, they may rapidly become established. Crop plants, such as oilseed rape, occasionally occur and Ragwort is a regular invader of gardens (it is very poisonous to horses).

*A garden fence completely overrun by Japanese Knotweed.*

# 13 Attracting wildlife

The whole nature of the garden affects how attractive it is to wildlife. In general, the tidier the garden, the less attractive to wildlife and the greater variety within it, the more attractive. Different species of wildlife require different habitats and without a pond, a tree, a hedge, rough grass or dead wood, the species that live in these habitats will obviously not appear.

But within each of these habitats it is possible to create conditions that are more or less attractive to wildlife to visit or reside. These are described for ponds, lakes and bog gardens in Chapter 14 and for grass of all kinds in Chapter 6 but, even for lawns, the way they are maintained can make a big difference. This provides a good illustration of some of the more subtle influences.

For example, what is applied to a lawn, by way of fertiliser or herbicide, may affect the number of earthworms and ants. The numbers of earthworms will greatly influence whether Foxes, Badgers, Blackbirds and Mistle Thrushes find the lawn worth visiting. Of course, not all such visitors are welcome!

By and large, only Badgers are likely to do any damage and then only in dry weather when they may try to dig worms out: otherwise, the worms are simply removed, mostly at night, from the surface. Even the removal of dead tree leaves may reduce the supply of food for earthworms. Ants attract the Green Woodpecker which may only make a few circular holes.

*Keeping patches of grass relatively long encourages a wider range of invertebrate prey for birds like this Robin.*

*Young Hedgehog – a regular visitor to many wildlife gardens.*

Don't get rid of all your dead leaves – they are a perfect place for Earthworms.

Only the birds are likely to be seen in daylight hours, mostly making short runs and stopping to listen, before pouncing on a worm and pulling it out. Blackbirds may be seen stamping their feet to attract worms to the surface (as gulls do on grass, as well as on mud). This is thought to work because the worms think the pattering vibration is raindrops and they prefer to surface when the grass is moist.

Animals will come to your garden if it meets their needs, and these can be divided into (a) their preferred or necessary habitat, which can provide everything they need (food and water, shelter etc.), for relatively small animals and (b) the separate needs of larger species where no (or few – very large) gardens can provide everything. The complexity comes from the fact that needs vary with species, numbers and time of year.

So a garden with no pond can still provide for the needs of amphibians – except at the time of reproduction. A pond (see Chapter 14) can provide everything needed by its inhabitants if they spend their whole lives there, if they are not overcrowded or their enemies are neither too large nor too numerous.

Providing habitats is covered by Chapters 5, 6, 7, 14, dealing with the main garden components, cultivated plants, the lawn, trees and shrubs and areas of water. The number and variety of species attracted to live in the garden all round the year is roughly related to the number of different habitats provided, depending on their size and diversity. Having some trees, for example, will attract those that feed on them or nest in them, but only large (and especially dead) trees will attract woodpeckers to nest in them and only a very large number will supply their needs all round the year.

Most large animals will have ranges well in excess of all but the largest garden: in most gardens they are visitors and often infrequent at that. In general, habitats provide for breeding requirements (Fox and Badger holes, birds' nesting sites) but the second can be augmented by nestboxes of various kinds.

A series of bat boxes attached to a tree.

You can buy or build nestboxes specially designed for owls, tits, Robins and even woodpeckers, Swifts and House Martins, and these species use them fairly readily. Since Grey Squirrels regularly breed in my owl box, presumably they can be provided for too but few people would find that necessary or even desirable. On the other hand, many people would like to attract Dormice and there is a box for them too.

Nestboxes are also made for solitary bees (like the Red Mason Bee – see below) and for bumblebees, though these seem to be less successful.

For some small creatures, rather special habitats may be needed for breeding (e.g. areas of suitable bare soil for some digger wasps, dead wood for powder post beetles) and for hibernation or over-wintering. Bat boxes and hibernation boxes for butterflies and ladybirds can be purchased, but ladybirds and lacewings seem to have no difficulty in finding cracks in window frames and dense hedges in which to spend the winter. Hedgehogs need piles of wood (but not bonfire material!), leaves or compost heaps to hibernate under and dog and cat food can be used (but not cow's milk) to fatten them up for the winter. There are 'houses for hedgehogs' on the market but they are intended for summer use only.

## Nestboxes for the Red Mason Bee

This attractive mason bee, which is not the slightest bit aggressive, will readily nest in specially constructed boxes, filled with horizontally placed tubes, not more than 1cm in diameter. These are usually made of bamboo but can also be of other materials. For example, removable glass tubes can be used to observe what is going on in the cells that the bee makes inside the tube.

I have also constructed an artificial nest out of dried hedge parsley stems, fastened with elastic bands inside a plastic sheet.

I have found that the best sites for the boxes are on south- or south-west-facing walls, at least 75cm from the ground. In the spring (as early as March) the females start delivering balls of mud with which to construct the cells and then pollen with which to stock them. When the tube is filled with cells, a final cap of mud is used to seal off the tube. But the first to appear are the males, which fly agitatedly around last year's nests waiting for the females to emerge, in order to mate with them. The males (6–11mm) are smaller than the females (10–16mm) and have a tuft of white hairs on the front of the head.

They are quite aggressive towards each other and, in their attempts to mate, may appear to be attacking the females, but only live for 3–4 weeks. The nests are vulnerable to parasites (flies, mites and wasps) waiting to enter when the bee is absent but there is one spectacular insect, an ichneumon fly, that uses its long ovipositor to insert its egg through the mud cap.

Purchased nestbox.

Home made nest.

Ichneumon fly on nestbox.

## Plants for insects

### Very early

Lungwort (for bumblebees)

### Early

Polyanthus

Aubretia

Honesty

Sweet rocket

Buddleia

### Later

Lavender

Thyme

Ivy

Petunias

Michaelmas daisy

Tobacco flowers
(for hovering moths at night)

The largest winter provision activity is represented by bird tables and feeders and guidelines are issued for their design (invulnerable to cats and squirrels) and for the kind of food to put out, in what form and in what containers. Birds, and Foxes for that matter, will rapidly get accustomed to regular feeding times, and may only visit the garden at these times.

More frequent visitors can be attracted by growing attractive plants. Plants such as stinging nettles can be used to attract butterflies (Peacocks on nettles (below) and the Garden Tiger moth on dead-nettles and dandelions) to lay their eggs and for the caterpillars to eat. In general, though, gardeners do not particularly want to attract creatures to feed on their plants except for flowers providing pollen and nectar, both of which are mainly collected by flying insects. You can imagine the energy required by a non-flying insect that had to climb up and down each plant! The Table, left, lists some of the early and later plants that attract insects.

Of the wild plants that attract nectar feeders, the umbellifers (such as Hedge and Cow Parsley) are the most easily observed and a wide selection of beetles and hoverflies can readily be seen on their pale, flat flowers. Examples of plants that attract British butterflies are given in the Table, opposite.

*A Peacock butterfly on its favourite foodplant – the nettle.*

Plants can also be grown to attract birds, especially thistles for Goldfinches, but berry-bearing shrubs and fruit of all kinds, particularly if brightly coloured. Cotoneaster is attractive to bees and wasps when in flower and to birds for the fruit. Yew, ivy and holly berries also attract birds, as do hawthorn, spindle and elder. Unfortunately, they are also very fond of currant bushes. Herbaceous plants that provide seeds for birds include Sunflower, evening primroses, poppies and daisy-like flowers.

*Juvenile Sparrows amid Cow Parsley.*

## Plants that attract British butterflies for nectar

Aster

Aubretia

Bluebell

Buddleia

Bugle

Clematis ('traveller's joy')

Dahlia

Golden rod

Honesty

Knapweed

Lavender

Marigold

Michaelmas daisy

Scabious

Thistles

Thyme

## Food plants of common butterflies

| | |
|---|---|
| Bird's-foot Trefoil | Clover |
| Common Bent | Common Sorrel |
| Holly | Honeysuckle |
| Ivy | Lady's Smock |
| Sheep's Sorrel | Smooth Meadowgrass |
| Stinging Nettle | Toadflax |

# 14 Ponds, lakes and bog gardens

Having some kind of fresh water in your garden will increase the variety of wildlife that visit or make their homes there. Birds need water to drink and bathe, amphibians need it to complete their life cycles, and many invertebrates live for some or all of their lives in or under the water.

## Ponds

There are many different sorts of ponds, varying greatly in size and depth, both natural and artificial. The main kinds are dealt with below.

### Water-table ponds

Underneath the soil surface there is a great reservoir of water and its upper edge is called the water-table. Rainfall in excess of evapo-transpiration (i.e. including water evaporated from plant leaves) either runs off via ditches and streams to a river and thence to the sea, or it seeps down between the soil particles to add to the water-table. In some places the water-table is a long way underground but in some places it may be only a metre or so down. Wells source their water from the water-table.

Much of my garden is like this and, in the low-lying parts, the water-table appears above the surface to form a pond. In one case, I have a pond some 30m across and, when full, 1.5m deep. It is usually full for all the winter but may dry out completely in a dry summer.

When it rains heavily, the water level in these areas rises by about 6–8 times the depth of rainfall, because, although there is now a pond, its depth is reflecting the whole underlying water table, most of which is below ground. So the water table goes up and down according to the rainfall, but not in a simple fashion. Clearly, 5cm of rain causes most bodies of water to rise by 5cm but this is not so for the water table, since the rain only has to fill the spaces between the soil particles.

To visualise this more clearly, imagine two glass tanks, one with 6cm of water in it and the other filled to the same height with gravel. Now, enough water is added to the first tank to raise the level by 6cm: the level will rise to 12cm. In the second one, however, if the same amount of water is added, it has to fill the spaces between the gravel and will rise from zero to at least 12cm. So the level has risen in the gravel by twice the rise in the other: the exact height will depend on the size of the pebbles and will be different (less) if soil replaces the gravel (see Chapter 22).

Water table pond: while full in winter (top), the pond dries out over the summer months.

Bulrushes – common on the edge of many ponds.

When my pond is full, it contains many insects and crustaceans – in fact, a fairly typical pond fauna but with some special features. The plants, however, are mainly quite different. The most abundant plant life grows round the edges, typically Yellow Flag iris, bulrushes, reed mace and rushes. Many of these species encroach into the pond, by extensive root and rhizome development and, in shallow ponds, may take over completely. When such ponds dry out, most of them can survive for months in damp soil and many will grow under quite dry conditions, though the only plant that I have found to almost require these conditions is water starwort. These species are thus well-suited to water-table ponds, but that does not mean that they are less at home at permanent pond edges.

However, when a water-table pond dries out completely, the soil may become covered by a luxurious growth of species such as Redshank and Water Pepper which superficially look alike but, in fact, are quite different (see below left).

The fauna, too, have to be able to survive drying out but they do this in two different ways. Firstly, unlike plants, they can move to more suitable conditions. With insects, this is mostly done by flight. Beetles and water-boatmen can simply fly away to another pond. Amphibians are really only present at breeding times, although frogs may hibernate in the mud at the bottom of ponds – even those that dry out – and toads may be found buried in the mud at the bottom of ditches.

For breeding, adult frogs and toads may only stay in the pond for a few days but their tadpoles must remain much longer, usually about two months. Adult newts may stay for a couple of months or more and their 'newtpoles' may be found from April to early October. Newts are therefore not generally found in ponds that dry out in the summer, but frogs and toads have sufficient time in the spring to complete their reproduction. In fact, frogs seem able to anticipate the time of drying out, to the extent that they may spawn at particular water depths or where the water is sufficient to last for the required time.

Water pepper (above) and Redshank compared.

The non-mobile invertebrates have to remain and mostly seem to survive in the mud as eggs or in specially resistant capsules. Indeed, some plants, such as duckweed, do the same. So, if you remove some of the dried or drying mud from the pond edge and place it in a bucket of water, all kinds of little creatures will emerge, the most common being Daphnia and Cyclops, and within a week 'leaves' of duckweed will start floating to the surface.

## Artificial ponds

Ponds used to be made of concrete but small versions are now made in fibre glass and any size can be created with linings of plastic or butyl sheets. Linings are best laid on a bed of sand, to avoid punctures by projecting stones, and are best secured at the edges by slabs, paving stones or earth, which can be planted with small plants, including those that will creep along. One of the advantages of creeping plants is that they can be rooted in deeper soil but cover the thinner areas which, covering the plastic sheet, are very vulnerable to drought.

Since artificial ponds are deliberately constructed for a purpose, their size, shape and depth should reflect that purpose. If a pond is primarily for fish, it has to be big enough for the kind of fish to be kept and should be fairly deep in order to avoid overheating in the summer and excessive icing in the winter. Cold-water fish need a minimum of 60m² of surface area for each 1cm of body length of fish (excluding the tail).

Bottom feeding fish, like Tench (right), prefer a pond with a muddy bottom that will become filled with small creatures, such as water lice and bloodworms. More active, schooling type fish, such as golden orfe, need a greater area which, in any case, helps to keep the water aerated. Of course, flowing water, whether fresh or recycled by a pump, and fountains enormously help with aeration. Siting is important, too. If a pond is sited under trees, leaves will fall in and, as they rot, they use up oxygen and cause problems. This applies to all kinds of tree: non-deciduous trees also drop their leaves, simply not all at once.

Larger ponds will attract water birds, attractive in themselves but less good for the inhabitants of the pond. It is true that wires can be stretched across the water, to discourage ducks and Grey Herons, but they are not themselves very attractive. Ponds for wildlife other than birds are better relatively small – after all, there is a limit to how far away you can actually see small creatures – and more creatures will be present without fish (with the exception of sticklebacks and Minnows).

Some ponds are mainly to grow attractive plants, such as water lilies and irises, bulrushes, reed mace, rushes and Amphibious Bistort. These are very good for small creatures but less so for actually seeing them. Some creatures actually benefit from water lily leaves to rest on and some, such as the China-mark Moth, need them to rear their larvae (below right). Aquatic plants are, in any event, essential for their aerating qualities, as food for some creatures, protection and nest sites for others.

Tench seek out food in the mud at the base of a pond.

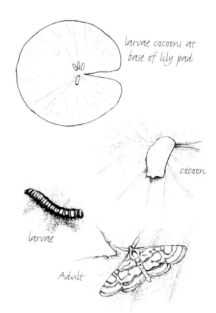

larvae cocoons at base of lily pad

cocoon

larvae

Adult

China-mark Moth larvae form cocoons on the base of lily pads.

A Coot on a water lily pad showing its uniquely adapted feet.

Blackbird taking a bath.

If the idea is to use the pond to show others what lives there, the construction has to take account of the age, capacity and number of those involved. Children like to get their faces close to the water; old people may find this more difficult. Children also enjoy catching and handling creatures and these needs can be catered for, to some extent, in the construction of the pond. I have been showing primary school children round my garden for 17 years and have built a pond specially for them (see Chapter 22).

Finally, any pond should be constructed and sited with safety in mind. Small children can drown in remarkably shallow water and thought needs to be given to ensure that this cannot happen.

## Inhabitants

Only very small invertebrates and fish live their whole lives in the water, though the Water Vole spends quite a lot of time in it. Many more visit the water, to drink, bathe or breed. Those coming to drink include a few of the mammals (such as deer and Hedgehogs) but many species of birds. Only the latter seem to deliberately bathe, as long as there is a sufficiently shallow area in which they can stand whilst they use their wings to fling water over their backs. Blackbirds (centre left) seem to do this most frequently (at least in my ponds).

Ducks spend a lot of time on the water, feeding, bathing and mating, but tend to nest on land (or, in some species including the Mandarin duck, in hollow trees). Although the Mandarin duck only nests in trees, Mallards occasionally nest in hollows in trees or even on top of clematis-covered pergolas. Mallards may take 1hr 20 min to lay an egg but tend not to hang about near the nest afterwards. Incidentally, when the eggs of these ducks hatch, the ducklings simply jump down from the nest (up to 2m). Their light weight and large surface area makes this a perfectly safe operation (just as mice and beetles can drop safely from considerable heights).

Coots (top left) and Moorhens also spend much time on the water, mainly feeding on weed but also grass and other vegetation on land. They consume invertebrates to some extent (Coots about 10 per cent and Moorhens about 20 per cent of their diet), though the newly hatched chicks eat more of these. Both species usually build a substantial nest in clumps of rushes or water iris, or on overhanging branches that trail in the water.

A few other birds feed on fish and amphibians. The Grey Heron needs easy access to water of appropriate depth for it to wade but usually visits gardens only occasionally, unless they are very large with good supplies of fish. The Kingfisher uses the water for diving to catch fish but is generally confined to rivers deep enough for this purpose. Around the water but not actually in it, Pied (top, opposite) and Grey Wagtails hunt insects.

Mother Mallard with ducklings at her nest.

All the amphibians (see Chapter 11), by definition, spend some time in the water, mainly for breeding, but one reptile, the Grass Snake (below), is a good swimmer and in warm weather will hunt prey even in relatively small ponds.

Wild fish only occur in substantial bodies of water (lakes and rivers) but the Three-spined Stickleback can be found in quite small streams. It is a small (5–7cm), brownish attractive fish, with fascinating breeding behaviour. The male has a bright red 'chest' in the breeding season (spring) and builds a barrel-shaped nest, 2–3cm long, made of small bits of weed (see page 168). It then persuades females to enter and lay their eggs within. A nest may contain from 300 to 1,000 eggs. The male guards the nest and eggs and keeps the latter aerated by using its fins and tail to fan a stream of water through the nest. The young hatch in 5–27 days, depending on the temperature, and are protected by the male for the first week or so.

Sticklebacks have rather small mouths and so live on some of the smallest inhabitants of the pond, water fleas (*Daphnia*) and Cyclops (pages 41). These are easily distinguished by their jerky movements and from one another by the positioning of the eggs that they carry. Other very small inhabitants include pea mussels, freshwater limpets, freshwater shrimps and planaria, but these are very difficult to see, unless in an aquarium (see Chapter 22).

Among the larger full-time pond dwellers are the aquatic snails. The Pond Snail is grey with wedge-shaped 'feelers' and its shell turns quite pale as it ages. It can grow to several centimetres in length but this depends, apparently, on the volume of water it is kept in (and not, it seems, the food supply). Pond Snails lay their eggs in a ribbon or tube of jelly on almost any surface, from the glass side of an aquarium to the undersides of lily leaves. These snails are generally described as herbivorous but they are really omnivores and will eat dead animals, including insects that have fallen into the water (except for the wings!).

A Pied Wagtail prospecting at the water's edge.

A Great Pond Snail feeding at the surface of a pond.

Grass Snake swimming.

Whirligig beetles.

The other large snail is the Ramshorn or Planorbis, which is deep red in colour (both body and shell) and has thin 'feelers'. The red colour comes from haemoglobin (as in our own blood) and enables it to thrive in relatively stagnant water. Interestingly, water fleas in stagnant water, such as a rain butt, will often develop a pinkish tinge, for the same reason.

The smaller creatures that are most readily seen are the surface dwellers, the commonest being the pond skaters, whose specially constructed feet rest on, and slightly depress, the surface film (see page 70) and the whirligig beetles (top left), which skim rapidly on the surface, often in circles.

Others come to the surface to breathe, taking a bubble back down with them. The easiest to observe are the larger water boatmen (centre left), or 'back-swimmers', so-called because they spend most of their time upside down. This is because they feed on creatures that have fallen into the water, usually trapped by surface tension, and stab them with their piercing mouth parts from below. Other boatmen are smaller, herbivorous and swim the right way up. It turns out that water boatmen can use their air bubbles as a 'buoyancy vest' to regulate their depth.

The few spiders that live in the water also surface to collect air. However, one of the most common aquatic spiders is the misleadingly named Raft Spider (bottom left), which is called the 'fisher spider' in the US. It runs on the surface to catch its prey, usually from a lily leaf, with one foot resting on the water to detect vibrations.

Water beetles also surface to trap air at their tails or under their wings: the three most common are the Great Diving Beetle, which may be over 3.5cm long (below), the smaller Furrowed Acilius (16mm) and the Common British Water Beetle. The larvae of these beetles are aquatic and may take a year to mature: they then pupate, often at the side of the pond. The larva of the Great Diving Beetle, like the adult, is a fearsome predator that is capable of attacking (and killing and consuming) prey as large as newts and small fishes.

A Water Boatman.

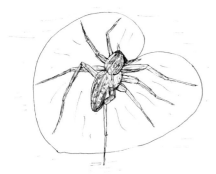
A Raft spider on a small lily leaf.

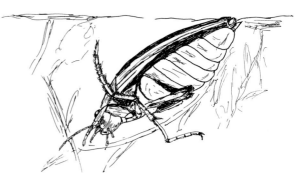
A Great Diving Beetle taking on air.

Bottom-dwellers are more difficult to see, though water lice are big enough (5–10mm) and active enough to be seen wandering over the mud. Bloodworms (tubifex) are also bottom-dwellers. They are often numerous, and feed on mud, spending most of their time with their heads in the mud and their tails waving about above them. These worms have bright red blood, reach 3–4cm in length and provide food for many fish.

Often on the bottom but rather more among the weeds are the larvae of caddisflies. These construct tubular cases of small stones, shells, weed fragments and small sticks and only their heads and legs poke out at the front (see top right) to pull them along. Even these can be withdrawn right inside, so the larvae are well protected. At their rear ends they are hooked to the case, so they are very difficult to remove. The cases are added to as the larvae grow and may reach 2.5cm in length.

Then there are the active swimmers such as the mayfly nymphs (centre right), beetle larvae and nymphs of dragonflies and damselflies (below). These are voracious carnivores and spend 2–3 years growing in the water before climbing up the stems and leaves of emergent vegetation when fully mature. This process can be easily observed as it takes some hours. The life cycles of these fascinating insects are detailed in Chapter 9.

All mosquitoes also have aquatic larval stages: their floating rafts of eggs seem to be unwettable and the emergent larvae (and pupae) wriggle up and down, sometimes resting at the surface (bottom right).

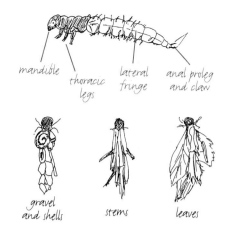

mandible
thoracic legs
lateral fringe
anal proleg and claw

gravel and shells
stems
leaves

Caddisfly larvae (top) and (bottom) larva cases.

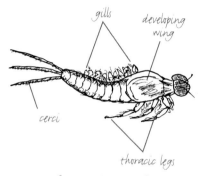

gills
developing wing
cerci
thoracic legs

Structure of a Mayfly nymph.

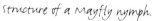
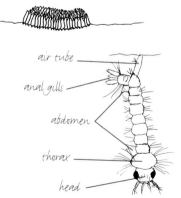

Eggs on water surface

air tube
anal gills
abdomen
thorax
head

Mosquito eggs and larva.

A Damselfly nymph showing its feathery gills – not a tail – which it uses to breathe.

One of the strangest larvae are those of the Phantom Midge (also known as the 'ghost' or 'glass larvae'). The midge itself is about 6mm long and is said not to feed at all. Fully grown larvae are 13–15mm long and hang motionless in the water, every now and then giving a sudden flick and reappearing a short distance away. They are transparent apart from the black eyes and quite difficult to see until you have 'got your eye in'. They are active even at low temperatures and spend the winter as larvae, feeding on small insects and crustaceans.

## Aquatic plants

As on land, plants are the basis of much pond life, although quite a few pond animals feed on the plants and animals that fall into the pond. Dead and decaying material is broken down ultimately by bacteria, releasing nutrients to the water. Green plants provide food for many organisms and support and shelter for even more, including sites for egg laying.

A major function of green plants is photosynthesis combined with the absorption of carbon dioxide and the release of oxygen, bubbles of which can be seen streaming upwards in warm sunshine (see below). But this only happens during the day and a pond can become quite short of oxygen during the night – another good reason why there is less animal life in the pond during the winter, when the days are shorter.

Several sorts of plants live in the pond. At the edges there are bog plants. In the pond itself there are both floating (see Table, top left) and submerged plants. Some of the floating plants are rooted in the mud, such as water lilies, whilst others float freely, such as the duckweeds (see page 223). The main rooted plants are listed in the Table on page 223. These species (including the water lilies) have preferred depths of water to grow in and many produce attractive flowers when they reach the surface.

### Floating plants

| | |
|---|---|
| Stonewort | Willow Moss |
| Water-milfoils | Water Starwort |
| Water Violet | Canadian Waterweed |

*Pondweed releasing oxygen bubbles during photosynthesis.*

Amphibious Bistort is one of these rooted but floating plants but has the added distinction of producing quite different sets of leaves, some of which only grow submerged, while others float and others grow up into the air. Like Yellow Flag and Loddon Lily, it will also grow well on dry land, when it looks quite different.

Totally submerged plants may still project their flowers above water. These plants tend to be rather limp and weak, since they do not have to support themselves – the water does this – and they have no stomata. Gaseous exchange takes place all over the plant surface.

Finally, there are the algae, many of which are microscopic (and may be very beautiful under the microscope) and form the food of many other creatures, including the tiny crustaceans like Daphnia and Cyclops. Unfortunately for the gardener, the green filamentous algae include such nuisances as blanket-weed, which can form masses of dense, often rather slimy greenstuff, entangling other aquatic plants. Although it is generally unwelcome, it does protect, for example, newt eggs and baby newts.

For aesthetic reasons, blanket-weed has to be removed, which is quite difficult without damaging other rooted plants. Sometimes a net works (where the algae is floating) and sometimes a rake will remove it from well-rooted weed, but probably the most generally-effective method is to take a stick with projections (e.g. small nails) and wind the blanket-weed round it. Cleaning it off the stick may be the next problem: sometimes tapping it sharply on the top of a fence post works well.

It has been found that rotting barley straw checks the growth of algae and quite a small amount will do (e.g. 10g per m³ of water, although more – 20–50g – is recommended). However, it takes at least a month to work and then increases in effect for about six months.

Fungi and bacteria also occur in water, but are not usually noticeable.

### Rooted plants

Water Horsetail

Water crowfoots

White Waterlily

Yellow Waterlily or 'brandy-bottle'

Mare's-tails

Amphibious Bistort

Fringed Waterlily

Water-plantains

Arrowheads

Broad-leaved Pondweed

A Common Frog on a waterlily pad in the midst of a sea of duckweed.

*A Great Crested Grebe on its floating nest.*

## Lakes and streams

It is perhaps not very logical to group these together, since the water is static in the one (apart from currents and waves in very large lakes) and moving in the other. However, in the main, it is only very large gardens that have either, and, for that matter, rivers. The latter combines the larger water volume of lakes and the movement characteristic of streams.

The plants and animals of lakes overlap with those of ponds, with the exception of water birds. Ducks, geese, Moorhens, grebes, Coots and even Mute Swans can find homes on lakes, nesting on the bank (ducks and Mute Swans), on reeds and trailing branches (Coots and Moorhens), on floating masses of weed (grebes). Reedbeds may support still more birds, such as warblers, but these do not normally find enough suitable habitat around garden ponds. Birds of rivers may have some additional species, such as Kingfishes and Dippers but large rivers have similar populations to those of lakes.

The most obvious of the vertebrates are the fish, the species varying with the size of the body of water and the locality. Mammals are not so common and even the Water Vole, which is more of a 'garden'-sized mammal than most, is now quite rare. The invertebrates include all those found in ponds, except that fast-flowing water has a much more specialised fauna because they have to be able to hang on to the underlying rocks or weed.

*The introduced signal Crayfish.*

Many, like the caddisflies (see page 221), have species whose larvae are adapted to streams, with structures that enable them to hang on to the stream bed. Some do this by spinning a web over the surface of a rock and then hooking on to it. Others stay close to the banks and, amidst reed beds, most of the aquatic organisms can thrive.

By contrast, lakes also contain organisms that thrive in deep (dark) water or in thick mud at the bottom. Some much larger species occur, including mussels and the White-clawed Crayfish – the largest native British freshwater invertebrate, although it is outsized by the introduced Signal Crayfish (above).

The plants of the lake and river's edge are similar to those that are found near ponds and in boggy areas: reeds, rushes, Yellow Flag, sedges, Marsh Marigold and horsetails. Floating plants vary according to the speed of flow of the water and are scarce in fast-flowing steams.

# Bog gardens

Bog gardens simply have to have wet or damp soil that never dries out. Some occur naturally, where the water-table is high or the soil waterlogged, but they can easily be constructed by placing a plastic sheet in a hollow and filling it with soil that can then be liberally watered. Sometimes such an area can serve as an overflow area for a pond, a stream or even a drainpipe.

Characteristic plants of the bog garden are grasses, sedges and rushes, the most prominent of which are the Common Bulrush, the Common Club-rush and the Common Reed, all of which bud from rhizomes to form dense beds of vegetation. These form protection for many small creatures, including amphibians. Amongst the most attractive are the Yellow Flag iris and the Marsh Marigold or 'kingcup' (right). A more complete list is given in the Table, right.

*Marsh Marigold.*

# 15 Enemies and friends of the gardener

It is said that the average garden may contain as many as 2,000 animal species, most of which have no real effect on garden plants or are beneficial. However, most gardeners tend to see this issue in black and white terms: organisms are either friends or enemies and the former are more interesting.

Biologically speaking, this is not always the case and, whether they are friends or enemies, it pays to know how garden animals function – what they eat, who eats them, what kind of habitat they require (light or dark, dry or humid), how they reproduce and how long they live. The issue is usually seen in terms of animals: wild plants are not really thought of as friends, although they can be on your side in what you are trying to do (this is discussed first in Chapters 5 and 10). Plants as enemies are usually thought of as weeds (see Chapter 6). So, here, we will first consider animals that help or hinder what we are trying to do.

## Enemies of the gardener

Since gardening is mainly about growing plants, the gardener's main enemies are those that destroy those plants – their seeds, their vegetation, their flowers or their fruit.

Seeds are cleverly designed to survive until conditions are right for germination – in the case of ash, 18 months. They usually have tough coats, even able to survive passage through the digestive tract of a bird – indeed, some require this before they will germinate. In addition, they are often produced in vast numbers: examples of wild plants illustrate this very well (see page 103).

However, most gardeners buy their seeds in packets rather than collecting them from their parent plant, so the enemies of concern are mainly those that eat or damage the seeds after sowing. In the case of small seeds, this could include many herbivorous or omnivorous soil-dwelling invertebrates, such as earthworms, slugs and millipedes. With larger seeds, such as those of peas and beans, the enemies include Wood Mice, voles and pigeons.

Somewhat akin to large seeds in this regard are seed potatoes and other tubers. Slugs are the main culprits, although a potato intended to grow into a plant does not necessarily require all the starch reserves provided, as long as its buds ('eyes') are not damaged. It is a different matter for the potato crop, where any damage is undesirable.

*Weeds – adaptable and opportunistic – but not always welcome in the garden.*

## Snails and slugs

There are many species of both snails and slugs to be found in gardens (about 20 snails and 12 slugs); none of them are popular with gardeners simply because of the damage done by a few of them. Most, in fact, are harmless or even beneficial in some way, so it is important to be able to distinguish the 'enemies'. They are described below.

### Snails

1. The Garden Snail is the commonest and the largest (about 3.5cm). It mainly damages low-growing vegetation and such fruits as strawberries.

2. Banded snails (page 296) are smaller (about 2cm), with attractively colour marked shells. They feed mainly on grass but also on tender plants, such as lettuces.

3. The Strawberry Snail (1–5cm) is the least desirable, particularly fond of strawberries and seedlings. The body is grey but the shell is usually reddish-brown.

### Slugs

There are some subterranean slugs that damage root crops and potatoes. Otherwise the two most damaging are as follows:

1. The Netted Slug is small and fawn-white and is one of the few slugs to eat green leaves. It is the commonest and most damaging slug although most prefer decaying vegetation: in tidy gardens, it is forced to eat live plants. Some are carnivorous.

2. The Garden Slug is the most destructive. It is small, smooth, dark brown, grey or black but has a yellow or orange sole. It feeds on seedlings, strawberries, lettuces, low-growing crops and potato tubers.

3. The Great Grey Slug feeds on fungi.

4. The Large Black Slug, though it eats anything, is rarely damaging in the garden.

There is actually one carnivorous slug. It is easily distinguished by the fact that it has a small remnant of a shell, carried on the upper surface at the rear (below).

A carnivorous slug showing its shell remnant.

# Vegetation

The larger herbivores (such as Rabbit and deer) are the most damaging, especially if they are able to reach precious cultivated plants. Voles and mice usually operate in long grass or wilder areas but, like pigeons, can be very damaging amongst seedlings.

Moles are usually disliked because of 'unsightly' molehills, which is how the Mole disposes of the earth from its tunnels – these could displace sown seeds. If the 'hill' is removed, it is not replaced, but new 'hills' arise as more tunnels are formed. However, the Mole destroys many subterranean insect pests, as well as vast numbers of earthworms.

Invertebrate damage is dominated by slugs, snails (see Box left) and caterpillars, all of which can cause problems. Snails can climb quite high in bushes but slugs are usually found lower down. Of course, in a sense, they are not 'usually found' at all, since they are nocturnal and some species hide in the soil.

Though they are endearing, a persistent Mole can devastate a lawn.

Caterpillars may be of butterflies or moths, and sawfly larvae also eat vegetation (and look very caterpillar-like). They may be camouflaged or hidden under webs, sometimes holding folded leaves together. Minor damage may be done by leaf-cutter bees and some gall wasps (see Box, page 65) but some of the worst pests are not leaf-eaters but sap-suckers. These are dominated by the aphids of various species, most noticeable as greenfly on roses (and many other plants) and blackfly on beans. These insects are protected by ants which 'milk' them for their sugary secretions.

A different kind of damage is done by leaf miners, such as caterpillars of the moth *Stigmella aurella* on blackberry leaves, and on lilacs the caterpillar of the moth *Caloptilia syringella*. More recently, the Horse Chestnut Leaf-miner has been causing serious damage. Generally, tunnels are made between the two surfaces of leaf (in between the two epidermal layers) and show up as pale wiggly lines (below). Sometimes these merge or are found as blotches with several caterpillars operating as a group, as in hazel leaves damaged by caterpillars of the moth *Phyllonorycter coryli*.

Leaves are also susceptible to damage by fungi (see Chapter 9), occurring as dark spots or blotches. Very often insects transmit the fungus (as they do viruses) by feeding. For example, Blackleg or *Phoma lingam* on cabbages is transmitted by the larvae of the Cabbage Root Fly (top right).

The larva of the Cabbage Root Fly.

Tunnels caused by the actions of leaf miners on a Burdock leaf.

# Weeds and poisonous plants

Weeds are often defined as plants out of place (or in the wrong place) but this only means that they are not what the gardener wants in a particular place. One cannot therefore talk about weed species because a plant you may not want in a bed of roses may be deliberately encouraged elsewhere.

Meadow flowering plants are good examples of wild flowers that are perhaps only wanted in meadows (see Chapter 6). Conversely, Perennial Ryegrass – a major component of agricultural grasslands – is regarded as a major weed of a wildflower meadow. The Table left gives a list of species that are generally regarded as garden weeds.

Nor are weeds only wild plants: cultivated plants can also be in the wrong place. Indeed, most species are only wanted in particular parts of the garden. Honeysuckle would be unwelcome in a rose bed and tall plants like hollyhocks and Foxgloves are never wanted in the front of a flower-bed even when they are wanted at the back. One of our favourite spring flowers, the Bluebell, is a weed in my gravel drive, where it thrives, but would take over all of it if not controlled.

So why discuss 'weeds' at all? Well, most gardeners are very concerned about them and spend a lot of time and effort getting rid of them. Then there is the related concern about methods: should we be using such large amounts of weed-killers? What are the effects on wild animals, of all sizes, that eat the weeds: will they be poisoned or simply deprived of food?

It can be argued that there is no need for noxious chemicals, that weeding by hand and hoe can always be used and we simply use weed-killers to save time and labour. However, there are many plants that are not easily removed in this way. It is quite hard to remove all the roots of, for example, Blackberry and Periwinkle, even by digging, and quite often a small amount of root will regenerate whole plants quite rapidly.

*Wild blackberries are a mixed blessing: their fruits are delicious but their rampant growth and thick roots can be a problem if they become established in the garden.*

*The highly efficient Creeping Thistle.*

*Dandelion clock releasing its seeds.*

If we wanted to nominate a plant that no-one wants at all, anywhere, most people would choose Ground Elder. It does not seem to suffer noticeably from pests and diseases, though I have seen Rabbits eating it when other plants were available. Another group that most find troublesome are the thistles. These are often beautiful in flower but difficult to get rid of if allowed to seed. Perhaps the worst is the Creeping Thistle (above) which will regrow from any part of its root. It is very important to prevent thistles setting seed. So, sometimes, weed-killers have to be used to clear an area which can be hand weeded subsequently.

Although weeds are a nuisance to the gardener, they are quite interesting plants in themselves. Take one of the commonest of them – the Dandelion. Did you know that the seedhead (the 'clock' children blow away) only releases its seeds when the air is relatively dry and will not do so in humid conditions? Have you ever wondered how the seed manages to detach its 'parachute' when it has landed? (As all parachutists have to do!)

Here's another example. The common Stinging Nettle (below right) is probably one of the most disliked weeds, partly because of the painful stings it can inflict by simply brushing against bare flesh (or even through light fabrics) and partly because of the difficulty in getting rid of it. It spreads by seeds and by underground rhizomes. It is said to require relatively fertile soils but is common on wasteland and rubbish sites. However, nettles contain fibres that can be used to make cloth, rope and paper: the processed fibre can be used for spinning. They are also used as a green vegetable when very young.

There are two forms of hair (or trichome) on nettles, made of silica: shorter ones trap insects (as a protection against those that would eat the foliage) and the longer ones contain toxic materials and deliver the sting. The tips of these hollow hairs break off on contact and release such chemicals as acetycholine, histamine and serotonin.

One could fill a book with the fascinating detail involved in the structure and life-cycle of these 'useless' plants we call weeds!

*Hairs on the stem of a Stinging Nettle.*

## Skin irritants, eye irritants and poisons

Some plants and fungi come into more than one category. In some cases only certain parts are harmful.

| Plant/fungus | Poisonous part |
| --- | --- |
| Lupins | All, especially seeds, except for sweet lupin |
| Daffodil | Bulbs |
| Yellow Flag | Leaves and rhizomes |
| Hellebores | All parts |
| Marsh Marigold | Sap |
| Aquilegia | Possibly all |
| Foxglove | All parts |
| Lords-and-ladies | All, especially berries |
| Tobacco | Leaves |
| **Herbs** | |
| Buttercups | Sap |
| Lily-of-the-valley | All parts |
| Celandine | Sap |
| Bluebell | Bulbs |
| St. John's Wort | Leaves and flowers |
| Rhubarb | Leaves |
| Ragwort | All parts |
| Yellow Vetchling | All, especially seeds |
| Tomato | Stem and leaves |
| **Climbers** | |
| Ivy | Leaves and berries |
| White Bryony | Roots and berries |
| Black Bryony | Roots and berries |
| **Fungi** | |
| Boletus | Not certain |
| Agaric | Not certain |
| Ink Cap | Not certain |
| **Horsetails** | |
| *Equisetum* spp. | Probably all parts |
| **Ferns** | |
| Bracken | Especially the rhizome |
| **Shrubs** | |
| Broom | Seeds |
| Mistletoe | Berries |
| Rhododendron | Leaves and flowers |
| Privet | Berries and possibly leaves |
| **Trees** | |
| Holly | Berries |
| Yew | Leaves and seeds |
| Laburnum | All, but especially bark and seeds |
| Oak | Leaves and acorns |
| Beech | Nuts |

# Poisonous plants

Children, particularly, need to be aware of the possible harmful effects of handling plants but especially eating any parts of them. Obviously, plants normally grown for food are safe to eat, though they may need to be cooked. (The fungi are dealt with separately, in Chapter 8.)

What are known as 'contact hazards' may take one of three forms: a) irritant sap; b) allergens to which only some people are susceptible; and c) sap that renders the skin excessively sensitive to strong sunlight. Anyone affected should be taken to the nearest hospital A&E Department, with a sample of the plant concerned. Although most garden plants are perfectly safe, the list of harmful plants is quite long (examples are listed left).

## Why are some plants poisonous?

The most obvious answer is that it is to protect themselves from animals that would otherwise eat them. Poisonous leaves will prevent them being eaten, especially if they taste unpleasant, and poisonous seeds or fruits will allow more to survive and produce more plants. Of course, animals may evolve to cope with this. Some are simply unaffected by the poison and some (for example certain caterpillars) actually make use of the poison in the plants they eat to protect themselves. Many of the compounds that plants use to protect themselves are now used by us either as medicines (see Chapter 16) or industrially.

An interesting example of the latter are saponins, which are used to make soap. The Soapwort, a riverside plant with pink flowers, is only one of hundreds of soapy plants. It used to be cultivated by wool mills and the leaves boiled to produce a soapy lather for washing the wool. To the plant, however, the saponins provide protection against fungal attack: this it achieves, apparently, by combining them with the sterols in the fungal membranes (of the hyphae – see Chapter 8).

When plants (such as tomato plants) are attacked, say by caterpillars, they send a signal to the as yet undamaged parts which initiates the defensive mobilisation of chemicals (such as protein inhibitors) to protect them. This may take up to an hour and may not kill the caterpillars but severely affects their growth and development. Damaged plants may also produce salicylic acid to act as an antiseptic at the wound sites. This may explain why aspirin (salicylic acid) is often added to the water of cut flowers.

One of the interesting findings from research into such processes is the discovery that similar reactions occur in both plants and animals, leading to the recognition that much of the chemistry of different organisms is shared.

It is worth remembering that whether something is poisonous or not depends on the amount taken. Paracelsus (1493–1541) famously pointed out that: "Poison is in everything, and no thing is without poison. The dosage makes it either a poison or a remedy."

## Pests of the gardener

The main pests of the gardener are biting flies – horseflies, mosquitoes, gnats and midges. They can occur in large numbers and they sneak up on you, attracted by scents (some hair colouring has been known to draw them in), human odours, carbon dioxide and heat. Some of them can bite through clothing and most are chiefly active at night or at dusk. They are worse under trees and in low wind. It is mostly by homing in on exhaled carbon dioxide that mosquitoes locate you!

These are all flies: they bite or pierce, they do not sting. The main stinging insects are bees, wasps and Hornets – in order of increasing aggression. Honey-bees and bumblebees rarely sting unless attacked or disturbed, especially at their nests. Wasps also defend their nests but may also sting when disturbed at their feed (or your picnic!). They seem readier to sting than bees, since their stings are re-usable, whereas bee stings pull out when used and the bee is fatally injured (see Box, right).

Hornets, in my experience, are by far the most aggressive and will attack without provocation: their sting is also much more severe. Solitary wasps and bees are much smaller and not aggressive but may sting if handled. However, the sting is rather weak and does not penetrate the skin very easily. The only dangerous vertebrate is the Adder and this only when accidentally trodden on or otherwise violently disturbed. It is the only large animal in this country that is venomous.

## Pests of plants

Most garden pests are invertebrates that attack plants, either directly or by transmitting a viral disease. The smallest are largely unseen: they are eelworms (roundworms or nematodes) that burrow into the plant tissue. They survive as spherical cysts in the soil and are spread by mechanical movement of that soil. The potato eelworm is the most serious.

The next group are the 'true bugs' – insects of the order Hemiptera, all of which have sucking mouthparts with which they suck the sap from roots, leaves or stems. Well-known as 'greenfly' or 'blackfly', the aphids are the most widespread and damaging, but others include the whiteflies (on cabbage), the leafhoppers (e.g. on potatoes) and the froghoppers (below) (hidden in a frothy exudation – 'cuckoo spit'). The froghoppper species are usually not of major importance as garden pests.

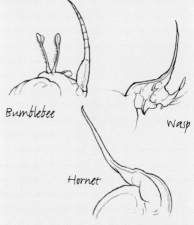
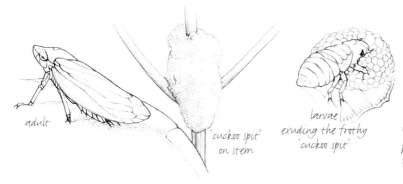

Froghopper adult and the larva that produces 'cuckoo spit' to protect and hide itself while developing into an adult.

Green Rose Aphids are a problem on many other plants.

Aphids, on the other hand, are a major problem, in themselves and as spreaders of viral disease. It was the latter that caused poor growth in potatoes grown for more than one season on the same land, a problem solved by growing seed potatoes in Scotland – where aphids are far less common. The best known aphids are the green Rose Aphid (which may also attack a great many other plants, such as cabbage and peas) and the Black Bean Aphid or 'blackfly' on beans. Lettuce is attacked by aphids on both the leaves and the root. Some bugs, however, such as the shieldbugs, do little harm, in spite of the fact that they can be quite big (about 1cm in length).

The butterfly that gives rise to the most serious infestations of caterpillars is the Large White, mainly on cabbages, cauliflowers and broccoli, but there is also a Cabbage Moth, whose caterpillars eat at the heart of the cabbage. The Pea Moth caterpillars are equally destructive of peas: they hibernate as cocoons in the soil.

Many beetles are carnivorous and thus helpful, such as the Ladybird and the ground beetles, but others (including the Pea Weevil and the Bean Weevil) damage vegetable crops, making the little round holes you see in broad and field beans. Peas and beans are also affected by weevils, which eat neat sections out of the edge of the leaves. The larvae of click beetles are the 'wireworms' that live on the roots of grasses. Another annoying beetle, the asparagus beetle, strips the foliage off the plant.

The craneflies or 'daddy-long-legs' produce larvae known as 'leatherjackets', which are well-known pests of grassland. A fly which is very specific to celery and parsnips but is most damaging to the former is the Celery Fly, the larvae mining the leaves.

Finally, we come to slugs, which hardly anyone likes, and snails, which few like but are not found as repulsive by most people. Slugs are widely thought to be very damaging and whilst some species can be so, especially to seedlings and tender young plants, few species are in this category (see page 228). Some species are actually carnivorous, others feed on fungi and many live on dead or decaying vegetation.

The most damaging ones are the Grey Field Slug and the Garden Slug. All slugs are more prevalent in wet conditions and more active in wet, warm weather. They feed mainly at night and hide away in dark damp areas during the day. They may therefore be found under almost any cover, especially an upturned tray or bucket. They like manure and will lay their eggs in it. Hedgehogs prey on them but they appear to be too slimy for most tastes. Frogs and toads eat them and can be seen wiping the slime off their mouths with rather clumsy movements of their front feet.

Snails have similar habits to those of slugs but their shells somewhat limit their access to hiding places and help to prevent desiccation. Snails will gather under upturned trays and buckets, however, if there is enough space for them to crawl under the edges. The most damaging snails are the largest (Garden Snail) but even these feed mostly on grass and weeds. Shrews often feed on snails.

We began this brief survey of plant pests with eelworms and it is fitting to end with them, simply because there is probably no plant without them and their numbers are vast.

It has been said that if all life was killed off except for the eelworms, we would be left with a shadow world in which eelworms traced out all the plant forms with their bodies!

## Diseases in the garden

Diseases can be caused by infections (by bacteria, fungi, viruses), infestations (by parasitic worms) or by nutritional imbalances. They occur in both plants and animals, both of which have defence mechanisms (immune systems) and physical barriers to the entrance of infectious organisms. Animal skin, often covered in fur, hair or feathers, acts as a barrier, as does the epidermis of plants, which are often covered in a waxy cuticle which is resistant to water and enzymes.

So pathogens enter through existing apertures (plant stomata, animal air and food intakes) or damaged tissue (wounds). Plants then mobilise tissues, such as lignin, cork, gum or resinous layers, and a group of proteins, called lectins, that may attach themselves to viruses and bacteria.

All kinds of pathogens may attack garden plants but some may also be used more helpfully in biological control. Many more are involved, unseen, in the control of garden pests: others are responsible for the reduction in the numbers of wild animals, such as the recent outbreak of a fungal disease in the Common Frog.

However, two species of fungi are effective at controlling Varroa mites on Honey-bees. The effect of these mites has been devastating to the UK's Honey-bee colonies. It has been said that, without pollination by Honey-bees, there would be no onions, carrots, water-melons, apples or strawberries, quite apart from the effects on wild plants.

The most important mite (*Varroa destructor*) feeds on the bees' haemolymph, causing weight loss, malformation and shortened life span: bee mortality can reach 100 per cent and colonies can perish within a few weeks. The fungus is not only effective but persistent and can be carried by bees between hives. So, pathogens, like all other organisms, may be good or bad, depending on the species and its target.

*Though snails chew holes in leaves, they rarely cause wholesale damage to plants.*

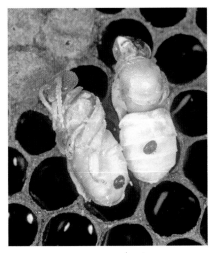

*Varroa mites on Honey-bee larvae.*

*Ichneumon fly showing its ovipositor in operation. They may parasitise the larvae of solitary bees.*

## Parasites and predators

Both live on other living things but 'predators' is a term used only for animals that kill and eat other animals. There are insectivorous plants, such as sundews, with sticky hairs that bend over to trap insects, which are then digested, but these are not described as predators.

Not very logical, you might think, since not all animal predators actively hunt their prey but lie in wait – the so-called 'ambush' predators (frogs and toads do this at least part of the time).

Parasites may be internal or external, animal or plant, and live on their hosts, usually without killing them. Those that always do kill their hosts are called 'parasitoids', but parasites such as the intestinal roundworms that infect most mammals may result in the death of the host if they become numerous enough.

However, also rather illogically, lice and fleas that live on the outside of animals are classed as external parasites (or 'ectoparasites') whereas aphids that live on the outside of plants (and also suck out their internal fluids) are not called parasites, but pests! Nor is it the case that, whilst aphids move to other hosts at times, animal parasites do not. Even internal animal parasites ('endoparasites') may spend part of their lives in other species.

All the important predators and parasites are described in other chapters, where they are most relevant. Whether they are friends or enemies of the gardener depends, not on whether they are predators or parasites but on what they eat. If predators prey on pests they are friends, if they prey on creatures that are beneficial in one way or another, they are enemies. Thus ichneumon flies (above), with their elongated ovipositors, able to penetrate a long way into tissue, may parasitise the larvae of solitary bees that are useful pollinators.

Similarly, parasites are friends if they parasitise enemies and enemies if they parasitise friends or valued plants. Thus ground beetles and centipedes that feed on slugs and other unwanted invertebrates are friends but toads that eat ground beetles are less helpful. These predators need places to hide and centipedes, which are not waterproof, need cover. Incidentally, centipedes are often venomous but harmless in the UK – their jaws are too weak to penetrate our skin.

However, few (if any) animal predators rely on one species of prey, since it is in their interests to be able to live on a wide variety of species, so they are sometimes friends and sometimes enemies. Furthermore, many predators (such as Foxes and Badgers) are often omnivorous and also feed on dead animals and a range of plants. Insectivorous birds feed on a wide variety of invertebrates, without regard to whether they are useful or damaging from a gardener's point of view!

Parasites, by contrast, are often highly specialised and confine their activities to one species of animal or plant. The unfortunate host plant or animal, of course, may also be parasitised by many other species, just as prey animals are eaten by many different predator species. Although eelworms, for example, occur in most plant species, different species tend to infect particular plants.

All these represent a complex web of interactions, so it is not a simple matter to designate all species as friends or enemies.

A Blackbird with an earthworm meal.

## Biological control

Biological control simply means the control of the numbers of one living organism by the deployment of another species. Of course, this happens all the time in the natural world, most of it unseen and unknown to us, but the term implies the deliberate use by humans of one species we regard as beneficial to control one that we consider harmful to us or our interests.

This may be achieved by introducing, protecting or culturing enemies of species considered undesirable by gardeners. It is as opposed to chemical or physical control (for example weeding or picking off caterpillars) and is often employed in order to avoid the use of pesticides and weed-killer.

Both plants (weeds) and animals (pests) are problems to be tackled but, mostly, only animals are seen as the controlling agents. However, fungi may be used, as in the case of *Verticillium lecanii* to control aphids, and some plants are used as barriers, putting off pests just by their presence. Tansy (sometimes called 'buttons' because of the flat round yellow flowers) is an example. Apparently its camphor scent puts off wasps, butterflies and aphids, and it was even used in mediaeval times to ward off the plague by its off-putting effect on rats.

Tansy – a protective barrier plant.

Rosemary can be used as a natural barrier to slugs.

It is claimed that aromatic herbs, such as Rosemary (above), Peppermint and Tarragon put off slugs, and extracts of them reduce their feeding by 60 to 80 per cent. Genetic modification could be used to incorporate the aromatic compounds into valued, including food, plants.

However, most of the unseen biological control is probably done by spiders, which are extremely numerous. It has been estimated that, in long grass, there are up to 5 million per ha and that the total number of insects eaten by them greatly exceeds that eaten by birds. A recent example of deliberate use of organisms is the culturing of a nematode (*Phasmarhabditis hermaphrodita*) to kill slugs. Viruses and bacteria are also used. In fact, the nematodes carry bacteria that actually kill the slugs. Ducks have also been used to control slugs.

Recently, a fungus has been identified that can control the Varroa mites that are currently decimating our Honey-bee populations. It appears to be effective against mites but does not affect bees, humans, fish, mammals, amphibians or other wildlife. The bacterium Bt, or *Bacillus thuringiensis*, is regularly used now to control Tomato Moth, Cabbage Moth and Silver-Y moth.

However, we now have to contend with the aggressive Harlequin Ladybird (originally from Japan) which competes with, and even attacks, our native ladybirds. Of course, it does feed on aphids, so is also useful. This is in addition to the problem of a big increase in a small parasitic wasp (*Dinocampus coccinellae*) which lays an egg inside the ladybird. The developing larva eventually kills the ladybird and weaves a cocoon beneath its body and pupates, continuing to benefit from the host's protective colouring.

'Integrated pest management' (IPM) is based on the combination of biological control and selective use of chemicals. Apple trees have many pests (more than pears, for example), amongst them several mites that feed on the undersides of leaves and cause 'russeting' in the fruit. But another mite, *Typhlodromus pyri* (or 'typhs'), is a major predator of the others and has become resistant to several major pesticides. So these can be used to control other pest species whilst leaving the field free for 'typhs'.

The Silver-Y Moth, whose caterpillars feed on the leaves of a wide range of low-growing plants.

# Friends of the gardener

It is interesting that most of this chapter has been devoted to 'enemies' of the gardener: this reflects a common assumption that gardening is a constant struggle against pests of one sort or another. The enormous contribution of insectivorous birds and rodent-eating owls tends to go unrecognised, because it is largely invisible and certainly unquantified. What is noticed is the occasional depredations of Woodpigeons amongst seed beds.

Few mammals do significant harm, except for Wood Mice on seed beds and, in some cases, Rabbits (and even deer) nibbling herbaceous borders (and roses). The beneficial work of Hedgehogs (on slugs) and Foxes (on mice and Rabbits) is also unseen, but the odd scrapes in the lawn by Rabbits, Foxes and Badgers are still there in the morning.

Snakes, frogs and toads (and even newts) are wholly beneficial but almost wholly invisible to most people. Frogs are now being badly affected by a fungus (*Batrachochytrium dendrobatidis*): indeed, amphibians generally, and worldwide, are suffering. In recent years, another disease has hit frogs: this is the vanavirus and it is fatal. Fortunately, neither of these diseases is harmful to humans.

Centipedes are carnivorous, with a venomous bite but harmless to humans, and eat slugs, which is good, but also spiders, which is not. This is because spiders are one of the gardener's best friends. They do no harm at all but, because of their vast numbers, are responsible for the destruction of enormous numbers of insects. Most of the latter are garden pests, either of plants (see above), or of people (mosquitoes, midges, gnats). Wasps, although annoying at times, catch many insects to feed to their grubs.

Slugs are also eaten by the glossy ground beetles you see scurrying over the ground and under logs and stones. Ants are most often seen where they are not wanted (kitchens, looking after aphids) but, away from our view, they consume a great many insects. Ladybirds are certainly 'friends' and concentrate on aphids, which are also eaten by hoverfly larvae. Bees are wholly beneficial and are extremely important for pollination.

Valuable services are also rendered by earthworms, including those in the compost, millipedes recycling dead vegetation, and woodlice eating rotten wood. Among our best-hidden friends are fungi, not the toadstools, the fruiting bodies that we see, but the fungal threads (mycelium) that we can't see, underground or permeating dead trees. They are invaluable recyclers. The fact is that our friends greatly outnumber our enemies but the latter, in order to survive (and feed the former!), are very good at reproduction.

Birds destroy vast numbers of pests, and the vast majority must count as 'friends'. Even the Cuckoo, which always seems to be welcome, in spite of its unpleasant habits (ejecting its host's eggs and offspring), is notable for eating hairy caterpillars rejected by other birds. Many people have an irrational dislike of Magpies, because they occasionally take nestlings, and in the mistaken belief that they are responsible for the decline in bird populations. Less objection seems to be taken against Sparrowhawks, which take large numbers of small birds.

## Beneficial invertebrates

| | |
|---|---|
| Ladybirds and their larvae | eat aphids, scale insects, leafhoppers, whiteflies, mites and potato and tomato beetles |
| Hoverfly larvae | eat aphids, mealy bugs and grasshoppers |
| Lacewings and their larvae | eat aphids, caterpillars, thrips, scale insects and mealy bugs |
| Centipedes | eat various small invertebrates |
| Millipedes | only attack dead or dying plants |

# 16 Medicinal plants

It is often pointed out that all medicines (indeed most substances) are potentially poisonous and many poisons are good medicines. It was known in the 16th century that it all depends on the dose (see Chapter 15). Historically, plants were the source of most medicines and 80 per cent of the world's population is estimated still to rely on herbal medicines, largely because the cost of drugs is beyond the reach of many people. It is claimed that natural products isolated from higher plants account for 25 per cent of the number of drugs in clinical use today.

It is also claimed that the £11 billion global herbal medicine industry is endangering 4,000–10,000 herb species worldwide as some two-thirds of the 50,000 medicinal plants are harvested from the wild. It is estimated that over three-quarters of a million plant species are awaiting investigation of their therapeutic potential.

In the UK we spent £87 million on herbal remedies in 2004 and one company (Weleda UK) is growing more than 300 species in Derbyshire. The main compounds of pharmacological importance are glycosides, phenols and various alkaloids. It has been suggested that many people could contribute by growing herbs in their own gardens as, indeed, used to be the case in what was called the 'cottage garden'. This adds extra meaning to the idea that a garden should be 'a place of healing'.

Common examples are: morphine and codeine from the Opium Poppy; cardiac glycosides from Foxglove; quinine from South American cinchona trees; vincristive (for treating acute leukaemia) from the Madagascar Periwinkle; and paclitaxel (cancer treatment) from yews. Aspirin, one of the commonest pain-killers, is based on salicylic acid originally derived from the bark of the White Willow. The genus name of the willows, *Salix*, comes from the Celtic word meaning 'near water' which is, of course, where willows thrive. The same constituent is also found in Meadowsweet.

Apparently there are over 80,000 medicinal plant species in the world! This chapter will concentrate on garden plants that are, or have been, of medicinal use.

Lucerne (or Alfalfa as it is known outside Europe) has been used for at least 1,500 years, though not commonly in this country. It is commonly grown agriculturally and, as a legume, fixes its own nitrogen. Like many of these medicinal plants it is used in various forms to treat a wide variety of conditions or to promote health – even, it is claimed, to lower cholesterol.

Yew – used in cancer treatment.

Foxgloves – from which you can extract the cardiac glycoside digoxin.

Deadly Nightshade – though poisonous, it is claimed to have a muscle relaxing effect when used in controlled doses.

However, many of these long-established claims have not been proven, in the sense that modern drugs have to be tested and their benefits demonstrated.

Indeed, some of the remedies described in Anglo-Saxon times do not give rise to great confidence. For example, marsh crowfoots was used to cure warts and swellings but had to be "pounded well with pigs' droppings", and dandruff was apparently treated with a mixture of watercress seeds and goose grease. Of course, without goose grease, how would you keep the seeds on your head!

Equally, in those early times, one would have been desperate for a cure for toothache and it would have been well worth trying herbal recipes such as the roots of Chervil and Bishopwort (wood betony). The ailment that a plant was believed to cure or relieve was often reflected in its name. Feverfew actually reduced fevers and Fleabanes release natural insecticides when burnt.

Many species were named to reflect the 'Doctrine of Signatures (or signs)', which held that God showed you what organ a plant could treat by creating it to resemble that organ. This often required some imagination. Liverworts (see Chapter 8) don't look much like liver but lungworts (with their spotted leaves – see Chapter 5) are said to resemble a diseased lung. 'Wort' often denoted a herb with medicinal properties.

The early use of preparations from whole plants or parts of plants, gave rise to the term 'phytomedicines'. These contain all the plant compounds in the plant (or the part used): they were not single compounds. However, modern drugs, as used in conventional medicine, are isolated compounds.

Some of the garden plants for which health benefits have been claimed are: Angelica for treating high blood pressure and angina; Autumn Crocus for treating gout – although the active ingredient is colchicine, a powerful poison; and Deadly Nightshade (left), another powerful poison, as a muscle relaxant. Current research, it seems, is even exploring the possible liver function-enhancing properties of Dandelions.

By contrast, the Anglo-Saxons held Fennel to be sacred, bestowing strength, courage and long life on those who consumed it. Feverfew, as its name implies, was used to control fevers and to this day is used to ease the pain of migraines. Garlic is one of the best known herbs but it is one of the most ancient, going back 5,000 years. It was used to rid the body of intestinal parasites and for treating infections (bacterial, viral and fungal).

Hawthorn preparations have been used to treat high blood pressure and arteriosclerosis and its berries were eaten to prevent scurvy (caused by vitamin C deficiency). Carnation flowers were used against the plague (as well as to provoke lust: this report claimed it was ineffective!). Self-heal (also called 'heal all' or 'woundwort') is a common weed of lawns: its attractive flowers are much visited by bees. The Chinese used it 2,000 years ago to treat liver and kidney problems but it has also been used as a gargle for sore throats and mouth ulcers, to treat fevers, vertigo, mastitis, burns, bites, bruises, haemorrhage, convulsions, mumps and hyperactivity in children. It seems unlikely that one remedy could actually affect such a variety of conditions but you can see how it got its name of 'heal-all'!

self-heal – traditionally applied to wounds to help with healing.

This spectacular list of remedies is at least equalled by Hemp and this species has, if anything, even more names, including, of course, marijuana. The wild geraniums (Herb Robert, cranesbills, storksbills) contain a rather smelly essential oil as well as tannins which has been used as an antiseptic and an anti-inflammatory. The name 'cranesbill' comes from the shape of the fruit capsules and, indeed, geranium is derived from the Greek 'geranos', a crane.

Hops are well known as a constituent of beer but they also have relaxing, calming qualities. Originally, in Europe, before Hops were introduced, beer was flavoured with many other bitter herbs, including Ground Ivy! It is claimed that hop cones in a bag under the pillow will aid peaceful sleep, because of their sedative properties. If their somewhat beery smell is found unattractive, the hops can be mixed with crushed lavender.

Another fairly ancient species, the Balm or Lemon Balm, was used as both a drink and a sedative and for its antibacterial properties. Incidentally, its genus name *Melissa*, from the Greek word for 'bee', denotes its attractiveness to Honey-bees. It, also, has been used for a great variety of different purposes, including the treatment of cold sores.

A more recent arrival in Europe (in 1576), the Horse Chestnut can be used as an extract to treat varicose veins and cramp in calf muscles and these effects have been confirmed in trials conducted within the last 30 years.

A wide range of herbs have been claimed to have medicinal applications, including agrimonies, Anise, Balm, Bay, burdocks, calendulas, Caraway, centauries, camomiles, Chicory, Comfrey, Common Horehound, Dandelion, Dill, Fennel, garlic, Horseradish, horsetails, lady's mantles, Lovage, Marjoram, nettles, Parsley, Rosemary, Tansy, Thyme and Yarrow.

The only authenticated animal product with medicinal properties, as far as I am aware, is honey, but this should not be used in an untreated form which has not even been sterilised. In fact, it is said that *Clostridia* bacteria, present in some honeys, can cause gangrene. In any case, honey should not be used on people with a known allergy to bee stings or pollen.

Lemon Balm – a versatile medicinal plant.

# 17 Cats and dogs in the garden

It has to be admitted that the impact of cats and dogs on the wildlife of a garden is almost wholly negative, with that of cats being vastly greater than that of dogs. Of course, with both cats and dogs but particularly dogs, there are differences between individuals and also between breeds. Pekinese and bloodhounds are both dogs but their impact is obviously very different.

The total effect is partly a consequence of numbers but the difference is not, although, in the UK, cats now outnumber dogs (cats about 9 million and dogs about 6.5 million) or, as a recent headline put it, "Cats overtake dogs," suggesting a surprising increase in both speed and stamina!

In fact, of course, their hunting styles are totally different. Virtually all cats hunt by stealth and stalking, culminating in a relatively short burst of speed, while dogs hunt more by 'dogged' pursuit over long distances. Even the Cheetah shows nothing of the endurance displayed by dogs in Africa. Within the confines of even a large garden, it is clearly only the former style that is appropriate.

Curiously, wild cats tend to hunt only when hungry or in need of food for their young: this does not seem to apply to the domestic cat and, in this sense, dogs seem to be more 'domesticated' than cats. Domestic cats are more solitary animals than dogs and their relationships are not hierarchical. Cats are very watchful and many prefer to watch from a high point (or 'perch') or lie low in the bushes.

There is another important difference between dogs and cats in the garden. For dogs it is really only your dog that you have to worry about, whereas not owning a cat does not mean that you have none in your garden. I do not own a cat but I have at least three different cats that regularly patrol my garden, where, I may add, they do little discernable harm, mainly because it is 3.5 acres and has many wild areas where potential prey can easily conceal themselves. Dogs, on the other hand, are generally fenced in and this also keeps other dogs out. It is not impossible to fence cats in – just more difficult. The fence has to be about 2m high, close-boarded, and a well-placed hedge discourages jumping.

Cats consider a wide range of garden areas to be their 'territory' and can be hard to discourage.

Dogs enjoy gardens – but the plants may not appreciate their presence as much.

A sturdy gate is a good idea with a big dog like 'Blue' my daughter's German shepherd.

The presence of dogs does have a discouraging effect on the larger fauna (Rabbits and upwards, including wandering cats) but probably has little effect on birds and smaller mammals. Invertebrates are little affected by either dogs or cats, toads are unpleasant to the taste and are soon put down again (but so are shrews and cats still kill them, probably because cats often show little interest in eating their kill anyway), and frogs and snakes are more elusive. However, the special dietary needs of cats are not met by all the commercial cat foods available and they may need to eat more animal food. So, it may be possible, in some cases, to reduce this problem by changing the cat's diet.

The most vulnerable wild animals to cats are small birds (some estimates for the UK are as high as 20 million taken by cats annually) and small mammals, especially voles, woodmice and shrews (one estimate is 220 million killed annually but we don't really know). In Australia, the situation is taken very seriously because of the vulnerability of native wildlife to predators not present when it evolved. So there are strict regulations and all cats must be registered, wear an ID tag and bell and must be curfewed at night.

As with all animals, of course, there is variation and in a study of 1,000 cats (half wearing bells) carried out by the Mammal Society in 1997, 66 cats killed nothing at all. But the rest killed more than 14,000 mammals, birds, reptiles and amphibians – the majority of the observed victims were garden birds.

Of course, such surveys can be criticised on the time of year selected, the age of the cats and so on, but it is generally accepted that there is a problem. Cats Protection publishes a leaflet on 'Cats and Gardens' and some people find

A noisy bell may help to warn birds of a cat's approach.

that cats wearing collars fitted with bells or electronic 'bleepers' kill many fewer prey. However, some people find that collars may result in serious injury, or even death and Cats Protection does not support them. It is said that the problem is worst in the first three years of a cat's life, so shutting it in at night can help in these years.

However, gardens vary enormously, not only in size and design but also in the extent to which wildlife can hide from predators. Clearly, many low-maintenance designs, with lots of bare concrete and no untidy corners, are bleak environments for wildlife anyway but there is also little protective cover.

And it is in just these situations that birds may be attracted by food put out on bird tables and the like. Indeed, this may provide the only reason for birds to visit, though they are unlikely to take up residence and build nests. Some people have found that, even with cats present, Woodpigeons will nest regularly in a holly tree and it may be that other birds will use a variety of prickly or thorny bushes as safe nesting sites. Bird tables can easily be made cat proof and thus provide a kind of spectacle.

In general, the wilder the garden, the more wildlife it will contain and the more interesting it will be from the point of view of natural history, as well as offering wildlife more protection from cats. Much thought has been given to increasing the attractiveness of a garden to visiting butterflies (less so for moths) and the value of plants like Buddleia is well known. The value of nettles for Red Admirals to lay their eggs on is also well known but few people actually plant nettles (most would say they don't need to!).

Bumblebees can be encouraged to nest in moss-filled plant pots and various boxes have been designed for Dormice to nest in. Owl boxes can also be used to attract Tawny Owls (though mine is generally used for breeding by Stock Doves and grey squirrels – not, of course, simultaneously!) and keeping some aged trees, especially willows, will provide for woodpeckers and thus Nuthatches, well out of reach of cats. Little Owls and Stock Doves cannot create their own holes but need naturally developed hollows.

For small mammals, the problem of cats may be acute – though cats are often encouraged to hunt them. They include Wood Mice, voles and shrews. Often dismissed as vermin, they are mostly harmless and, in the case of shrews, consume large numbers of pestiferous insects, slugs and snails. Cats can detect small mammals by sight, smell and sound. Apparently a cat can detect the footsteps of a mouse 9 metres away and their sense of smell is some 30 times as good as ours.

Seed beds can suffer from attack by Wood Mice and voles but in rough grass and orchards they are quite harmless. In fact, you will not know they are there – but your cat will (and so will Foxes). The use of dustbin lids (described elsewhere, see Chapter 4) provides protection, especially for breeding, and allows you to view these attractive little neighbours. The same is true for Grass Snakes and all the other creatures that are attracted to dustbin lids.

Place nestboxes high up on trees to deter possible predation by cats.

This kind of protection has been little explored but it seems clear that the wildlife that use such things do so mainly because of the protection they offer. For garden birds, the equivalents are nestboxes, designed to accommodate different species, by virtue of size, position and entrance hole. These can easily be placed in safe positions and allow splendid opportunities for seeing the commoner species (especially Blue and Great Tits) without exposing them to the risk of cat attacks.

However, the more secretive nesters – birds like finches, Long-tailed Tits, Dunnocks and Goldcrests – are not so easily satisfied and for these, as well as thrushes and Blackbirds, tall, impenetrable hedges are the best answer. The value of such birds to pest control in the garden in incalculable. Blue and Great Tits, for example, consume enormous numbers of aphids (and do not touch ladybirds) and continue to do so in the colder months when other predators are inactive.

Ponds are about the only part of the garden more vulnerable to dogs than cats. Dogs usually mean no harm but can do a fair amount of physical damage: cats have predatory intentions (especially towards fish) but achieve very little, being decidedly averse to water. Fish can be protected by surrounding accessible parts of the pond with a wet, boggy area. Raised ponds can have protective walls to make them dog-proof and also safer for children.

In general, the boisterous behaviour of dogs is rather like that of children and wildlife can get accustomed to both. My garden abuts onto a primary school playground and it is quite clear that birds such as Mallards get quite used to the periodic bursts of noise. This is not surprising, as a walk through St James' Park in London well illustrates. Even Carrion Crows, very cautious and alert in my woodland, hop about in groups near people in Hyde Park.

*Teach your dog to behave near wildlife and discourage it from digging.*

The quieter behaviour of cats and their seemingly inexhaustible patience make them very difficult for wildlife to adjust to, although birds and squirrels are quite good at calculating whether a cat is at a safe distance or not. Cats Protection has published a design for a 'cat-friendly' garden. However, as mentioned earlier, none of the invertebrates are seriously affected by cats, so cats in a garden still leave vast areas of natural history unchanged by their presence.

There are some additional problems for gardeners that are posed by cats, associated with scratching and toilet behaviour. The former simply needs a scratching post and the latter needs loose soil (in a secluded corner) where cats can bury their faeces, instead of using your latest seedbed. It is recommended that an area of freshly dug ground be provided but fallen leaves, grass cuttings, sandpits and even gravel will be used as toilets. Cats also eat grass, but are unlikely to do any damage to your lawn. Providing a patch of long grass is a good idea, especially for cats prone to hairballs.

Dogs also defecate in the garden, of course, but, however, unpleasant, they do not do the same kind of damage as cats. Dogs, however, can be trained to use a particular area – another reason for a patch of long grass. One feature not often provided for cats in a garden is a platform placed in a tree, easily accessible to a cat. They like this kind of 'look-out' facility and it has the added advantage that everything else knows where the cat is.

Pet lovers may perfectly well regard gardens as being for their pets and 'pet friendly' garden designs are available (from Cats Protection for cats and from The Blue Cross for dogs). In any event, it is important to have regard to the safety of pets in gardens. For example, the British Veterinary Association Animal Welfare Foundation recommends keeping pets away from: areas where pesticides or fertilisers have been recently used; stores of pesticides/herbicides; buckets or watering cans full of mixed chemicals; oily puddles; and plant bulbs.

My neighbour's cat uses this tree stump as a favourite look-out post.

# 18 Houses and sheds

You might think that buildings are not really part of the garden but the animals see no such distinction. Plants, if allowed, also climb over buildings and, indeed, many are deliberately planted to do so, for their flowers, to give a softening effect on the appearance of bare walls, for their scent and to deter burglars (prickly or thorny shrubs). Ivy is rarely used, as it is difficult to control and leaves unsightly marks when removed, but climbers such as wisteria and roses are quite common.

Actually, ivy roots do little harm, since they do not penetrate but simply serve to attach the plant, and ivy that is already in place can be killed off by cutting through the stems at the base, whether on buildings or trees. The dead plant can be left in place, without the trouble of removing it.

Climbers are used by birds as nesting sites: Chaffinches and Blackbirds will do so, if the vegetation is thick enough. Otherwise, the outside of houses and, to a lesser extent sheds, are occupied mainly by invertebrates. The main exception is the House Martin, which builds its clay nests under the eaves (below), often in considerable numbers.

House Martins are summer visitors, arriving in April and leaving again in September or October. The nests are built with pellets of wet mud (some 2,500!), lined with grass or feathers, and the four or five eggs are incubated for three weeks, with fledging taking a further two or three weeks. Two broods are quite usual.

*House Martin nest under the eaves.*

*A Zebra spider catching its prey.*

*A Red Mason Bee in a crack between bricks in a wall.*

Apart from invertebrates, such as bumblebees and butterflies, that use the walls to bask (and warm up) in the sun, the most common to be seen on walls are the mason bees and wasps and the Zebra Spider (top left). The Zebra Spider is well-named (for its black and white stripes) is small (2–3mm) and lives in crevices in the walls or window frames. It is completely harmless and catches small insects by jumping on them (it is a member of the jumping spider family, Salticidae).

The Red Mason Bee nests in holes or crevices in the walls (left) and constructs a tube of cement (masticated soil) cells in each of which it lays one egg, placed on a supply of pollen. The adult bees are orangey-brown, about 1cm in length and, very noticeably, carry their pollen not on the hind legs (as bumblebees do) but on the underside of the abdomen. The bright orange or yellow pollen makes them easy to spot. They can be attracted by specially constructed nest boxes (see page 211).

Crevices in walls are also used by some species of mason wasps to nest in. Like the mason bees, they also provision their cells for the developing larvae to feed on, not, however, with pollen but with living prey. Each wasp species sticks to one sort of prey: some catch spiders, some solitary bees, caterpillars or weevils, all of which are stung to paralyse them. The venom injected is also antiseptic, so the prey is kept alive and fresh for the larvae to feed on. It is easy to identify these wasps by the kind of prey they can be observed delivering to their nest sites. However, as with most creatures, there are others that prey on them and if brick walls are observed on a sunny day, brightly-coloured parasitic wasps can be seen searching for nests of mason wasps. The most noticeable are the ruby-tailed wasps (see Box, left).

Some solitary wasps and the powder-post beetles bore holes in old wood and Honey-bees, social wasps and Hornets may nest behind wooden cladding on buildings. The holes made by powder post beetles are quite small (1mm across) and a small pile of powdery wood is often found beneath them. Wasps, bees and hornets also nest inside the house, usually in the roof-space, particularly in old houses where access is easy between tiles. The main difference between these species is that Honey-bee colonies survive the winter, whereas in wasps and Hornets all the workers die at the beginning of winter and only the queens survive, hibernating – usually in the roof space. Wasp nests can be quite large, up to 60cm across, entirely made of papery wood-pulp.

All three species can be very aggressive in defence of their nests but Hornets are by far the most damaging. I have had a small Hornets' nest in the wall of my cottage, within 20cm of the font door and thus impossible to ignore. Any attempt to deal with Hornets should be undertaken in full protective clothing – their stings are very painful.

Within the main house, depending on its age, may be found honey ants, hibernating Two-spot ladybirds, lacewings, house flies, small moths and, if you bring in logs for the fire, woodlice and some beetles. But the most frequently found invertebrates are spiders. Many people heartily dislike spiders, but rarely want to kill them.

Tiers of hexagonal cells in the massive wasps' nest that I found surrounding water pipes in the attic of my cottage.

Here's an interesting question: since the spiders must be eating something (mostly flies and other insects), would you rather have the spiders or the creatures they live on? We wouldn't notice them so much if they didn't spin webs, except for those found in the bath! Mostly, they are there because they have fallen in and can't climb out: if you hang a towel, or even string, over the side of the bath they will climb out when you are not looking and disappear – at least for a time.

Another little fellow found in the bath and elsewhere is the Silverfish. This slippery, wingless insect feeds on starchy materials, including paper and glue. It belongs to a primitive group, called bristletails, and you may find its relatives in the garden compost. The Silverfish is the only one commonly found indoors and, apart from its silvery scales, it is characterised by its three tails: it is harmless.

The only birds found in houses are those that have strayed in or fallen down a chimney but some mammals, mainly House Mice, may take up residence. Pipistrelle bats (see Chapter 11) may roost in the roof space or behind wooden cladding, if they can find access. Occasionally, Wood Mice or Yellow-necked Mice may come in for the winter. Attics may also be used by Grey Squirrels at times and their 'chewing' damage can be much more serious than that of mice.

Sheds, similarly, provide excellent quarters for a range of invertebrates, including larger spiders with bigger webs. Large, open-fronted or otherwise accessible structures, including barns, provide nest sites for birds, such as the Robin, Wren, Swallow and, in large barns, Barn Owl.

The biggest invertebrate nuisances inside the house are flies – Houseflies, bluebottles and greenbottles. The last two are usually only serious if they have access to meat, on which they lay their eggs. The most dangerous to human health is the Housefly because it can transmit disease agents to food or surfaces it settles on.

Silverfish – seen on wood here but you'll often encounter them in the humidity of the bathroom.

The Housefly – a major spreader of germs in the home.

# 19 What's going on in the winter?

Very little you may think, as far as the garden is concerned. I have heard gardening experts react to this notion with remarks like "There's a lot to do: clean out the shed …", which rather reinforces the idea that life is at a standstill.

## Animals

Very few British mammals hibernate (only the Hedgehog, Dormouse and some bats) and no birds do. Some birds spend the winter elsewhere, but in their place others come here as winter visitors (for example, Fieldfare and Redwing). So they all have to keep on eating and therefore stay active and although feeding the birds may help, most birds do not of course, depend upon handouts – the insectivorous ones are rarely catered for!

However, Badgers and squirrels spend much time asleep in their setts and dreys, emerging perhaps once a week. Birds are more easily seen in winter, because there is less foliage about, but this makes little difference for the smaller mammals which hide in long grass, in hedge bottoms or come out mainly at night. In consequence, so do their predators, Foxes, owls and, of course, cats.

We tend to use the term 'predators' rather selectively. For example, we certainly include Foxes and owls but not always Badgers (which, admittedly, only eat some live prey) or Moles, which, like Badgers and Foxes, eat a lot of earthworms (Badgers can eat 200 worms a night).

However, we do refer to hoverflies and ladybirds as predators of aphids. We refer to the Sparrowhawk as a predator of small birds but not the Robins, tits, thrushes and Blackbirds that eat earthworms, insects of all kinds and, in the case of the Song Thrush, snails. We could call them all carnivores, although some, like the Badger, eat plant material as well. The Badger is therefore really an omnivore (as well as a scavenger of carcases).

The fact that many prey, and therefore their predators, are nocturnal, means that the latter have to be able to detect the former in very poor light. Some, like owls, use their acute hearing as well as their large eyes; some, like Badgers, have an acute sense of smell (some 800 times as powerful as our own). In addition, it has recently been found that a few animal species can see in colour at night, which is something we cannot do (hence the German proverb: "At night, all cats are grey").

Chilly Rooks at their winter roost.

*A Fieldfare puffs up its feathers to keep out the cold.*

Fox tracks in snow.

Duck tracks in snow.

Winter nights are, of course, longer though sometimes brightly moonlit, so animals that continue to be active in winter gain from being nocturnal. Another characteristic of winter is snow and, surprisingly some invertebrates, such as springtails and the wingless scorpionfly, actually move on the surface. One of the advantages of snow (to the observer) is that even quite light snow may reveal the tracks of animals that travel over the ground.

Many birds leave tracks very early in the morning, though few are on the ground at night, but this does not generally apply to the larger predators, such as owls and Sparrowhawks. Tracks may be found at other times, where there is soft mud but snow shows them very clearly. They not only show where animals went and, sometimes, a hint of what they were doing, but they are characteristic of each species, so these can be identified. See page 89 for some of the most commonly found bird tracks and mammal tracks.

Cold-blooded animals, such as frogs, toads, newts and snakes, depend upon ambient temperature and their activity is governed by this. So, even those that do not actually hibernate have their metabolism and thus their activity greatly reduced in the winter. Happily, this also greatly reduces their need for food and many of them have laid down fat reserves to tide them over. This reduced activity includes fish although, because of the way ice forms, their temperature remains above freezing. Land animals seek sheltered places to retire to, including underground burrows.

Invertebrates vary in their adaptation to winter. Those whose food sources disappear, such as butterflies and moths, ladybirds, lacewings and Houseflies go into suspended animation and often hide in your house, in cracks round window frames and so on, from which they may startlingly appear, in surprising numbers, when we have a warmer spell. Some overwinter as pupae, larvae or eggs.

My Berkshire garden after a heavy snowfall.

However, one stonefly is active in February, Drone Flies, Houseflies and bluebottles may be found basking in any sunshine that is going, winter gnats keep dancing and some moths are about (for example the Winter, November and Early Moths as well as the Spring Usher).

Many insects reduce their numbers to a few overwintering adults, except in the water, where nymphs of dragonflies, damselflies and mayflies survive while the adults that die out. Small aquatic crustaceans actually thrive better in cold water and Daphnia and Cyclops are often present in greatest numbers in January. Greenfly is a good example of an insect whose food source (for example bean leaves) may disappear and it is a special generation of winged adults that overwinter on, for example, the Spindle tree.

Many small invertebrates remain surprisingly active: this is especially so for the detrivores that live on decaying vegetation, fallen logs and leaves, for example. They choose protected spots where frost does not penetrate and which remain moist, favourites being under logs, even better between heaped-up cut logs, and large stones. Here may be found woodlice, Brandling Worms and the predatory centipedes. You may also find mice and Hedgehogs (below): the latter may hibernate in heaps of material prepared for bonfire night, so these should be examined carefully before being lit.

Reproduction rarely occurs in winter – there being no point in increasing the numbers to be fed – but mammals like deer and Foxes may be pregnant during part or all of the winter period. This is so that mammals with long gestation periods can give birth in the more favourable springtime. Surprisingly, some cold-blooded invertebrates continue to breed and I commonly find clusters of spherical white slug eggs in January. They are always in protected places, underneath rotten logs being the most suitable, providing protection, insulation and humidity.

Similarly, under logs (rotten or otherwise), woodlice may be found in sizeable clusters, since their food supply is secure and plentiful.

The Spring Usher moth is active in winter but supremely well-camouflaged.

A Hedgehog hibernating in dead leaves – take care to check for them if you are planning a bonfire.

*Early Horse Chestnut buds.*

# Plants

Most seeds overwinter, partly because conditions are unsuitable for growth and development and partly because, in annuals, no other part of the plant does. Deciduous bushes and trees simply lose their leaves (see Box, left) but many perennials overwinter as bulbs, tubers, rhizomes or corms while above ground their vegetation completely dies back. All these, of course, remain alive and woody plants often have well-developed buds resistant to frost by virtue of outer casing, waxy coverings or simply because the buds contain very little water. They consist of densely packed cells, which only have to take up water, when temperatures rise, to expand and elongate very rapidly.

Quite early in the winter, some of these buds are extremely well developed (notably those of Horse Chestnut and lilacs), sometimes enclosing coloured petals and distinct anthers (for example, camellias). In the ground, in spite of periodic frosts, cold winds and snow, growth of many plants continues and shoots begin to appear early in January (depending, of course, on location).

The appearance of the first leaves of Bluebells, Lords-and-ladies and daffodils illustrate how they are bunched or, in the case of Lords-and-ladies, twisted, to form a rigid point able to penetrate even hard-packed soil. This rigidity is only possible because of the low water content and as soon as the leaves absorb water they cannot be pushed through anything! Seedlings often achieve a strong enough structure to push through soil by emerging with the stem curved over, so that it is the strong rounded part that comes up first, with the leaves or cotyledons hanging down.

Snowdrops, winter aconites and violets are well-known for actually flowering in winter, but leaves of daffodils and hyacinths appear at the same time and weeds, such as nettles, though small, appear to thrive. This gives them a head start in the competition for space and light. Flowers tend to come up as pointed buds protected by the leaves (for example, daffodils) or bent over (as in violets) so that it is the curved stem that pushes through the soil.

Other plants, such as Blackberry and willowherbs, have well-developed shoots just below the surface and these, too, are sharply pointed. This is especially true of the Great Willowherb: if the old stem is pulled out of the ground (which is quite easy to do) the roots will be found to have generated a number of pale (often pinkish) fleshy shoots (see right).

# Frost damage

Unlike animals, plants cannot seek shelter to protect themselves from cold. Some plants are frost-hardy: frost-susceptible plants typically evolved in areas where frost does not occur, but even frost-hardy species usually need to be pre-conditioned to low temperatures (1-7°C) for 7-14 days prior to freezing (this is called 'acclimation').

Leaves, unless protected by thick or waxy cuticles, are the most susceptible to frost damage because of their large surface area to volume ratio. Roots are also susceptible but, of course, are less exposed. Buds are protected by low water content and overlapping scales that trap air between them.

In some cases, the ability to survive low oxygen supply (in ice-encasement) or low light is important and, often, plants suffer from inundation with water in winter. I have noticed on flooded land some species survive better than others (see Table right).

However, plants also have to avoid being startled into premature growth or even flowering by a warm spell during the winter. This is achieved by 'vernalisation' – the requirement for a certain amount of exposure to cold conditions before the reproductive response can be triggered. The length and severity of the cold period differ between species and are an adaptation to their particular climate.

*Great Willowherb showing pink underground shoots.*

*Snowdrops may emerge and survive even a heavy snowfall.*

### Prolonged inundation

(at least 2 months)

| Survivors | Casualties |
| --- | --- |
| Docks | Elder |
| Blackberry | Nettles |
| Sycamore seedling | |
| Burdocks | |
| Gypsywort | |

# 20 What to look for each month

The following account is based on observations of my own garden over some 18 years. Looking back, the most impressive features are, on the one hand, the consistency with which certain events recur every year and, on the other, the marked differences between years. This is very evident in such things as whether House Martins and Spotted Flycatchers return. They may do so every year for a long time and then stop.

Sometimes, as with frogs, the changes I observe may reflect widespread changes in such things as disease incidence: others appear inexplicable. So, one must not be surprised at such changes. However, they can work both ways and regular, close observation may suddenly reveal a plant or animal (or a behaviour pattern) that you have not seen before. In fact, part of the excitement is that a standard walk round your garden is quite likely to surprise you with something new.

Of course, what you see will also vary with location and, in the future, with any changes in the climate and, consequentially the weather (see Chapter 21).

Loddon Lilies – one of the earliest plants to emerge in winter.

*Frost-encrusted hips of the Dog Rose.*

# January

What happens in January depends greatly on the weather which, in the UK, can be extremely variable. Sometimes this only affects what is visible. Changes that are least affected by the weather occur in the water or underground (or even on ground well covered by leaf litter).

## Plants

Most flowering plants flower in particular seasons (apart from gorse, which has the reputation of flowering throughout the year), mostly in warmer times. However, in January, in many places, in many years, snowdrops are in flower: how do flowers at this time of the year get pollinated? In the south of the country, the first leaves of the Loddon Lily are already about 10cm high and snowdrops, Bluebells and daffodils may be about the same height and even in bud.

Leaves are absent from deciduous trees, although they often remain recognisable on the ground, but the evergreens, like hollies, yews, ivy and all the conifers (except Larch) remain much the same. Do their leaves live for ever? If not, when do they fall? Many trees and bushes have also lost their fruit but some may remain (some rose hips and some haws, for example) but some of the most numerous, though certainly not the most conspicuous, are on ivy. What has happened to those that have fallen? Many have been eaten and, with some fruits, the seeds will have passed straight through the animal and will germinate later: such seeds are almost impossible to find now.

Others, notably Sycamore and limes, can still be found lying on the ground with their 'wings' still attached. Acorns and conkers can easily be found under the dead leaves and close examination may find that some acorns have begun to put down roots. Some aquatic plants continue to grow slowly (for example Canadian Waterweed), others may be relatively dormant (water lilies, Water Starwort). Plants of the water's edge start pushing their leaves a few inches out of the soil, especially Loddon Lily and Yellow Flag, and the buds of Primroses may be visible (in some places they may flower).

Buds, of course, are the main winter features of deciduous trees and, cut open, will reveal tightly packed green leaves and, in the case of pussy willow, contain recognisable silvery-grey catkins. On some shrubs and trees, the first catkins may actually be exposed. On Hazel, for example, the (male) catkins are well-developed but the small female flowers appear later. Occasionally, the female Silver Birch catkins (which stick upright) may even appear earlier than the pendulous male catkins. Camellia flower buds actually contain clearly visible petals (some already pink) enclosing well-developed stamens and style. Most of these buds are protected by tough, often leathery, scales – none more so than the sticky buds of the Horse Chestnut. The green buds of lilacs are good examples of tightly packed green leaves.

Grass continues to grow, much to the regret of gardeners, whenever the temperature gets above about 4°C. This must also be the case for many of the herbaceous plant leaves (Wild Strawberry, Foxglove, lungworts, evening primroses, hollyhocks and, especially, some cyclamens) and weeds such as Dandelion, Daisy and nettles.

*Early Primroses in bloom.*

Even when it's this cold, a cock Pheasant will let potential mates know of its presence.

## Animals

Birds and larger mammals become more visible, because there is less vegetation, as do last year's nests. A covering of snow gives the additional opportunity of seeing their tracks (see pages 88 and 256), many of which are quite distinctive for footprint and pattern. These tell you something of what has been going on, mostly at night, but some sounds help as well. Foxes may begin their mating noises and even Pheasants try calling to tell potential partners where they are.

Small animals tend to be more difficult to see. A few of the mammals hibernate (Hedgehogs, Dormice) and others are relatively inactive (bats): all the adult amphibians and the reptiles also hibernate. But some small mammals remain active and have to keep eating. The voles and mice often store cut grass, fruits, nuts and seeds, to cover the most difficult periods and hide away in burrows or other protected spots (including mice in your loft). However, under the dustbin lids, voles, mice and shrews can still be found and feeding them shows just how much activity is taking place. The food is often removed or partly eaten within hours of putting it down.

Very occasionally, woodpeckers can be heard starting to drill new holes. This is a quite different sound from the territorial drumming but it has to be distinguished from the slower, less regular and softer strikes that represent searching the bark or the wood for insect grubs. When drumming, they are usually high up in the trees; they usually seem to contrive to be on the opposite side of the trunk to you!

The deer most usually seen in gardens is the Muntjac (in the south-east), the smallest of our deer, a bit like a large dog. It is difficult to spot unless it moves, because its colouring is so like the background vegetation at this time of year – mainly brown. However, its shape is quite characteristic (see right) and, if encountered in the open, it may stand and stare at you. It is said that the Muntjac is rather short-sighted and it does appear that, provided you are quiet and stand still, you can be quite close. It seems to be unaware of you in these circumstances.

A Muntjac deer – easier to spot in a snowy garden.

*Rooks can hunt out food in almost any situation.*

When the weather is cold, Blackbirds spend less time on lawns – since earthworms stay deep underground – and more time turning over dead leaves in more wooded areas. Quite often, you can see the leaves flying about before you see the birds, especially at a distance. Curiously enough, Song Thrushes do not seem to do this but Redwings do, in just the same way as Blackbirds. Moorhens also turn over dead leaves, whether on land or floating on the water, but it is more deliberate, less vigorous than the others.

Many birds, especially those that nest in holes, can be seen exploring potential nest sites. Those that build nests in trees and bushes may also be prospecting but, apart from Rooks and crows, it is hard to be sure.

Underground and underwater winter has much less effect and the typical invertebrates continue their lives, albeit at a slower rate (especially reproduction). In the pond, and in small pools, larvae of Phantom Midges seem almost as numerous, shrimps and Water Lice scuttle about, mosquito and midge larvae wriggle about and Daphnia and Cyclops are often more numerous at this time or year. Even in the coldest weather, mayfly nymphs and Phantom Midge larvae may be very active but they are hard to see underneath thick ice. They derive their oxygen from the water – the mayfly nymphs having three tails they use as gills – so do not need to come to the surface. Beetles and water boatmen, which do come to the surface for air, usually rest at the bottom and reduce their need for oxygen.

Cyclops tend to appear a little earlier than Daphnia, both of them thriving at low temperatures. This should not surprise us, since it is well known that the marine invertebrates on which whales and fish feed are most abundant where cold currents well up bringing a greater concentration of nutrients to the surface. If you look very closely at the smaller creatures, you may detect the first tiny stages of water boatmen and dragonfly nymphs (less than 1mm long). Surface dwellers, however, such as pond skaters, are unsurprisingly not evident.

Intermediate between exposed soil and both underwater and underground are the places, under leaves, bark, logs and stones, where invertebrates hide. They remain active, woodlice and millipedes feeding on dead and decaying matter, and predators (such as centipedes) continue to feed on them. Smaller slugs and snails also hide in such places but the larger snails cannot squeeze in or go underground (like many slugs): so they seal up their shells and hibernate, often in large groups (of up to 30) wherever they can find space. If you put down a dark cover (perhaps a flower pot, upturned tray or corrugated iron sheet) they will congregate under it, as long as they can creep under the edges. Here they leave circular marks when they depart, which seems to happen with some of them even when the temperature is less than 6°C. They will commonly return after each foray but not necessarily to precisely the same position.

# February

What happens in February is very dependent on the severity, or otherwise, of the winter. Violets, Primroses, crocuses, Rosemary and Cowslips may flower, while daffodils and Loddon Lilies push both leaves and buds well above ground, flowering towards the end of the month. Weeping Willow twigs start to turn green but these develop catkins, not leaves, at this stage. However, the leaves of Elder are already well advanced by now.

Voles, shrews and Wood Mice remain active, as do Foxes and Rabbits (but mostly at night). Grey Squirrels are very busy and may even start nesting; bats appear on mild nights. Under dustbin lids, you may sometimes find earthworms disabled by shrews, as a live food store. Woodpeckers start their territorial drumming, high up in the treetops. They are hard to see or even locate as their drumming carries a long way, but their dipping flight identifies them when they fly.

Under logs, woodlice, centipedes and Brandling Worms are as numerous as ever but are probably not breeding: on the other hand, slug and snail eggs may be found. On the walls of old houses Zebra Spiders start to emerge on sunny days.

Aquatic plants grow slowly and can be seen even under the ice, but water lilies wait for warmer weather. Also in the pond, invertebrates are not so visible or numerous, except for cyclops and water fleas. Some newts appear in the water.

Sweet Violet is the first of the violets to flower.

Winter crocus blooming vigorously in the snow.

*If they are in a sheltered spot that avoids the frost, Camellias may start to flower in February.*

Acorns, at least those that have not been eaten, put down roots but the shoots wait for higher temperatures. Sycamore seed litters the ground and looks dead but if you open up the swollen seed, you will generally find the bright green, curled-up cotyledons (first leaves) ready to emerge. They may actually do so later in the month. Voles know all about these seeds, collect them and eat the green parts. Camellia buds in protected positions may actually flower and hyacinths and Bluebells push up their leaves and flower buds.

Ants remain below ground but will emerge under dustbin lids if food is put down. Their movements, however, are much slowed down – so they are more easily observed. Indoors, queen wasps, ladybirds and lacewings suddenly start appearing. Jackdaws start nesting in the chimneys after having inspected them regularly throughout the winter. Magpies start building their roofed nests, mainly in tall hedges.

Hazel catkins (male) and their small crimson (female) flowers appear, though the latter have to be searched for, and 'pussy-willow' catkins emerge (page 267, top), the male ones bearing golden pollen. Very few tree buds burst as early as this, but Sycamore may do so in some years.

Ferns already have well-developed but tightly curled up, brown fronds waiting to unfold when the temperature rises. Nettles and Cleavers start vegetative growth very early, although the latter does not have extensive root reserves. This early start gives them a tremendous advantage as weeds, competing with their neighbours.

Mallard ducks and drakes begin to appear as pairs on isolated stretches of water where they may nest, and the first newts and frogs migrate to the water. In fact, frogs may spawn in February (see Chapter 3) even if ice occasionally forms on the water. Last year's newts, still about half size (or less) and 'velvety', start appearing under logs.

*Mallards begin to pair up even when conditions are still harsh.*

# March

One of the most noticeable things about March is the appearance of catkins shedding pollen, including those of the Alder tree, where new catkins appear alongside last year's cones shedding seed.

The most obvious catkins are those of 'pussy willow' (right), those of males bearing highly visible golden pollen on silver catkins: the female catkins occur on a different tree – as do those of yews. But, in the yews, the contrast in size is enormous: female yew flowers are quite hard to see and the males are only easier because of the large quantities of very fine pollen they shed. This happens if you brush against them but the pale yellow pollen can be seen as a dusting on adjacent leaves.

Hazel catkins may be over by this time, depending on temperatures, and Blackthorn is usually in full flower. All this happens before leaves appear, one of the most unusual being Ash. This tree normally flowers early, some bearing male catkins, some female and some mixed. The old prediction that: 'If the ash comes before the oak, we shall have a soak: if the oak comes before the ash, we shall only have a splash,' appears to refer to the leaves – which normally appear first in oaks.

The typical pussy willow furry buds of Goat Willow.

Alder catkins, flowers and last year's cones in my garden.

In the Ash flowers emerge before the leaves appear.

*An early baby Rabbit.*

Where there is relatively bare ground, the holes of Wood Mice stand out and, in the warmer weather, bumblebee queens may be seen exploring them as potential nest sites. Voles start making nests for breeding. Rabbits and Badgers are often very active digging out new burrows and setts or simply removing old bedding. Indeed the first baby Rabbits often appear above ground for the first time. Rabbits, as is well known, are efficient breeders and females mate again some 12 hours after giving birth. The young are suckled only once a day (for about 5 minutes) and remain in the burrow (for safety), often with the entrance blocked up with soil. Weaning is at about 28 days when the young suddenly appear on the surface.

If the weather is favourable, many birds start nesting, especially those that are not so concerned about hiding their nests: those that are and nest in trees, bushes and hedges may wait until leaves develop (though this does not apply to coniferous hedges like yew and cypress). In fact, thrushes and Blackbirds will often nest in March, choosing honeysuckle or those kinds of clematis that have leaves at this time. Ducks also start nesting but the nests are usually just circular depressions at ground level.

Stock Doves nest in holes in trees, so the nest is not visible, but the birds themselves are very careful about revealing the site. This is also true for Blue and Great Tits. Crows are big enough to defend themselves and Rooks benefit from the protection afforded by their quite large colonies.

Squirrels are very active and, because of the absence of leaves, can be clearly seen. One of their curious behaviour patterns at this time of year may be seen in 'pussy willow' bushes: the squirrels appear to be licking off the pollen from the male catkins. I have only seen this occasionally but it is well known, of course (especially to bees!) that pollen is an excellent source of protein. Pond life becomes more active and frog spawn appears.

*A Blue Tit nesthole, well hidden in a hole in a tree.*

# April

Everyone, rightly, associates April with a surge of spring growth and a whole range of spring flowers, including many catkins, such as the spectacular 'pussy willow', Alder and Hazel (top right) and the less familiar ones on Silver Birch. 'Pussy willow', which usually refers to the Goat Willow, is so called because of its large and rather spectacular catkins, 'catkin' being a form of 'kitten'. Male and female catkins are borne on different trees, the males distinguished by their bright yellow pollen and the females by their green pistils. The silvery hairs that are so noticeable and attractive before actual flowering are sometimes used by Blue Tits as nesting material and they can be seen 'combing' the catkins with their bills to collect them.

April is also a month when, depending on the temperature, insects become both active and noticeable, the most prominent being queen bumblebees. Not so noticeable, however, are the small (5–8mm) solitary bees emerging from their burrows – especially in paths and other patches of bare earth.

I used to find it odd that large numbers of these bees made their burrows in a brick path outside my front door, only a metre or so from those of the solitary wasps that prey on them! However, the bees cannot know this, as they emerge in April and the wasps not until July and, looked at from the wasps' point of view, it makes a lot of sense.

Coots and other water birds start nesting but April is the best month for observing the activities of hole-nesting birds, since they are busy nesting and there are relatively few leaves on the trees. This is not so true for the woodpeckers, which make new nests each year and behave very secretively. But the ones that use old nest holes and larger holes in trees (caused by rotting) can be seen exploring and defending their choices. This latter process may go on for some time and I have observed Stock Doves and Jackdaws particularly perching near a nest hole and popping in and out for

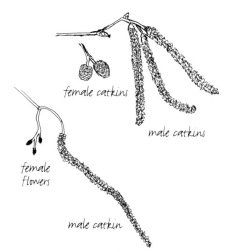

female catkins

male catkins

female flowers

male catkin

Top: Alder catkin; below: Hazel catkin.

Male Silver Birch catkin.

arder Bee emerging from its nest under
ustbin lid.

A Little Owl – a welcome visitor and much smaller than you would imagine.

Orange Tip Butterfly.

Holly Blue butterfly.

The most common of these hole-nesting birds are Jackdaws, Starlings, Stock Doves and Nuthatches but, in some parts of the country, Little Owls occur. These are attractive birds and often appear in daylight. They are quite small, about 21cm long (compared with 25cm for a Blackbird). When viewed from the front, there is no doubt about their identity but seen flying about in foliage they look like rather chunky brown thrushes, although the head is noticeably blunter.

The comparison of length illustrates the difficulty of describing size. Doubling the length of an animal may reflect proportional increases in all dimensions and result in an eight-fold increase in volume and possibly weight. However, in the case of the Little Owl and the Blackbird, the difference in shape is crucial. Part of the Blackbird's length is its tail and its relatively slender neck and head, whereas the Little Owl (above) has no discernable neck, with a substantial head and only a very short tail. If you think of it in human terms, you know that a man who is twice the height of a child is, in fact, very much bigger and heavier but a shorter man can also be much heavier than one who is taller.

On the ground, it is about this time of year that molehills appear, although Moles remain active throughout the winter, simply operating in deeper burrows. In this, they are also following their food, many burrowing insects and worms also avoiding the cold surface layers of soil. It is often said, as it is of the shrews, that the Mole has to eat at least its own weight of food every 24 hours. However, this has not been found to be the case and half its weight is more usual. Furthermore it can actually endure starvation for up to 48 hours.

On warmer days, insects and other invertebrates now appear in large numbers. The first butterflies are usually those that overwinter as adults, such as Brimstone and Peacock, followed by species that overwinter as pupae, like Orange Tip and Holly Blue (left). On sunny walls, the solitary Red Mason Bee and the Zebra Spider are very noticeable.

On the water surface, pond skaters can be seen mating and, below the surface, water boatmen are also mating. They 'row' about joined together and thus appear much bigger than normal. The first baby boatmen can also just be seen (with practice), but they are very small when they first become visible. Pond Snails start laying eggs on the underside of emerging water lily leaves.

April is usually the month in which newts start their courtship (top right). None of the species in our gardens actually mate: the male deposits a 'spermatophore' and the receptive female picks it up. To get the female to this receptive state, the male, which is crested to some extent and has a broad vertically-flattened tail, performs a courtship display which usually includes curving the body in view of the female and rapidly vibrating the tail. Although newts are nocturnal and are most easily seen after dark by flashlight, courtship displays can often be seen in daylight at this time of year.

A pair of Smooth Newts courting. The male is below.

Sometimes the courtship takes less usual forms. For example, one night, by flashlight, I observed each newt passing closely beneath the other when, so mightily stimulated, the female contorted her body very vigorously and ended upside down with her bright orange belly showing clearly and her legs spread, in which position she remained motionless, as if dead. The male, either fooled by this or startled by this unorthodox behaviour, promptly pushed off. I saw this twice, after which the male returned (some time later) but on a third repetition, we both lost interest and left her lying there. Females may also lie still at odd angles when laying eggs in blanket weed, where there are no leaves to curl round the egg.

In some years, however, rather to my surprise and even before I had spotted any newt eggs, I have found tiny newt larvae (sometimes called 'newtpoles'). At this stage they are only a few millimetres long and are a bit difficult to distinguish from the much more numerous mayfly nymphs. On closer examination, however, they not only lack the three feathery gills that mayfly nymphs have at the tail end, but they are more sharply tapered towards the tail and do not keep jerking about like the nymphs.

Sampling nectar, especially of Green Alkanet, Bee-flies (below right) appear to hover but they are actually holding on to the flower with their legs. Mating is quite spectacular, coupling back to back in flight, always with their long tongues extended prominently in front. They are not bees but have an orange/brown furry coat that resembles that of a bee – hence the name. They parasitise ground-nesting solitary bees but are far too big to get in their burrows, so they simply drop their eggs nearby and, when the grubs hatch out, they find their way down the burrow, where they live on the bee larvae. Another of their curious features is that they readily settle on the back of your hand, especially if it is angled to the sun, and do not seem at all alarmed by placing your hand near to them. This also works sometimes with dragonflies, although not as often.

A Bee-fly hovering, prior to feeding.

Many migratory birds make their return in this month, including most Swallows and House Martins. At some point in April, the first Cuckoos are seen – or, more often, heard.

Grass Snakes mating. In my garden they use the protection of a dustbin lid for this purpose.

## May

May is often quite warm and in late April or early May Grass Snakes begin to appear. However, they are quiet and unobtrusive and will largely pass unobserved in most gardens. I have found two exceptions to this. The first is under my dustbin lids, which provide not only protection and concealment but also warmth. The second, but only in quite warm spells, is the pond, where they readily swim about looking for food and are very noticeable. In fact, you can easily watch them in the water but notice how quickly and totally they disappear when they come out. Grass Snakes will mate at this time of year – sometimes under the dustbin lids.

With the emergence of large numbers of insects, this is the time for birds to be feeding their young. Many can be seen with bills full of invertebrates and can be watched to see where they go. Great Tits and Blue Tits will often go straight to their nests, perhaps because they are usually in inaccessible holes and thus not vulnerable to watching predators. Blackbirds and thrushes, by contrast, approach their nests very cautiously, usually indirectly but often by the same route each time (but different for the two parents).

Mistle Thrushes can often be seen in pairs on the lawn collecting food, but disguise their route to the nest in quite complicated ways, flying to a tree and remaining there for some time (observing the scene) before making the next move. Others, such as Jays, are even shyer than usual at this time and hide their nests very effectively – and also their presence, although they may be heard 'chattering'.

Grey Squirrels, on the other hand, are not at all shy at showing themselves but hide their dreys very well, in spite of the fact that they are really quite bulky. They seem to do this either by siting them in thick ivy or high up in the angle formed by large branches and the trunk. In one case, I had to have a very large, ivy-covered, dead oak felled and it was not until it was on the ground that I discovered no fewer than five large dreys built amongst the ivy.

A shy Jay, well camouflaged in dense leaves.

By the end of the month, the young of many birds have fledged and can be seen feeding or waiting to be fed. Birds whose young leave the nest immediately, or very shortly, after hatching, such as Pheasants, Moorhens, ducks and Coots, are capable of very rapid movement and, except in public parks, hide very effectively. They are able to feed themselves from the outset, although they may be guided to food and have it held out for them to show them what is suitable. And Coots, for example, will dive down for weed that the young cannot reach.

Those species that feed their young for several weeks after hatching, until they are fully feathered, work very hard during this time, making up to 138 feeding trips a day. When the young are fledged, they may still be fed, sitting on branches fluttering their wings to attract attention. (This is a common signal in many birds, also used by females to indicate readiness to mate.)

In some species, notably Robins and Green Woodpeckers, the young are coloured differently from the adults. Young Robins are speckled and lack the characteristic red breast. Young Green Woodpeckers lack the crimson crown and the bright green and yellow colours; before developing these they are paler, brownish, spotted and with chests barred with black. The stance and flight are just the same, however.

Of course, this is only the start of the breeding season: some bird species produce several successive broods. House Sparrows tend to be treble-brooded, Starlings may be double-brooded, Blackbirds and thrushes may be treble-brooded or even have four. Larger birds like crows, Rooks, Jackdaws and Jays are generally single-brooded but Mallards, for example, will often breed again if their eggs are destroyed.

Although insects are very active at this time of year, they are mostly very temperature-dependent. Aphids abound, however, and aquatic insects are not so affected by ambient temperatures. Water boatmen (or back-swimmers), for example, produce large numbers of young at this time. At first, they are hard to distinguish from Daphnia but, as they grow, they can clearly be seen as miniature adults, diving upside-down with strokes of their oar-like legs. In some ponds, the first larvae of the China-mark Moth cut cases out of water lily leaves.

Early bumblebees and some carder bees start nesting. Garden Spiders, like insects, are also temperature-dependent but on warm days can be seen in large numbers. Many female wolf spiders can be seen carrying cream-coloured egg sacs, usually at their rear ends.

Plant growth is very vigorous in May and, as is well known, nettles grow mightily from their network of tough yellow roots. Those who cut the lawn may also observe that, in general, the fastest growth is in May and about half the year's growth may be produced in six weeks around this month. The pattern may be modified by fertiliser and irrigation, however. Less noticeable, of course, is plant root growth, but shoot elongation can be enormous, especially in trees and climbing plants like the Hop, White Bryony, Cleavers and convolvulus. Lesser Celandines die off.

A Moorhen with chicks in its nest hidden amongst the reeds.

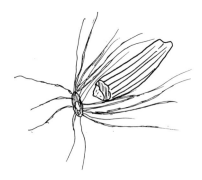

Seed of Crack Willow viewed under a microscope.

Cleavers growing vigorously up a bank.

# June

Towards the end of May or the beginning of June, different willows do two strange things. One is that Weeping Willows appear to be prematurely shedding their leaves but these yellow 'leaves' seem to be smaller than the main crop that remain green all summer. The second is that Crack Willows shed their seed and cascades of grey 'fluff' float down and about in the wind (even in very light wind), often in great quantities just for a few days. The seeds are tiny and attached to tangled masses of hollow threads: they do not have individual 'parachutes' like dandelions but each seed does in fact have its own fluffy 'sail'. However, the detail (see left) can only be seen under a microscope. Such materials are often used for constructing nests, especially by Blue and Long-tailed Tits, but willow fluff is probably too late for most.

Plant growth is very rapid and this is a good time to notice the range of methods plants use to climb mainly up other plants (see Chapter 5). One method is simply to twine round them: this is used by convolvulus (bindweeds). Many plants have developed stout hairs with a kind of 'velcro' effect, making them feel sticky to the touch and tenaciously adhering to clothing. Cleavers (or 'goosegrass') is the most common example, climbing up anything, including hedges, to heights of 2 metres.

Hops, similarly, have backward-pointing, stiff hairs on their stems, so that they feel smooth in one direction and as if they are cutting you in the other. These hairs are very short and difficult to see – but very easy to feel. Hops are very effective climbers and will go up 5 to 6 metres.

Another group of plants have tendrils, simple, quite delicate 'feelers' that twine their ends round anything they encounter (vines do this). Many legumes also do this, including peas, beans and vetches, as do White Bryony and Passionflowers, but these last two have a special additional trick. Once attached, their tendrils then develop, along their length, a coiled spring mechanism which tightens the attachment in a way which allows movement in the wind (see page 107). These tendrils then become quite tough and, although most of these climbers die down long before the winter, the dried tendrils may remain for a long time.

The range of techniques is very wide, from simple twiners, like honeysuckles, to those that grow on the support (wall or tree), such as ivy which forms small adhesive roots all along the stems. These roots do little more than anchor the stems and even ivy that has grown 30 feet up a tree will usually die if its thick basal stems are cut. The plant is really getting its water and minerals from the roots in the soil: the damage it does comes from covering the leaves of its support (more common with bushes than trees), denying them light, or by the sheer weight it imposes, which may cause branches to break off or even trunks to topple over.

Another event to look out for in June is the first formation of galls (although 'currant' galls are present in May), especially on oak trees. These are caused by small gall-wasps and there are a great many species, each causing a different kind of gall. The most noticeable at this time of year are the developing marble galls, oak apples and the various spangle galls: the first

*The Spotted Flycatcher – a rare but welcome garden visitor.*

two are formed on the small stems at the outer edge of the tree and the last occur on the underside of the leaves. Knopper galls are amongst the most spectacular but do not occur until acorns are being formed.

Prominent amongst other insects are damselflies, Stag Beetles, shieldbugs and, perhaps, bush crickets. Many of the larger animals still have young about and in the water 'newtpoles' grow rapidly, still with their red feathery gills. Emerging from the water, in the night or on fine days, are dragonfly nymphs: they climb up vertical leaves, such as bulrushes and water irises but, in the absence of these, will use flat water lily leaves or even the sides of the pond. Their empty cases remain behind, after the adults have emerged, for several days, as a record of what's been happening.

Spotted Flycatchers and warblers will have arrived and those fortunate enough to have House Martin nests will be able to watch the birds repairing their nests and beginning their first broods.

On a larger scale, snakes shed their skins and often a complete skin can be found, where the snake has wriggled out of it (see page 87). The most noticeable features are the large scales of the underside, on which the snake moves along, the smaller hexagonal scales on the upperside (sometimes compressed into a near-oval shape) and the lens-like eye coverings. Since snakes have no eyelids, their eyes are protected by this thin, transparent outer skin.

Also, on hot sunny days, digger wasps begin to push up little conical mounds of earth, to reveal their circular burrows, often between bricks on a path. Often their little yellow faces can be seen just inside the burrow entrance, waiting to emerge when it is warm enough. Then they can be seen retiring with their paralysed prey, with which they provision their eggs down in the burrow. I am regularly astonished by the problems they have in remembering where their burrows are and which one it is out of the dozens that may lie within a metre or so. They frequently explore the wrong one and, sometimes, put down their prey in order to dig out the entrance: on occasion they then apparently forget where they left the prey!

Top: Gooseberry sawfly larva; below:
Large White Butterfly larva.

# July

One of the features of July, although by no means confined to this month, is the appearance of web-building caterpillars. Some, like the Red Admiral (on Stinging Nettles) fold a leaf (or two) together with silken threads to provide a relatively safe tent-like hiding place. This actually makes it easier to find them than if you had to look under every leaf: I wonder if insect-eating birds have worked that out, too!

Others, like the Small Tortoiseshell (especially on the Small Nettle) and the Peacock (on Stinging Nettles), spin a communal web, under which tens of small caterpillars feed. When they get older, they tend to separate and feed individually.

Some larvae of sawflies look very similar to those of butterflies and moths but, although they all have six true legs, just behind the head, they differ in the number of 'false' or 'pseudolegs' under the rear half of the body. Lepidopterans (both butterflies and moths) never have more than five pairs of these stumpy legs (including the terminal pair), whereas sawflies all have at least six pairs.

Distinguishing different species of caterpillars is quite difficult and a magnifying glass makes a tremendous difference. This is because hairs and spines (and whether they are branched or not) can be important characteristics. The presence of caterpillars can be given away by their webs, but also by their droppings (known as 'frass'): these look like little black dots and are very numerous on leaves and caught in the webs. Another sign (especially on oaks) is the complete removal of the leaf tissue except for the skeleton of veins. Of course, the most complete examples show you where they've been, rather than where they still are. Some spiders also make tents for breeding.

Digger wasps are at the peak of their activity. Another warm-weather phenomenon is the swarming of Black Garden Ants. Under a dustbin lid, where the ants think they're underground, pupae are brought to the surface, apparently in response to rising temperature (and taken below again if it falls). These are of two kinds: those of the sexual generation being several times as large as those of workers. These pupae are often sold, misleadingly, as 'ants' eggs', as food for fish. The real, whitish eggs are, of course, much smaller – obviously, since no ant could possibly lay an egg the size of even the smallest pupae!

When the winged queens and males (produced from unfertilised eggs) emerge, they mill around in large numbers before embarking on their mating flight, thereafter for the queens to found new colonies. Why some colonies in the walls of houses suddenly swarm indoors is baffling, as well as pointless. This may be the only time ants are seen inside.

Incidentally, although everybody can recognise an ant, hardly anyone considers how they do it. It has been pointed out that, whilst most adult insects have wings, ants – as generally encountered (i.e. the workers) do not. A succinct statement has also been used to summarise the characteristic features: 'Any insect with no wings, a waist with nodes and elbowed antennae is an ant.' Most people, however, are struck by the sheer numbers usually present in a small area. Even when spread out on a plant, 'milking' the aphids, there are usually a lot of ants about.

Much less numerous are Stag Beetles, commonly encountered in July. Sadly, I often find them drowning in a pond. However, even after several hours' immersion, they frequently recover – but this may take several hours while they dry out (especially the tiny tubes that carry air throughout the body), so one must not give up too soon. Sometimes, parts of chewed up stag beetles are left by Foxes.

The Stag Beetle is probably the largest of our terrestrial beetles (the aquatic Great Silver Water Beetle may be larger) and the most spectacular (right) because of the large jaws of the male, which give it its name. In spite of appearances, the female is said to have the more powerful 'bite', but I have certainly had a finger grasped by a male, which managed to draw blood. It is quite hard to remove such a beetle with one hand unless you have forceps (or scissors) to prise the jaws apart.

A smaller species, the Dor Beetle, also occurs in much the same way, on logs or fallen in the water. Both Stag and Dor Beetles often walk about on the ground and stumble into the water in this way.

Ichneumon flies may be seen, usually quite large, with the females sporting long ovipositors. The larger dragonflies are also very evident at this time of year and may be seen emerging from the water. In the pond itself, there may be half-grown newts. At this time of the year, on warm days, Grass Snakes will often be swimming in the pond and baby snakes about 15cm long appear.

## Dustbin lids

Actually seeing small mammals under the lids is largely a matter of luck. One of the ways of finding out what is going on, in between sightings, is to place food under the lids and see if, and how quickly, it is removed. Suitable foods include bread, fruit, grains of all kinds and nuts. The advantage of nuts, including acorns and cherry stones (available at different seasons), is that, in opening them, small mammals reveal who was responsible. This is because different species have different characteristic ways of gnawing through the shell (page 46).

The presence of empty snail shells indicates the feeding of thrushes and shrews, which are carnivorous: the range of shells also illustrates the range of snail species in the area.

Male Stag Beetle.

A Young Song Thrush – you can still see the yellow 'gape flange' at the side of its beak.

Snail remains at a Thrush's 'anvil'.

A Juvenile Green Woodpecker (left) with adult male. It will not develop the brighter adult markings for several months.

## Bird life

This is an interesting month for noticing juvenile birds that differ in appearance from the adults. Some species do look very similar to their parents, but when newly fledged still have rather short tails and still show the yellow 'gape flanges' at their mouth edges.

Others differ from the adults in specific ways. As already mentioned, young Robins have speckled rather than red breasts, Green Woodpeckers only gradually develop the full red top and bright yellow green colours and have barred or spotted chests (below), and young Woodpigeons, even when full-sized, lack the typical white collar for several months.

Many birds are still feeding their young, indeed some will be laying eggs in a second or third clutch. In small birds feeding usually continues for at least a few days after the young are fledged. Song Thrushes may be seen feeding their young on snails. Adult Song Thrushes choose quite prominent 'anvils' on which snail shells can be shattered. Sometimes this is done on a brick path or steps but often a favourite stone is chosen, which becomes stained and surrounded by broken shells (not unusually, 15 or more). At the anvil, thrushes can be seen feeding bits of snail to their newly fledged young.

I have not observed how they find the snails but some of the snail hiding places are accessible to birds. Not the flat stones or other flat surfaces which attract substantial numbers – I have often found up to 25 in one place – but behind ivy against walls, for example.

In very dry weather, snails seal off the entrance to their shells, just as in winter for hibernation: when animals become inactive for a spell in the hottest part of summer, this is called 'aestivation'. On oak leaves, many small spangle galls appear: currant galls are largely over.

## Plants

Flowers of all kinds flourish but the most interesting developments are the ingenious mechanisms for delivering seed produced by vetches (spiral dehiscence) and cranesbills (see Chapter 5).

An Emperor Dragonfly female laying eggs in the water.

# August

Even as late as this, some newts remain in ponds and many 'newtpoles' still have gills and are confined to the water. However, the older ones have already left the water and may be found some metres away, under logs or large stones where they are protected from predators and find a ready source of small invertebrates as food. At this stage, they have lost their gills and their skin has become dry and velvety. Although only about 2.5–3cm long, they can travel a long way in search of food and shelter. Dragonflies continue to lay eggs, which will produce nymphs that emerge the following summer.

I had not realised that moorhens may still be hatching eggs this late until a pair nested in the Yellow Flag on our 'office' pond (and thus within constant view). I observed that both parents remained close to the nest (and each other) the whole time. Also, presumably because of exceptionally warm weather (c. 34°C on most days), the sitting Moorhen spent hours off the nest. I imagine that the eggs needed little extra heat during this time. Unfortunately, all 10 or so eggs disappeared and only one broken shell remained. Probably Grey Squirrels were the culprits. The Moorhen pair, however, remained for many weeks close to the nest. Pigeons and doves may still be building nests in August.

Digger wasps remain very active and can be seen carrying their paralysed prey down into their burrows. A close encounter with one of them demonstrated that, while not aggressive, they can deliver a sharp, and briefly painful, sting! Their behaviour on arriving back at their own tunnel entrance (once they have found it!), is often very interesting. I have seen a wasp clasping its bee prey discover that that it could not fit down the hole while holding its victim. So the bee was left at the entrance while the wasp went down the tunnel head first, turned round and popped up to drag the bee down behind it. The side tunnels make this manoeuvre possible, and, indeed, the wasp always both enters and leaves the hole head-first.

An immature Smooth Newt still bearing gills.

Common Wasps, nesting in holes in the ground, can be observed carrying particles of soil away, to be dropped some 20 metres from the nest.

Many galls are now at their most obvious. Oak trees harbour more than any other plant and the undersides of leaves are often covered with spangle galls, their stems adorned with oak apples and artichoke galls and the developing acorns may be almost enveloped by the extraordinary knopper galls (all caused by minute 2mm gall wasps). If these galls are opened (very carefully to reveal the spherical inner chamber) they may reveal grubs or fully developed adults, capable of flight after a short interval to dry out.

August is a good time to look for seed dispersal mechanisms (see page 104). All this seed production is characteristically autumnal. What is not, is the presence of the beginnings of catkins – typically a spring phenomenon. These can be seen on hazel twigs and on Alder, tightly packed green cylinders about 1cm in length. Since we do not expect to find catkins in August, we probably do not see them – as we often only notice what we are looking for, because we know it to be there. Similarly, we may not notice the buds on 'pussy willow' twigs. However, many plants reproduce in the autumn by runners (Wild Strawberry), stolons (irises) or immensely long shoots rooting many metres away (Blackberry).

Some plants only make their first appearance and flower in August. Wettish waste land often has Gipsywort, which appears several months earlier, mixed with Common Gromwell which waits until August.

*Wild strawberry growing amid the grass. In my garden it grows close to the edge of the pond.*

# September

When knopper galls fall off, in the autumn, they are dark brown, almost black, and quite hard to distinguish from the dark earth so common under big oak trees. In some years, however (for example in 2003), they can be found in enormous numbers, carpeting the ground beneath the tree. There are, of course, good and bad years for both acorns and knopper galls but the two cannot be closely related, because the galls are caused by gall wasps from the previous year's crops.

Many other big trees are also shedding seed, two of the most well known are Sycamore and limes, both have 'sails' or 'helicopter blades' to assist their spread on the wind. Expecting hard seeds to be inside the seed case, which is what you find in the case of lime, the seeds of sycamore are full of surprises. The lime seed case is very hard and, not the sphere that it first appears to be, but ridged. Inside this (which has to be cracked open with pliers) is another seed coat and within this a small (4mm) brown seed. If this is broken open the creamy coloured seed content is revealed. All rather what you might expect. However, the easily opened Sycamore seed, as we have already seen, contains its first leaves right from the start.

Later in the month the Horse Chestnut begins to shed its well-known 'conkers', protected by their spiky green capsules. Doubtless the latter protect the developing seeds but soon split to reveal the shiny 'conkers', most of which (if not collected by schoolchildren) seem to remain on the surface of the ground, relatively untouched by wildlife.

Another feature of September is the shedding of seed from the Great Willowherb (right). The seed pods split open to reveal masses of fine white hairs and embedded in these are very small dark seeds (speckled and slightly spiky under a microscope). You really need a magnifying glass to see that each seed has a tuft of hairs at one end – very similar to the willow seeds shed much earlier in the year. They are a sort of miniature version of the willow seeds – a sort of reminder: I wonder if that is why they are called willowherb!

One of the less attractive sights at this time of year is the appearance of 'mangy' Foxes. The condition is called 'sarcoptic mange' (after the sarcoptic mange mites that cause it) and it results in such irritation that the animals scratch, removing fur and causing skin lesions, notably over the flanks. Adult Foxes exhibit this condition in the autumn and it not only looks (and doubtless feels) unpleasant but it contrasts so markedly with the beautiful, quite brightly coloured fur seen at other times. The condition may sometimes even kill the victim, perhaps due to exposure to cold in the winter.

Dragonflies and digger wasps may still be active into September, and butterflies will still be active on warm sunny days.

*Fruit and seeds of the Lime tree.*

*Great Willowherb seeds.*

*Purple Loosestrife.*

*An Oak tree in autumn.*

# October

There are some interesting features that can only be seen at certain, limited times. For example, seed-dispersal mechanisms, pollen production, mating, nesting and reproduction in animals. One of these is in October, when deciduous trees are shedding their leaves.

The leaf stalk (petiole) has a special (abcission) layer where it joins the stem, designed to give a clean break for the leaf to fall. This is best seen in large-leaved trees, the most spectacular being the Horse Chestnut (page 153). If the stalk of the compound leaf of a Horse Chestnut that has turned brown and is beginning to shrivel is snapped off where it joins the stem, the remaining scar will be the shape of a horseshoe complete with seven 'nail-holes'.

Indeed, the end of the petiole, where it is snapped off, mirrors this shape but is green where the stem scar is a deep chestnut colour. After a short time (some minutes) the leaf also begins to show these same, matching 'nail-holes' – they become visible as they darken on exposure to air. The number of 'holes' does vary somewhat and in small leaves may only be four or five while in large leaves there may be eight. Even clearer old scars may be found on the stem, generally at the base (outer edge) of a small branch.

Similar scars may be found on many deciduous trees but, as the leaves get smaller, the scars tend to be shallower and triangular. Interesting scars are best seen in larger-leaved trees such as mulberries and balsam poplar (where the large leaves tend to occur at the top of the tree).

Although the discovery of fresh, colourful scars on Horse Chestnut twigs can only be observed at this time, the old scars can be seen at any time and especially clearly in mid-winter (when it is often assumed that there is nothing to look at, particularly in plants). All this is obvious if you actually look carefully at twigs. Most of us don't, most of the time: why should we, not knowing that there is anything interesting to be seen.

Even less does it occur to us to look in the soil but here is an example of what can be seen. In the spring, Lesser Celandine is a common and recognisable plant, with bright yellow flowers and dark green heart-shaped leaves. In shady places, it often carpets quite large areas but dies down completely by the end of spring. Just before it does so, however, cream-coloured tuberous growths may be observed in the axils of the leaves. These are 'bulbils', small bulbs that are outgrowths of the stem and serve as reproductive organs, from which new plants grow the following spring.

In the autumn, however, they can be found in the soil but may easily be confused with detached bunches of tubers on swollen roots each up to 1.5cm in length, just below the surface of loose soil where the celandines grew. They can be transplanted to a new site but will not grow until the following spring.

The most noticeable change in the autumn countryside is the loss of leaves from deciduous trees (which is why this season is called 'Fall' in North America). In many cases this is preceded by quite spectacular changes in leaf colour. Some just go yellow or brown but others (especially maples) turn bright red or mixtures of red and yellow.

It is not known for certain why they do this. In general, for reasons of economy, the green chlorophyll is withdrawn from the leaves before they fall, thus avoiding wasting it. This then reveals the yellow colour that was there all the time. But this does not account for the spectacular reddish colours, which are associated with a wide range of chemical compounds.

Many competing theories have been put forward to explain them, from protection from frost and pests to excretion of waste products. The latter seems to make more sense since the leaves are about to be lost anyway but there appears to be some evidence that trees with the most brightly coloured leaves actually suffer from fewer pests in the following year, the colour acting as a signal to insects not to lay their overwintering eggs on those trees. All this is accelerated by frost and actual leaf-fall is, of course, greatest after strong winds, characteristic at this time of year.

Some invertebrates are especially noticeable in October, such as Drone Flies feeding on ivy flowers, and harvestmen.

Autumn leaves on the turn.

Evening Primrose flowers remain open even in the dark.

*Hibernating small Tortoiseshell butterfly.*

# November

Like the winter months, November can be full of surprises, largely because we don't expect much to be happening at this time. But even when the ground is covered by dead leaves or even snow, more will be going on than you might think. For example, although Loddon Lilies are not the first to flower in the spring (snowdrops are much earlier), the dark green leafy shoots may be showing up to 5cm above ground, mainly in wettish areas.

Buds of all kinds are well developed, there are catkins on hazel bushes and plants like lungworts seem to continue leaf growth almost throughout the year. All these tissues seem to be frost-resistant, probably because they consist of small cells packed with sugars but little water. Only in the warmer, spring weather do all these structures fill with water and expand to their final size.

Many small animals die and food is short for both carnivores and herbivores. Some hide in sheltered places, protected from the weather, others live on their fat reserves. A few seek refuge in our houses, getting in through tiny cracks but others, such as Small Tortoiseshell butterflies, which one would have thought too big to do this, still manage to get in, in order to hibernate. Unfortunately, in warm spells or in response to central heating, they may become dehydrated, or become active prematurely and perish, because there is no supply of nectar to sustain them.

The smaller forms of pond life seem to thrive as winter advances and after a period when Phantom Midge larvae have been scarce, they suddenly start appearing again, less than full size and in rather deeper water (>15cm). These larvae illustrate another survival mechanism for the winter months. The adult insects die (such as dragonflies, and mayflies, which only live a day or so after they emerge, and many other flies which lay their eggs in

*Nuthatch with acorn.*

water) but their eggs may stay in the water for some time before hatching and, in any case, the larvae survive the winter perfectly well.

The reason is that, below any ice that may form, the water temperature does not fall below 4°C – the ice forming a protective layer between the water and the outside. Cold-blooded animals – including fish – simply move about less at lower temperatures and, because they are expending so little energy, do not need to eat. So a shortage of food is no great problem either. Cold-blooded soil animals like earthworms do the same but retire to greater depths: there, too, the temperature remains more stable.

Warm-blooded animals cannot do this, though some do use deep burrows, so they must either continue to feed, live on their fat reserves, hibernate or store food for the winter. The latter include squirrels which can be seen digging up acorns they have buried in the autumn. Jays do the same and Nuthatches (opposite, below) also store acorns.

Squirrels also construct 'dreys', usually quite high up in the forks of large branches, commonly in oak trees. These dreys consist of small branches and dead leaves lined with dried grass and may be built in big trees because they move less in the wind. Sometimes these dreys are built in thick ivy. Apart from those, the dreys are more easily seen at this time of the year, because there are few leaves left on the trees, but, because they tend to be placed in the fork of a major branch and the main trunk, they can often be spotted by looking straight up the trunk.

An obvious feature of the autumn and early winter is the leaf litter that accumulates on the soil surface. Where a leaf falls on a lawn and there are earthworms, leaves can be found pulled down into their burrows, usually by the stalk. This incorporation of leaf litter into the soil is also carried out, but less obviously, by smaller invertebrates and fungi and left alone it will all disappear. Whilst it lasts, during the winter, it serves to protect small creatures (and plant shoots) from frost and predators. However, Blackbirds, especially, but also Redwings, know this and spend a lot of time flicking over the leaves and searching underneath. A similar behaviour pattern can be seen on ponds where large leaves have fallen in. Moorhens can be seen turning them over, to see what small animals are on the underside of the leaf.

Among the fallen leaves of oak trees may be found the spangle galls so common on the undersides of the growing leaves during the summer. The adult gall wasps emerge from many galls long before this but not, it seems, from the spangle galls, which fall with or from the leaves with the galls intact. It is a delicate operation to open one (by lifting off the 'pimple' in the middle) but, if this is done, a small (1mm) grub will be found, waiting to emerge as a gall wasp in the spring.

In some years, one leaf may have up to 20 spangle galls and thousands of leaves may carry them, so the total in an oak wood must be many millions. However, like so much in animal and plant biology, all these phenomena vary enormously from year to the next.

A squirrel drey set high in a tree.

# December

One of the features of December is the absence of leaves on deciduous trees. Most people tend to use these leaves to identify the trees: this is no longer possible, although fallen leaves may serve the same purpose whilst they are present and not blown about in a confusing fashion.

However, this is a very good time to learn how to distinguish tree species in other ways, chiefly by the shape of the tree, the bark (left) and the buds (below). Buds alone are sufficient to mark out several species, notably Ash, Horse Chestnut, balsam poplars, Alder and Common Beech, by a combination of colour, shape and texture. Shape of the tree is sufficient by itself for Weeping Willow and Lombardy Poplar but others are greatly affected by their neighbours and how closely packed they are. The bark is very clearly different for Cherry, Common Beech, Silver Birch and, to a lesser extent, Ash.

Of course, coniferous trees still have their leaves and, often, give-away cones, and other evergreens, like holly and ivy, not only have leaves but also berries. Some deciduous trees and shrubs like Hazel and Alder may already have catkins, though not yet expanded.

On fallen oak leaves, many spangle galls remain attached – though others have fallen off – and mainly contain tiny grubs. Knopper galls, on the other hand, though rather harder to find amongst the leaf litter (because they are now almost black) seem to contain fully developed gall wasps.

Left: bark of (top to bottom) Sycamore; Oak; Willow and Cherry.
Above: buds of (left) Horse Chestnut and (right) Lilac.

In some years, some birds can be seen selecting nest sites as early as December. I have observed Jackdaws fighting over the ownership of a chimney, ducks choosing nesting sites in pond-side vegetation and hole-nesting birds exploring existing holes (though tits and Wrens are often just searching for food, or a place to roost). Many birds feed on berries at this time, notably Woodpigeons and Blackbirds on ivy and cotoneaster. On warmer nights, where the temperature reaches 10°C, bats fly at dusk.

As in November, buds may contain well formed leaves and flowers. Horse Chestnut buds are very difficult to dissect because the very sticky gum (which is, naturally, not soluble in water) seals the outer scales very tightly, so that it is difficult to see where they join. However, if opened, they reveal grey fluffy spikes that will later develop into flowers or leaves. Camellia buds are even more spectacular, containing pink petals, fully-formed orange anthers and a green style.

Hedgehogs may be seen – or more often heard – snuffling about amongst the dead leaves and shrews stay active, even at 4°C.

Camellia bud.

Jackdaws may start preparing to build new nests even in the depths of winter.

# 21 The impact of climate change

Weather is the state of the atmosphere at a given time: climate is the average weather over a period of time. The climate of the earth has always changed, often from extremely cold (ice ages) to much milder. What is different now is that rapid, potentially irreversible changes, in directions unfavourable to many living things including us, are predicted for the future as a result of human activity, mainly the burning of fossil fuels.

## Plant growth and fossil fuels

Plant growth is carbon-neutral: plants when they die and decay liberate exactly the same amount of carbon (as carbon dioxide) that they fixed in life. About 50 per cent of the dry weight of a piece of wood, bread, apple or paper is carbon and about 90 per cent of all carbon in plants is in forest trees. Plants take up about one seventh of the atmosphere's carbon dioxide, but a similar amount is released in their respiration, only less by the amount retained in growth.

Over vast periods of time, however, huge quantities of plant and animal material have been buried, under pressure, as fossil fuels (coal, gas and oil) where the carbon has accumulated and not returned to the atmosphere. A similar process has happened in the sea, in the form of tiny animal shells, later forming chalk and limestone. It is these vast stores of buried carbon that are released to the atmosphere, as carbon dioxide, when we burn fossil fuels for energy.

Coupled with the development of technologies that use fossil fuels – and nearly all electricity comes from them – the human population has also greatly increased. The total useage of these fuels has become enormous and is still increasing. There is now a clear and overwhelming scientific consensus that the consequent release of carbon dioxide is resulting in uncontrolled global warming.

# Global warming

This simply refers to the fact that the energy from the sun that reaches the earth is, in part, trapped by the earth's atmosphere and not all merely reflected back into space.

As we all know, cloud is very important in this – it is the clear nights that are cool or even frosty. It is not only cloud, however, that prevents heat escaping; the so-called 'greenhouse' gases (carbon dioxide, methane, ozone) also serve to trap heat. This gives rise to global warming, without which the earth would be uninhabitable. Most life, and certainly human life, requires the retention of some solar heat.

The problem is 'enhanced' global warming because of the steady increase in the concentration of greenhouse gases in the atmosphere. This may seem extraordinary since the actual carbon dioxide content is 'only' 0.038 per cent (i.e. 380 parts per million – ppm), but for most of evolution it has been closer to 250ppm. However, it is said to be increasing rapidly.

Similarly, the predicted temperature rises may also seem small: in southern England, for example, an increase of 2.7°C in summer and 1.6°C in winter – but this could eliminate frost!

There remains considerable uncertainty as to the extent and rate of any changes but the current estimate of the likely change in Europe's climate by the end of the 21st century is for hotter summers, wetter winters, summer drought and water-logged soils in winter. For example, rainfall in summer down by 30 per cent and, in winter by 10 per cent, but changes in wind speed, storms, floods and drought could be of greater significance.

*Beyond the clouds we need to reduce the greenhouse gases to stop the earth from overheating.*

Lavender – a potential beneficiary of a warmer climate.

## The impact on gardens

In detail, this is impossible to predict. Not only will the reaction of plants depend on the species, it will vary between varieties. In general, higher carbon dioxide levels and higher temperatures result in more rapid growth, but they may also shorten the period of growth. So ornamental hardy annuals would probably grow and flower more rapidly but also senesce earlier. Roses and rhododendrons could grow much bigger.

On the other hand, the absence of low winter temperatures will affect fruiting plants, such as apple and blackcurrant, where chilling is required to break dormancy or initiate and expand flower buds. Earlier flowering would also apply to spring bulbs.

All these considerations also apply to weeds, of course! However, drier, hotter summers, whilst suiting lavender (above) and Rosemary, would greatly affect fibrous-rooted perennials and plants like delphiniums, hollyhocks and phlox which are very susceptible to drought, and the general rule may be to avoid surface-rooting plants which, of course, include our lawn grasses. Grass may continue to grow – and need cutting – throughout the winter and just go brown in the summer. The use of coarser, more drought-resistant grasses makes for more difficult mowing and a less dense turf. Water shortages will reduce any opportunity to solve our problems by irrigation.

Of course, other species can be selected for the lawn, such as clovers and Lawn Camomile, as for the rest of the garden, suited to drier conditions. Indeed, many Mediterranean species are already being tried.

Trees and hedges are also likely to be greatly affected, especially Pedunculate Oak and Common Beech. Other susceptible trees include birches, Cherry, holly, Leylandii and spruces. However, there are less familiar oaks that would serve, such as the Holm Oak and the Mexican Oak, though other species might suit heavy soils, for example. Leguminous trees such as acacias and Gleditsia have advantages, and deeper-rooting species are more drought-resistant (like Ash, chestnuts and Field Maple). Hedges and shrubs can also be selected for drought resistance, including Blackthorn, Hazel and *Cupressus arizonica*.

Climate change will affect animals in several ways. Warmth-loving animals could expand their ranges – crickets and grasshoppers and the Comma butterfly appear to be doing so already. Butterflies whose caterpillars can feed on a wide range of plant species will be better able to adapt than those that are highly specialised. There will be opportunities for alien pests to arrive and thrive, in the absence of their native predators, and many invertebrates could multiply more rapidly.

Aphids and mites could increase very rapidly indeed and more survive in mild winters but whether their predators (for example ladybirds and hoverflies) would benefit similarly is not really known. Alien predators could also greatly affect some of our native animals, as the New Zealand flatworm, which preys on earthworms, has already done in Northern Ireland and parts of lowland Scotland. Already 13 of our 35 species of slugs are recent invaders but with no noticeable effects on existing invertebrate and plant communities.

*Blackthorn bushes with spring flowers.*

The number of butterfly and moth species that migrate to Britain for the summer has apparently increased fourfold in the last 25 years and for every 1°C increase in temperature (a big increase) due to global warming, a further 14 more are expected. However, butterflies and moths represent only a small proportion of the migratory insects and, of course, some, such as malarial-carrying mosquitoes, could be really undesirable. Regular butterfly visitors include Clouded Yellow, Red Admiral and Painted Lady, although the Red Admiral now also winters in Britain.

Amongst the regular moth visitors are the Hummingbird Hawkmoth, Hoary Footman, Small Thistle and, unfortunately, the Gypsy Moth, whose caterpillars can devastate forests.

These are only a few examples of the kind of things that may happen but there are already indications of much more complex effects. Birds like the Blue Tit time their breeding so that the hatching of the chicks coincides with the abundance of small green caterpillars (mainly on oak trees) that they feed on. If these two events get out of phase, due to climate change, it could have a devastating effect on Blue Tit populations.

With migrating birds the situation could be even worse with different effects on the trigger for activity in countries. It is thought that the arrival of the cuckoo may no longer coincide with the nesting activity of its usual hosts, and it seems that the arrival of the Pied Flycatcher from West Africa no longer coincides with the peaks of caterpillar production on which it feeds its young.

The best hope for gardeners is to be prepared to innovate and experiment to adjust to climate change: some will see this as exciting – others will take a different view.

Two examples of the Harlequin Ladybird – an ever-proliferating immigrant species.

Gypsy Moth caterpillars.

# 22 Ideas for garden wildlife-watching

This chapter looks at particular projects that you could undertake as part of your garden wildlife-watching studies, to further your knowledge and enhance your enjoyment of the time you spend in your garden.

## Unsolved problems

First of all, I need to be clear that these are problems to which I do not know the answer. That does not, of course, mean that there isn't one or that the answer is not already known to others, but the fact that these things puzzle me probably means that I am not alone. Anyway, it is no bad thing to try and work out for yourself why things happen.

So, to start with, here are some very general puzzles. Animals are often quite difficult to see until they move. Yet many of them make characteristic movements all, or much of, the time, for no apparent reason. Since it seems unlikely that they do them for no reason at all, the puzzle is why, when it gives them away so readily.

For example, all wagtails seem to wag their tails almost continuously and it is hard to see what purpose this serves. Grey Squirrels flick their tails and jerk their whole bodies about quite a lot. Some see this as a sign of anger or fear, in reaction to the presence of people, dogs or other animals, including other squirrels, but I have seen them do it when I could see none of these things. In the case of wagtails, the same applies and, in any case, why all the time? Wrens exhibit jerky movements that reveal their presence, apparently for no special reason.

The biology of animals and plants has been studied for so long, you might think that everything was already known, but that is not the case. Even at the level of natural history, never mind the more fundamental areas of molecular biology, the number of unanswered questions is endless. One should never lose the curiosity of childhood and the observation that gives rise to it.

*Wrens make a characteristic vertical movement with their tails.*

*Children can be encouraged to explore the garden and respect and enjoy its inhabitants from the earliest age.*

Night-time garden exploring may yield a sighting of more nocturnal animals like this Common Toad.

A banded snail on the move – you could try discreetly marking it to see if it returns to the same spot.

Simple questions, like "what is it doing?", "how does it do that?" and "why does it do that?" can be asked by anyone at any time. You don't have to be especially knowledgeable but you do have to have some confidence. As people grow older, they often become afraid to appear ignorant or to look silly, but if you don't know the answer, it is sensible to ask the question. As the Chinese proverb says: "He who asks is a fool for five minutes. But he who does not ask remains a fool for ever."

It comes as a surprise to many people to discover that the answer is not known, or not known with certainty. Of course, you cannot ask a question if you do not see anything to ask a question about. That is why it is important to observe what goes on around you.

Bear in mind that you cannot actually do this all the time: you would suffer from information overload. The example I have used to illustrate this is of driving along a busy road. You cannot possibly take notice of every car you encounter and you (sensibly) ignore all those that are not relevant to your driving. But the same is true for a passenger. Yet if you are thinking of buying a car, you may take much more notice, and, if you are already thinking of buying, say, a Vauxhall car, you will soon find that you get to know what different kinds of shape, size and colour there are. In other words, observation flows from interest.

So, biologists should observe the plants and animals they encounter. The trouble is that many of these plants and animals are very small and hidden from view: in the case of animals, they may only come out at night. It is difficult to take an interest in what you cannot see and impossible if you do not even know it is there (or even exists).

That is why this book aims to describe what is (or may be) there, and where and when it may be there. All based on the most easily accessible part of your environment – an ordinary garden. Even here, and without any special effort at observation, there is no shortage of unanswered questions. Better still, they are questions to which you might find an answer and there are problems that you may be able to solve.

One way of approaching this is to think of possible answers or solutions and then to think of ways in which they can be tested. This is the essence of any science, to observe, to identify a question, to formulate a hypothesis and then to test it by experiment. Of course, even if some of the answers are known (and it is worth checking on this first), it is much more interesting and exciting to read reference books when you know what you are looking for and why you are doing it.

So, here are some unanswered questions (as far as I know) that can be investigated in an ordinary garden. Of course, not all will be found in any one garden but you will find some that are relevant.

## Snails and woodlice

Snails and woodlice occur in nearly all gardens. Both are vulnerable – to predation and desiccation – and need to seek refuges. Woodlice usually hide under things – logs, bricks or any object resting on a flat surface – where the space is very narrow. Snails, with bulky shells, need more space and will therefore hide under ivy, or an upturned bucket, or any cover that gives them sufficient access.

I have found that large numbers of snails will gather under a sheet of black plastic, for example. Woodlice can be found above the ground, in crevices on trees or under loose bark but I have even found them under a flat tray resting on a wooden platform 1 metre above ground.

My question is, how do they know these refuges exist? How do they find them? and how do they find their way back to them, after making feeding expeditions? After all, if they did not wander about, how would they find the refuge in the first place? You can easily establish refuges and see if they become colonised. Any object that lies flat on the ground will probably attract woodlice (even if it rests on brick). Sheets of black plastic or dark covers will probably attract snails (of several species).

I have tried paint-marking snails under a refuge to learn who travels away and whether they return (indeed, by marking their resting place, to find out whether they return to exactly the same spot).

Behaviour of this kind will only occur when the weather is warm enough (when is this?) and may not occur in very dry times. So it varies with the time of year and actual movement may only occur after dark. If they are under a completely dark cover, how do they know when it's night-time?

A related question is "when do they breed?" Snails and slugs, in my experience, lay their eggs in late autumn (up to November), though I have found some throughout the winter (in the south). Since they are cold-blooded, why do they do this? When do the eggs hatch?

Woodlice breed when it is warmer and the females carry their eggs with them on their undersides – how long for? How many eggs do they produce at one time? If they are only carried for protection, would they hatch away from the adult? Woodlice are easy to keep and feed on decaying vegetable matter, such as dead leaves, bark and rotten wood, so you can watch them under controlled conditions.

## Puffballs

These fungi appear in the autumn, as near-spherical, grey-brown balls which, when ripe, emit clouds of brown spores when the fungus is touched. They are among the most easily recognised fungi, growing on the soil and leaf mould. As they grow (usually to 2–5cm in diameter) and ripen, they develop a hole at the top, through which the spores emerge. The spores are minute and their numbers are enormous.

*This Puffball is emitting its spores quite discreetly – sometimes they are dispersed in a great explosion.*

So, here's a challenge: how many spores does a given-sized puffball contain? How would you go about finding out? Here are some useful hints. In most such problems only a sample can actually be measured – in this case counted under a microscope. So the sample size has to be large enough to be measured (weighed?) but small enough to be countable: and you have to know what proportion of the whole is represented by the sample.

A similar but much simpler problem is to answer the question "how many seeds does a Dandelion produce?" In this case, it is possible to count directly the number of seeds (though they also blow away easily), picking them off one at a time. Or is it simpler to blow off all the seeds and count, under a magnifying glass, the little pits left behind? These are easily seen but hard to count systematically – how do you know which you have already counted? (A spot of ink on each – from a biro?)

A further problem with counting fungal spores is that they are carried away on the slightest air movement (one sneeze and you'd better start again!). It will be necessary to fix them in some way on a microscope slide, by something moist (and sticky?). Would they stick to a damp slide even after it dried out? Counting under a microscope usually involves a superimposed grid so that sample squares can be counted and multiplied up.

## Ducks

Here's a problem that only requires patient observation. It is said that only female ducks quack – the drakes are silent, or at least don't quack. Is this true? How early does a duckling start to quack? And can this be used to distinguish the sexes at an early age? Of course, not all species of ducks quack anyway, but the mallard (the commonest) does.

## Midges

On summer evenings, clouds of midges can be seen 'dancing' – often under trees. Why do they do this? What sort of evenings do they do it on? Do they avoid rainy or windy evenings? What temperatures are suitable?

Are both male and female midges involved? In what proportions? Does mating occur? What attracts them to form a cloud and where do they come from? What causes them to stop and disperse and where do they go? How long do they live after dancing? Can you think of ways of answering these questions?

## Water boatmen

There are two main kinds of water boatmen, both aquatic: a smaller dark species that swims the right way up, is heavier than water and is vegetarian, and a larger version that is lighter than water, is a predator and swims upside down (hence its other name of 'backswimmer'). The back-swimming species feeds on insects that fall into the water, which is why it makes sense to swim upside down, since it approaches its prey from below and stabs it with its piercing mouth parts, through which it sucks out their contents.

*Do your own observations to find out whether it's only female ducks that quack!*

*Warm summer evenings are the best time to watch midges.*

The question is how does it know when and where the prey are? It is said that it is attracted by the struggles of the trapped prey but you can easily observe its wariness if the struggles are very vigorous, indicating a dangerous creature, such as a wasp.

Small insects may struggle only a little (trapped and almost immobilised by the wings) and not for long. So, how do the boatmen (so-called because of the way they use their long, powerful middle pair of legs like oars) distinguish between prey, a small leaf or a rain-drop? Or do they investigate anything that could be of potential value?

## Solitary bees and wasps

Here are two different examples that give rise to the same question. The Red Mason Bee is a solitary 'mason' bee that appears in the spring and seeks out cracks in masonry in which to lay its eggs. It does this in a long tube of cement that it produces to form cells. It provisions each cell with pollen which it gathers from flowers and collects on the underside of the abdomen (not on its legs like bumblebees do). These bright orange undersides are very obvious and immediately identify the bee. On the pollen it lays an egg, closes off that cell and moves on to the next. At the surface, it seals the last cell with a cap of cement.

These bees will readily occupy specially-designed nest-boxes (see page 211) filled with tubes, so they can be easily observed. In the following spring, the next generation of bees emerges to repeat the cycle. Now, clearly, you might think that the last-laid egg has to be the first to emerge, otherwise the bees from the first-laid would have to burrow (destructively) through all the others. So, the question is: "How do any of them know when to emerge?" If it's temperature, why don't they all respond simultaneously?

Actually, the answer to the first part is already known. The first egg laid is the first to hatch and the resulting adult is the first to emerge. It then bites through the wall in front of it and nips the rear end of the bee in front. This then repeats the process until the last laid emerges.

Our second example concerns digger wasps. There are several species, so they vary in size and colouring, although most have a typical black and yellow banding. In about June, they emerge and then the females start excavating burrows in bare earth, often between the bricks of a path. They then lay their eggs in the earth tunnel, which may have branches, and provision each cell with a paralysed insect (small bees, caterpillars or flies) or a spider (wasp species are characterised by the prey they capture, so you can use this to identify the wasp). The prey is stung but remains alive as fresh provision for the growing wasp grubs.

So, here again, we have a sequence of eggs that hatch to produce grubs that mature into wasps, and again they have to emerge in reverse order to that in which the eggs were laid. The same question presents itself therefore: "How do the wasps know when to emerge – at the right temperature, when it's not raining (and perhaps not too windy?) and in the right order?"

A water boatman – how do they seek out prey?

Sand Digger Wasp starting to excavate a burrow.

*A school visit to the pond in my garden.*

## Leaf-cutter bees

Leaf-cutter bees make their nests in holes in trees or walls and line them with a tube made out of pieces cut from rose leaves (see page 87), some oval for the sides and some circular for the ends. I have noticed that the same rose bushes are used in successive years. Since the adults do not survive the year, it must be the new bees that emerge and go to the bush from which the nest was made. How do they know where it is?

# Things to do

Here are some ideas for features that you could develop to help the whole family experience biology in the garden. They are the result of my many years showing primary school children round my garden and trying to make it easy to see the plants and, especially, the small animals that live here.

## The construction of 'School Pond'

The first is the 'School Pond' (top left), which I made because most of the ponds available to the children were roughly circular, below ground level and relatively small. Such ponds are difficult to see things in, unless they are fairly large and then the animals can disappear quickly. Here's how it was built.

Ponds can be made in many different ways and for many different purposes. 'School Pond', as its name implies, was constructed in order to show school children what lived in the water. Its size was determined by the number of children who could sensibly fit round it and 30 is about the maximum number that can be shown what is there and what is going on.

The dimensions therefore turned out to be 7 metres long and about 3 metres across. There is no point in greater width since organisms cannot really be seen clearly if they are more than 1 metre away (unless an island is envisaged or, possibly, a bridge), and for most gardens a much smaller pond will suffice.

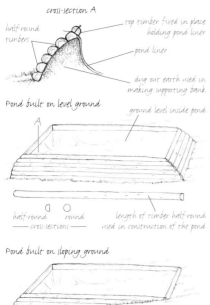

The construction details are shown left. For extra stability you can build a wooden frame (of green wood if you want to reduce the possibility that it will rot). Make sure it is securely supported in the ground. The easiest way to build the surround is to dig out the deep end and use the soil to form the banks. If the pond is built on a slope, the shallow end can be almost at ground level and the deep end above ground (see lower diagram). The banks can be covered in turf to keep them securely in place and a simple wooden framework can then be embedded into the banks, to which the split poles can be fixed.

To avoid stones or other sharp objects in the soil piercing the liner that will hold the water, use a base liner – this could be a piece of old carpet. Then line the pond with a liner of your choice – these come in a range of qualities and sizes. The liner can then be fixed (using flat-headed tacks) to the pole second from the top, so that the top pole covers the join. It is possible simply to trap the top edge of the plastic between the top poles (or rails), nailing them together.

*Constructing 'School Pond'.*

The whole idea is to provide an edge that children can sit or lean on, getting their faces close to the water surface. Whilst leaning up the slope of the sides, it is very difficult for anyone to fall in.

In order to make it possible for animals and birds to come and drink, without falling in and being unable to get out, it is necessary to have a shallow end with a sloping access. Vegetation growing round the edges (for example from between the poles around the sides and ends) or in pots can help small creatures (and even Grass Snakes) to get in and out. Animals that live in the water only to breed (such as frogs, toads and newts) need to be able to crawl in and out safely. Some of them may even hide under the sides.

Four sorts of plants are needed for a pond like this.

1. *Creeping plants* to grow round (but not covering) the sides. Many kinds of rock plants are suitable but the best, in my view, is Wild Strawberry (page 280). It creeps along, rooting in cracks at intervals, grows all the year round, has pretty flowers and safe, tasty fruits. It does not grow tall or get out of hand but, in any case, is easy to control.

*A Honey-bee sucking up water on the leaf of a floating plant.*

2. *Aquatic plants* are needed to aerate the water. In sunlight, they can be seen giving off streams of little bubbles of oxygen. Water plants are also needed as food for some creatures, especially Pond Snails, although most of these prefer grazing algae growing on the pond sides etc. Aquatic plants are also needed for small creatures to hide among and for some to lay their eggs on (including Pond Snails and newts).

3. *Floating plants* are useful to wildlife. Some, such as the various forms of duckweed are generally undesirable, since they multiply very rapidly, cover the surface and block out the light (needed by the submerged plants). But plants with floating leaves (such as water lilies and Water Starwort) are both attractive and useful. Water snails and China-mark Moths lay their eggs on the undersides of the leaves and many other insects use them as drinking platforms.

4. *Bog plants* have their roots in water, or saturated soil, but their stems and leaves grow erect in the air. Many, such as Yellow Flag iris, are very attractive and are worth having for this alone. However, their value for wildlife in the pond is mainly that they provide surfaces up which insects that live in water as nymphs can climb to emerge, usually as winged adults. The most spectacular are the dragonflies and their cast larval (or nymphal) skins are left attached to vertical leaves. However, the actual emergence of the adults can easily be observed, because they are in such prominent positions.

Both water lilies and the bog plants are best rooted in pots, otherwise the roots can spread all over the pond floor and cause considerable problems. Pots can be removed for any modification (replanting, repotting or pruning) but need to be placed on a flat surface and, because different plants (including different water lilies) need to be planted at different depths, these surfaces also need to be placed at different depths. Pots can be placed on bricks, of course, but the flat surfaces are best formed in the earth dug out under the plastic.

*Yellow Flag Irises.*

Freshwater Limpets are minute, usually only 2–4mm but some may grow larger.

## A garden aquarium

After many years of putting small creatures in jam jars, and passing them round so that children can see them closely and from the side, I decided it would be helpful to have a garden aquarium. It is often quite difficult to see small creatures in the pond and, indeed, unless you know exactly where to look you will not see some of them at all. This applies to most mud-dwellers and all those little animals that hide in order to survive.

A good example is the Freshwater or Lake Limpet (top left). I only knew about these when I found some on dead leaves that had fallen into the pond. They are very small (up to 3mm across) and roughly conical (or 'hood-shaped') with their flat undersides firmly attached to the substrate.

I placed a few in an aquarium and found that they multiplied rapidly and regularly appeared attached to the glass front, where their insides are clear to view. They are not always there and clearly wander about quite a lot but, at the time of writing, there are more than 60 on the front glass alone (43cm x 27cm). This is why I call it a garden aquarium, because it's simply an aid to pond observation, in which you can see creatures more readily than in the pond itself. It is not really practical to keep it outside, however: in summer it may get too warm and algae thrive on the glass; in winter, ice can crack the glass.

Any small glass tank will serve, filled with rain (or pond) water and planted with ordinary pond plants – Canadian Waterweed and Water Starwort do very well – using pond mud or fine gravel. It's a good idea to keep it stocked with snails (Pond Snails and/or Ramshorns) because they help to keep down the green algae which grows on the glass.

But for very small creatures, jam jars are even better, because it is easier to find the animals. Examples are seed shrimps (of the family Cyprididae) which are only about 1.5mm long, swim freely and often occur in large numbers. Less easily found and observed are the Pea Mussels, which can be felt (as tiny gritty bits – rather like rounded sand grains) in blanket weed. They can thus be collected when removing the weed.

These animals are not usually observed in the pond itself, even though they may be present in large numbers but the use of jars or tanks also makes it possible to see more detail of Freshwater Shrimps (below left), water lice (which are not lice at all!), baby snails, dragonfly and damselfly nymphs (especially when very small), Daphnia, Cyclops and the larvae of water beetles. However, it has to be remembered that dragonfly nymphs and water beetle larvae are carnivorous so can only be kept at the expense of the others mentioned.

As a result of having these small creatures confined and accessible it is possible to follow details of their life histories. For example, female shrimps can be seen carrying their eggs and offspring between their legs and, with a magnifying glass, eggs can be seen within the carapaces of Daphnia and in the egg sacs of Cyclops (page 41). This is an advantage of an aquarium as a magnifying glass can hardly be used with the pond.

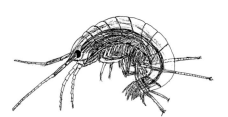

Freshwater shrimp.

As with the limpets, other little creatures periodically increase in numbers and move over the glass, presumably to graze on minute algae. However, this cannot apply to the flatworms or planarians because they are carnivorous. These are elongated, flattened animals (around 5mm in length) and they feed on such creatures as water lice (top right). They can be collected by placing a piece of liver or raw meat in the pond: this soon attracts them.

Among the larger creatures that can be studied best in an aquarium are caddisfly larvae. These grow up to 2cm long and are commonly encased in a tube, lined with silk and made of pieces of vegetation (stems or leaves), empty flat snail shells, small stones or grains of sand, depending on the species. However, a larva deprived of its case (a difficult operation since it tenaciously hangs on by hooks at its tail end) will build a new one of anything to hand. If you provide it with small, coloured beads and nothing else, that is what it will use to build its new case. The head and thorax, carrying the legs, protrude at the front of the case and drag it along behind them.

These larvae live for about a year, though the adults only survive for about one month, and may live on small insects and fragments of vegetation. The adults are more rarely seen and, although related to butterflies and moths, are rather dowdy, their wings covered by hairs (hence the name of their order – Trichoptera or 'hair-winged').

Two other larger pond inhabitants can be kept, water boatmen and pond skaters. Some smaller boatmen are vegetarians and live near the bottom. They swim the right way up and are heavier than water. The more common, and larger, back-swimming water boatmen are carnivorous and lighter than water, so they have to swim to descend and hold on to plants and stones to remain below.

They feed on insects that have fallen into the water so, in an aquarium, they have to be provided with food. This is simply done by using the aquarium as a disposal unit for dead flies and other insects found, mainly on window sills (not, however, those killed by insecticide).

Adult pond skaters tend to require a greater surface area than an aquarium provides and bump into the sides or fly off! I have had more success by introducing baby skaters, so that they get used to the area available. The same arrangements for food supply works for them. Both species simply suck out the body fluids, leaving the rest, but this is cleared up by Pond Snails.

Pond Snails, largely regarded as herbivorous, seem to be very fond of these dead insects and eat everything except the wings. I have yet to discover anything that eats these!

In general, an aquarium cannot actually be kept outside, unless the exposure to light is carefully controlled, as the glass usually becomes too encrusted with algal growth for even a dense population of snails to control. In addition, the water may go cloudy (not necessarily very green). I have found that this can be rapidly cured by introducing large numbers of Daphnia and Cyclops. A single Daphnia is said to be capable of filtering a litre of water per day! In any case, an aquarium cannot be left out in the winter, unless it is at least under a roof. An outdoor aquarium will freeze and shatter in winter.

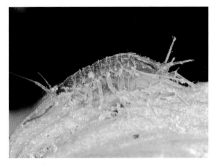
Water louse.

Caddisfly larva.

Pond skater with insect prey.

## Bog plants

Bog Arum

Bogbean

Branched Bur-reed

Brooklime

Bulrush

Common Club-rush

Common Reed

Conglomerate Rush

Celery-leaved Buttercup

Flowering-rush

Great Pond Sedge

Great Willowherb

Hard Rush

Marsh Horsetail

Marsh Marigold

Marsh St. John's-wort

Purple Loosestrife

Redshank

Reed Sweet-grass

Water Dock

Water Mint

Yellow Flag iris

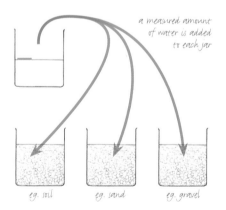

*a measured amount of water is added to each jar*

*eg. soil          eg. sand          eg. gravel*

*where are the water levels now?*

*The water table principle.*

## A bog garden

Plants that like to grow in boggy areas may not occur anywhere else, so there is little opportunity to see them, although some can be grown in or at the edges of a pond. The Yellow Flag iris is one of these. It will grow in water, even in up to 20cm of water, especially if the waters (as at the edge of some ponds) are not always as deep as this. But it will also grow on land that dries out in the summer.

Other plants will grow perfectly well on land that is only boggy some of the time. These include Water Mint, Loddon Lily, Redshank, Gipsywort, Common Gromwell and Water Pepper. Creating a bog garden is very simple, as long as the area can be kept damp. The easiest way is to line a shallow depression with black plastic sheeting. You can use an existing hollow in the land or simply dig out the area wanted. This can be of any size and depth but larger or deeper areas hold water for longer and can be replenished for much of the year just by rainfall.

Smaller or shallower areas either have to abut a pond (which can overflow into the bog area) or will need topping up occasionally. Then simply fill up the lined depression with soil and fill it up with water.

Typically, bog plants (not limited by availability of water or nutrients) grow very vigorously and spread quickly by extensive root systems or rhizomes. Bulrush, Reed Mace, Rushes, Bog Arum and Bur-reed are examples. Table (left) illustrates the range available and many of them are extremely interesting and represent a number of quite different groups.

## A water-table model

In Chapter 14, the way in which the water table rises was described and a comparison was made between two tanks, one containing just water and the other including gravel as well. The precise result depended on the size of the gravel pieces, so a simple experiment can be carried out to show what happens if the size of the particles is varied, from gravel to sand and determine which is the most absorbent.

The experiment is best done outside or in a sink, as there may be overflow from the water involved. Take a series of jars, the larger the better, although you can use jam jars and fill each with a different kind of soil, e.g. large and small gravel, earth and sand (left). Then using a measuring jug, or a jar marked with coloured tape, add exactly the same amount of water to each jar and measure the height that the water rises to in each case.

## A miniature wood

A quite different feature is a woodland in miniature, for children to explore. The idea flowed from noticing that it was difficult for small children to relate to big trees. Even the leaves were often out of reach on even the lowest branches. So I grew a wood specially for children.

The idea is to plant a variety of trees and keep them at a restricted height, say 2 metres. This means that the details of leaves, buds, galls, flowers, fruits and seeds are all within reach, even of small children.

*The hedge I created from a Silver Birch tree.*

Full-size trees can be seen anywhere and are very good for conveying the enormous size that they can achieve and details such as bark, but other features are very difficult to see. Who has seen the flowers of an oak tree? (Who knew that they had flowers?)

The first thing to realise is that most trees will grow to whatever shape you want, provided that you start when they are small. This is generally not recognised and people say things like "I couldn't plant a Silver Birch there because it would grow too tall and block the light/view". When my Silver Birch got to about 2 metres tall, I simply removed the top and allowed lateral branches to develop. I then cut it down again until the main trunk, 15cm across, was less than 25cm tall. Its branches grew out for 2 metres at one side and about 1 metre on the other, all controlled annually simply by cutting them to whatever shape and length I required.

So a small wood can be produced with all the trees at, say, 2 metres (or shorter), just by continually cutting them back to the desired height. The branches proliferate and can be shaped to make archways or bushes or whatever.

On a piece of rough grass, I planted saplings of willows, oaks, Ash, Common Hawthorn, Cherry, holly, Horse Chestnut and Laurel and kept them all to a height of about 2 metres. They all grow vigorously and nearly all the branches and their leaves are easy to reach. As a result, even in the winter, twigs, buds and bark can be examined and trees identified in this way. In the summer, all the pests, parasites and other inhabitants are easily accessible. All parts of the tree, except the roots, are accessible to children of all ages and sizes: the only feature missing is the typical structure and appearance of a full-grown tree.

Nearly all trees have non-visible, dormant buds under their bark, which only develop if the main stem is cut off. So a sapling can be kept short from the outset or a much larger tree, say 30cm in diameter, can be cut down to almost any height and the dormant buds will emerge and produce leafy branches.

## Looking at galls

The easiest galls to find and investigate are those of oak trees. Three of them are especially prominent: marble galls, spangle galls and knopper galls. Marble galls are caused by a gall wasp. The galls grow on the smaller twigs of the Pedunculate Oak and can first be seen in summer (the eggs having been laid in May or June), then they are small, round, green swellings. Inside there is an egg which hatches to produce a small white grub that feeds on the inside of the gall.

There are many questions you can investigate through studying marble galls. Can you find an egg? How big is it? When does it hatch? How big is the grub when the gall is full size (about 1.5cms across)? When does the mature wasp emerge? (This can be found by tying a small bag of muslin around the gall and seeing what emerges and when.) Do the galls turn brown before or after the wasp emerges? How does the wasp get out? Where does it go?

At this point, the life-cycle gets very complicated. The female wasps that emerge are asexual and lay eggs in the buds of a different oak species (the Turkey Oak). This can be distinguished by its acorns, which are half enclosed in cups covered in long, slender, hair-like scales. The wasp eggs develop slowly over winter in small, thin-walled oval galls between the bud scales, becoming apparent in March or April. It is worth looking for these but they are quite difficult to see.

Male and female wasps emerge from them in the spring and mate, the females going off to start the cycle again on oak.

Spangle galls (bottom left) in fact come in four kinds. They develop on oak leaves, and vary in detail but all are circular, 1–2mm across, with a small hollow or pimple in the centre of the disc (where the egg resides). The egg is laid by a gall wasp and the spangles occur on the underside of the leaf.

They are easiest to find in the autumn and they may be very numerous. Similar questions can be asked about these galls and the eggs/grubs inside them as for marble galls. But the end point is different because the leaves fall off in the late autumn (though not in some young trees). Does the gall fall off before the leaf? In any case, what happens to it? When does the gall wasp emerge?

Very commonly, as with the marble gall, there are sexual and asexual generations and the life-cycle may be very complex. What happens between the leaf/spangle gall falling to the ground and eggs being laid on leaves next year? Where do the wasps live and what do they live on? There is much still to be learned about many of these very numerous species of gall wasps.

If you look among the leaf litter in winter under an oak tree that had spangle galls, you can find the spangle galls still intact and you can look inside them. You could keep some in a glass jar and see what emerges.

When do the adults emerge from all these galls? You can find out by placing some damp soil at the bottom of a jam jar and keeping it moist, but not flooded. Place some oak leaves with spangle galls in the jar, just resting on the damp soil. Cover with a loose-fitting lid or a piece of gauze or muslin, just to let air in. Then wait.

Oak Apple gall.

Spangle gall.

I don't know when they come out: it may not be until the spring. Or, in a warm house, it might be earlier. You could try one jar inside and one outside. Don't forget that the wasps are only about 2mm long and may hide under the leaves (or the lid!).

Few people seem to have heard of knopper galls (top right), in spite of the fact that they are quite large (about 2cm across), quite prominent and, because they all occur on the acorns, you know exactly where to look. They are green and partially surround the growing acorn but when the acorns fall to the ground they turn black. They can still be found amongst the leaf litter in early winter but the wasp may have emerged by then.

*An elaborate knopper gall on an acorn.*

Has it? How many still have little white grubs in the middle and how many have fully developed wasps? Some of the latter, when you have carefully divided the gall, may fly off. (The gall gets very hard in winter and has to be cut part way from each side (or top and bottom) to avoid cutting through the grub or wasp.)

## A 'snailarium'

Snails and slugs are interesting creatures, though generally considered little more than a pest. In the garden, they are not very often seen, unless you look under logs, for example, mainly because they are largely nocturnal. What is seen is the damage done, holes in leaves and potato tubers and devastated seedlings. So there is a useful purpose in creating a place where they can be observed.

I have found that any large glass container will serve (bottom right). If water is placed at the bottom, plants can be grown as food and a high humidity can be maintained (essential for all snails and slugs to thrive), provided that a lid (or cork) is used to close the top.

By varying the plants, rooted in some soil with access to the water, one can observe which are being eaten and, by varying the species of snails and slugs, one can work out which are eating what. Eggs may be laid and, in the same way, one can learn to identify the species they belong to. There is one problem, it is surprising how quickly the container becomes fouled with snail droppings. Even small snails produce a lot of quite substantial pellets and fungal diseases could thrive in such a moist environment.

It is impractical to try and remove the pellets and the simplest procedure is simply to set up a fresh container whenever the fouling becomes excessive. This provides an opportunity to replace the vegetation with fresh (and, perhaps, different) plants. After the snails have been transferred and any eggs removed, the original container can then be totally cleaned out.

*A 'snailarium'.*

A different arrangement is necessary if the snails and/or slugs are to lay eggs because these are generally placed on or under the soil. Excessive moisture then has to be avoided to prevent damaging mould growth. The snails themselves will generally rest near the top of the glass sides and seem to enjoy each other's company.

*slug eggs of several species.*

Slug eggs (top left) are readily found under rotting logs and can be placed in jars until they hatch. If slug eggs are placed in such containers they will readily hatch and develop. When I tried different sorts of eggs, I thought I would be able to identify the species, but when they hatch they are too small to do this! They are mainly active at night but their tracks can be seen in the condensation on the glass.

## Why do flowers open?

Lesser Celandine buds appear in early spring and, on cold mornings, appear to open only after they are in full sunshine. They then close up again in the evening. This suggests that they respond to light and, especially, sunshine. However, if you keep a potted Lesser Celandine indoors, flowers will remain fully open all night, so it seems that light levels have nothing to do with it.

In fact, if you cut off a few tightly closed buds in the early morning and place them in a water-filled container, they will open fully within, say, a quarter to half-an-hour, depending on the temperature. Furthermore, if you then place them in the fridge for a short time, they will close up again. So, temperature appears to be the key: that doesn't mean, of course, that sunshine has no effect, because, as we all know, even on a cold morning, sunshine can substantially warm up the area it falls on. The flowers do not last many days, however, and, after a time, seem to lose their capacity to respond either way.

You could try this experiment with other common flowers, like Primroses, Cowslips, Dandelions, Daisies and hawkweeds. Of course, not all flowers can open and close, because of their structure. Daffodils, lungworts and Foxglove are examples of those not designed to open and close.

Even with those that can, do they all actually do it? Or is it only the early spring flowers – those that are likely to be affected by low temperatures? Among those that do, does rain have any effect?

## Seed counting

The size and number of seeds both vary enormously between plant species. Why is this? The purpose of a seed is to produce another plant but its chances of doing so depends on the numbers produced and their chances of survival.

Larger numbers clearly increase the chance that some will survive but, if they are very small, they have few food reserves to help them generate a new plant. There is also the question of who eats them. Big seeds may be more attractive to some animals. Squirrels like acorns, but what about conkers? Who eats these?

Goldfinches love thistle seeds (top right) but cannot cope with acorns, and who knows what small seeds are eaten by slugs, earthworms, millipedes and a host of minute organisms in the soil? It seems likely that there is a negative relationship between seed size and number, with larger numbers of seeds being associated with smaller size.

*Partially closed flowerheads on a Cowslip.*

To some extent this is obvious, though it also depends on the size of the plant species. Conkers and acorns are produced in very large numbers by big trees but for garden plants (cultivated and weeds) it seems likely that big seeds like peas and beans are produced in much smaller numbers than, say, Foxglove seeds, which are tiny but number several thousands per plant (see page 103).

It would be interesting to have more detailed information on seed production for a wide range of species. The great thing about this project is that different species produce their seed at different times, over a long season, and, in any case, seed heads can be stored (dry) for counting at leisure. If the seed can be weighed – no easy matter for very small seeds – then it would be possible to plot weight against number and see what relationships exist.

There are obviously two problems with small seeds, weighing and counting them. These are related, because the easiest way to determine average weight is to weigh a large number together. So, it really comes down to counting.

The easiest species to count is Honesty. The numbers of stems on a plant and pods on a stem are obvious and limited and, since the pods are transparent, the seeds can be seen and counted without dissection. In any case, there are only four or five per pod (bottom right). However, weighing them has to wait until they have ripened.

By contrast, if you open one seed pod (out of the hundreds) on a Foxglove plant, you will be astonished at the large number and small size of the seeds. It is easier to weigh the contents of, say, 20 pods but counting them is very difficult. I have found the best way is to spread the seed as uniformly as possible on graph paper with very fine divisions. On paper with the smallest possible squares, one seed just about occupies one square. Since it is numbers you are after, it does not matter whether the seed fits the square exactly, you simply have to count the squares occupied.

This is easy on graph paper, provided that you can achieve a uniform spread, such that, within an area, each square is occupied. Since the seeds from one pod will cover some 600 tiny squares (roughly 6 sq cm), it is quite difficult to count out the seeds of 20 pods! Of course, once you know the average number of seeds per pod, you can just collect and weigh the seeds of 20 pods.

It is important to consider how accurate you need to be. After all, all these numbers vary greatly. As someone once said, "It is better to be roughly right than precisely wrong." The problems will vary with the plant species and is very easy for those with larger seeds, except for trees.

Even when the seeds are very visible, for example because of their 'wings' (Sycamore and lime), tree seeds are not all visible and you need to see all parts of the tree. Probably the easiest are small trees with large fruits, such as plums and pears, with only one seed per fruit. For large trees, the Horse Chestnut is relatively easy because the conkers are readily visible and it is easy to count the 'seeds' in each.

*Honesty seed pods – you can clearly count the seeds without opening them.*

*Goldfinch feeding on thistle seedheads.*

For the purpose of studying a relationship, it is only necessary to collect a wide range of seed sizes and numbers. You can then see if there is any relationship between seed size and number and, if there is, which species do not conform: you can then try to work out why this is.

## A seed-growing facility

Many people, especially children, like growing plants and seeing seeds develop but little encouragement is usually given to growing wild plant seeds, including those of trees and bushes. Yet these seeds are often amongst the most noticeable.

Conkers and acorns are familiar to all, as are the 'helicopter' winged seeds of Sycamore, limes and Ash. Quite a wide variety are available and amongst the non-woody plants are vetches, cranesbills, Bluebell, burdocks, poppies, Dandelion, Daisy and a whole host of grasses. Furthermore, the seeds of these plants are interesting in themselves. However, children need to be guided as to which seeds are worth trying because they differ greatly in how easy they are to grow and the conditions they require.

Acorns and Sycamore are very easy – just place them on damp soil. Conkers are much more difficult, and Ash only germinates 18 months after ripening. Conkers need a single cold period to break dormancy but, if sown in autumn, they will germinate the following spring (if not destroyed by mice! – although they are extremely bitter). Most tree seeds are best sown in October.

Ash needs two cold periods: the first breaks the embryo dormancy then, in the intervening spring and summer, the embryo develops within the seed; during the second winter the cold breaks germination dormancy. Some very common species I have never tried, including the Dandelion.

So, a seed-growing facility can be simply a protected bed of soil outside or a tray or other (deeper) container inside, filled with fine soil or seed-growing compost. It is best to avoid seeds that are difficult or need special conditions (such as exposure to low temperatures or 'scarification' of the seed coat), in order not to disappoint or discourage children, unless they are deliberately experimenting. Two common plants whose seeds are easy to collect for germination are Daffodil and ivy (left).

It is also necessary to keep the soil damp but not waterlogged and this may best be achieved by rotating responsibility for watering round a group. Of course, a general (communal) facility can also house individual containers in which individual children can experiment.

## An invertebrate facility

You can also create an 'invertebrate' facility, with invertebrates kept in a collection of glass jars. One advantage of this idea is that it encourages children to take responsibility for their 'own' animals.

There are eggs to be hatched, to see what emerges. Those of slugs, snails, earwigs, spiders, ladybirds, butterflies and lacewings can be found and set

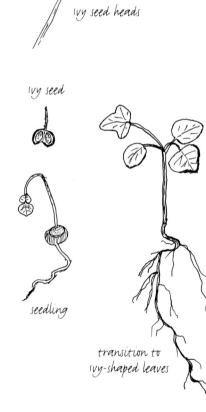

*ivy seed heads*

*ivy seed*

*seedling*

*transition to ivy-shaped leaves*

Different stages in the development of an ivy plant.

up within glass jars to observe what happens. In water, both Pond Snail and newt eggs are transparent, so development can easily be seen.

To do any of this successfully it is essential to know what conditions (especially of humidity) to provide and to work out how to do this. It is also necessary to know something of life histories, such as the parental care shown by earwigs and by many spiders. This leads to the use of reference and other books, with a specific purpose in mind. A real educational advantage is gained by going to books knowing in advance what you want to get out of them. This provides motivation to consult (people and books) and excitement is discovering what you wanted to know.

## Seeing root growth

You can also use glass jars for showing how roots grow and children can devise ways of holding the seeds they want to study (below).

Many ways can be devised for seeing things that cannot really be observed otherwise. This applies to small animals and to plants and can give rise to more problems for further experiments.

## Experimentation

The ideas in this chapter are really just an extension of the main theme of this book – that gardens are full of fascinating life, in addition to cultvated plants – if only you know what to look for and where to look.

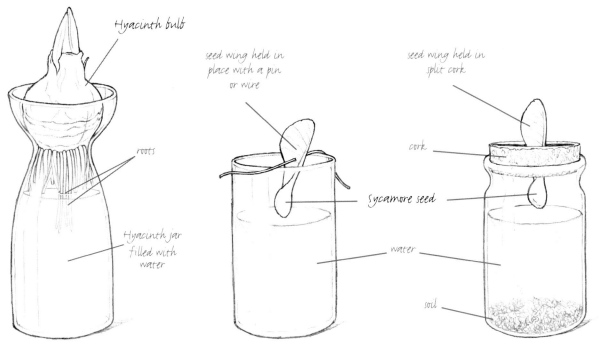

Observing seed growth.

# Scientific names of species mentioned in the text

11-spot Ladybird *Coccinella undecimpunctata*
14-spot Ladybird *Propylea quatuordecimpunctata*
Adder *Vipera berus*
Alder *Alnus glutinosa*
Alfalfa Leaf-cutter Bee *Megachile rotundata*
Alkali Bee *Megachile rotundata*
*Allolobophora longa*
*Allolobophora nocturna*
Alpine Mouse-ear *Cerastium alpinum*
Amphibious Bistort *Polygonum amphibium*
Anise *Pimpinella anisum*
Apple Grass Aphid *Rhopalosiphum insertum*
Apple Rust Mite *Aculus schlechtendali*
Apple Sawfly *Hoplocampa testudinea*
Apple Sucker *Psylla mali*
Apple Woolly Aphid *Eriosoma lanigerum*
Ash *Fraxinus excelsior*
Asian Giant Hornet *Vespa mandarinia*
*Aulax glechomae*
Autumn Crocus *Colchinum autumnale*
Autumn Hawkbit *Leontodon autumnalis*
Azure Hawker *Aeshna caerulea*
*Bacillus thuringiensis*
Badger *Meles meles*
Balm *Melissa officinalis*
Bank Vole *Myodes glareolus*
Barn Owl *Tyto alba*
Basil *Ocimum basilicum*
*Batrachochytrium dendrobatidis*
Bay *Laurus nobilis*
Bean Weevil *Acanthoscelides obtectus*
Bee-fly *Bombylius major*
Bee Orchid *Ophrys apifera*
Bergamot *Mondara didyma*
Betony *Stachys officinalis*
Bishopwort *Stachys officinalis*
Bird's-foot Trefoil *Lotus corniculatus*
Black Bean Aphid *Aphis fabae*
Black Garden Ant *Lasius niger*
Blackberry *Rubus fruticosus*
Blackbird *Turdus merula*
Blackcap *Sylvia atricapilla*
Blackthorn *Prunus spinosa*
Black-veined Moth *Siona lineata*
Bladderwort *Uticularia vulgaris*
Bluebell *Hyacinthoides non-scriptus*
Bog Arum *Calla palustris*
Bogbean *Menyanthes trifoliata*
Borage *Borago officinalis*
Bracken *Pteridium aquilinum*
Branched Bur-reed *Sparganium erectum*
Brandling Worm *Eisenia foetida*
Brimstone *Gonepteryx rhamni*
Broad-bordered Bee Hawkmoth *Hemaris
  fuciformis*
Broad-leaved Pondweed *Potamogeton natans*
Brooklime *Veronica beccabunga*
Brown Long-eared Bat *Plecotus auritus*
Brown Rat *Rattus norvegicus*

Brown-lipped Snail *Cepaea nemoralis*
Buddleia *Buddleja davidii*
Buff-tailed Bumblebee *Bombus terrestris*
Bugle *Ajuga reptans*
Bullfinch *Pyrrhula pyrrhula*
Cabbage Moth *Mamestra brassicae*
Cabbage Root Fly *Delia radicum*
*Cameraria ohridella*
Canadian Pondweed *Elodea canadensis*
Candle Snuff fungus *Xylaria hypoxylon*
Candytuft *Iberis sempervirens*
*Capitophorus ribis*
Caraway *Carum carvi*
Carrion Crow *Corvus corone*
Cat's-ear *Hypochaeris radicata*
Catmint *Nepeta cataria*
Celery Fly *Trypeta heraclei*
Celery-leaved Buttercup *Ranunculus sceleratus*
*Ceratostomella ulmi*
Chaffinch *Fringilla coelebs*
Chalk Carpet *Scotopteryx bipunctaria*
Cherry *Prunus avium*
Chervil *Anthriscus cerefolium*
Chicory *Cichorium intybus*
Chimney Sweeper *Odezia atrata*
China-mark Moth *Nymphula stagnata*
Cinnabar *Tyria jacobaeae*
Cleavers *Galium aparine*
Clouded Buff *Diacrisia sannio*
Clouded Yellow *Colias croceus*
Coal Tit *Peripatus ater*
Cockchafer *Melonotha melonotha*
Cocksfoot *Dactylis glomerata*
Codling Moth\* *Cydia pomonella*
Coltsfoot *Tussilago farfara*
Comma *Polygonia c-album*
Common Beech *Fagus sylvatica*
Common Bent *Agrostis capillaris*
Common Blue *Polyommatus icarus*
Common Bulrush *Typha latifolia*
Common Carder Bee *Bombus pascuorum*
Common Catsear *Hypocheris radicata*
Common Chickweed *Stellaria media*
Common Club-rush *Schoenoplectus lacustris*
Common Earthworm *Lumbricus terrestris*
Common Evening primrose *Oenothera biennis*
Common Fig *Ficus carica*
Common Frog *Rana temporaria*
Common Gooseberry Sawfly *Nematus ribesii*
Common Gromwell *Lithospermum officinale*
Common Haircap Moss *Polytrichum commune*
Common Hawthorn *Crataegus monogyna*
Common Hazel *Corylus avellana*
Common Hogweed *Heracleum sphondylium*
Common Horehound *Marrubium vulgare*
Common Lizard *Zootoca vivipara*
Common Lungwort *Pulmonaria officinalis*,
Common or Garden Field Worm *Allolobophora
  caliginosa*

Common Pill Woodlouse *Armadellidium vulgare*
Common Pipistrelle *Pipistrellus pipistrellus*
Common Reed *Phragmites australis*
Common Shrew *Sorex araneus*
Common Sorrel *Rumex acetosa*
Common Storksbill *Erodium cicutarium*
Common Sundew *Drosera rotundifolia*
Common Toad *Bufo bufo*
Common Vetch *Vicia sativa*
Common Wasp *Vespula vulgaaris*
Common Woodlouse *Oniscus asellus*
Comfrey *Symphytum x uplandicum*
Conglomerate Rush *Juncus conglomeratus*
Convolvulus Hawkmoth *Agrius convolvuli*
Coot *Fulica atra*
Cornflower *Centaurea cyanus*
Cow Parsley *Anthriscus sylvestris*
Cowslip *Primula veris*
Crack Willow *Salix fragilis*
Creeping Thistle *Cirsium arvense*
Cuckoo *Cuculus canorus*
Currant Clearwing *Synanthedon tipuliformis*
Daisy *Bellis perennis*
Dandelion *Taraxacum officinale*
Dark Sword-grass *Agrotis ipsilon*
Deadly Nightshade *Atropa belladonna*
Death Cap *Amanita phalloides*
Devil's Coach-horse *Ocypus olens*
Diamondback Moth *Plutella xylostella*
Dill *Anethum graveolens*
Dipper *Cinclus cinclus*
*Dinocampus coccinellae*
Dog Violet *Viola reviniana*
Dog's Mercury *Mercurialis perennis*
Dog-rose *Rosa canina*
Dogwood *Cornus sanguinea*
Dor Beetle *Geotrupes stercorarius*
Dormouse *Muscardinus avellanarius*
Drone Fly *Eristalis tenax*
Dunnock *Prunella modularis*
Emperor Dragonfly *Anax imperator*
European Yew *Taxus baccata*
Elder *Sambucus nigra*
Elephant Hawkmoth *Deilephila elpenor*
Fairy-ring fungus *Marasmius oreades*
Fallow Deer *Dama dama*
Fat-hen *Chenopodium rotunda*
Fennel *Foeniculum vulgare*
Feverfew *Tanacetum parthenium*
Field Bindweed *Convolvulus arvensis*
Field Scabious *Knautia arvensis*
Fieldfare *Turdus pilaris*
Five-spot Burnet *Zygaena trifolii*
Floating Pennywort *Hydrocotyle ranunculoides*
Flowering-rush *Butomus umbellatus*
Fly Agaric *Amanita muscaria*
Forester moth *Adscita statices*
Fox Moth *Macrothylacia rubi*

Fox *Vulpes vulpes*
Foxglove *Digitalis purpurea*
Foxglove Pug *Eupithecia pulchellata*
Fragrant Evening Primrose *Oenothera stricta*
Freshwater Limpet *Ancylus fluviatilis*
Freshwater Shrimp *Gammarus pulex*
Fringed Waterlily *Nymphoides peltata*
Fumitory *Fumaria officinalis*
Furrowed Acilius *Acilius sulcatus*
Garden Slug *Arion hortensis*
Garden Snail *Helix aspersa*
Garden Spider *Araneus diadematus*
Garden Swift moth *Hepialis humuli*
Garden Tiger moth *Arctia caja*
Gatekeeper *Pyronia tithonus*
German Wasp *Vespula germanica*
Giant Hogweed *Heracleum montegazzianum.*
Giant Wood-wasp *Urocersas gigas*
Gingko *Gingko biloba*
Gipsywort *Lycopus europaeus*
*Gracilaria syringella*
*Glomus intraradices*
Goat Willow *Salix caprea*
Goatsbeard *Tragopogon pratensis*
Goldcrest *Regulus regulus*
Goldfinch *Carduelis carduelis*
Grass Aphid *Metopophium festucae*
Grass Rivulet *Perizoma albulata*
Grass Snake *Natrix natrix*
Grass-leaved Flag Iris *Iris graminea*
Great Crested Newt *Triturus cristatus*
Great Diving Beetle *Dytiscus marginalis*
Great Grey Slug *Limax maximus*
Great Pond Sedge *Carex riparia*
Great Silver Water Beetle *Hydrophilus piceus*
Great Tit *Parus major*
Great Willowherb *Epilobium hirsutum*
Green Alkanet *Pentaglossis sempervirens*
Green Apple Aphid *Aphis pomi*
Greenfinch *Carduelis chloris*
Green Hairstreak *Callophrys rubi*
Green Hawker dragonfly
Green Oak Tortrix *Tortrix viridana*
Green Woodpecker *Picus viridus*
Green-veined White *Pieris napi*
Grey Cushion Moss *Grimmia pulvinata*
Grey Field Slug *Deroceras reticulatum*
Grey Heron *Ardea cinerea*
Grey Squirrel *Sciurus carolinensis*
Grey Wagtail *Motacilla cinerea*
Ground Elder *Aegopodium podagraria*
Ground Ivy *Glechoma hederacea*
Guelder Rose *Viburnum opulus*
Gypsy Moth *Lymantria dispar*
Hard Rush *Juncus inflexus*
Harebell *Campaula rotundifolia*
Harlequin Ladybird *Harmonia axyridis*
Hart's Tongue *Phyllitis scolopendrium*
Hazel *Corylus avellana*
Hedge Garlic *Alliaria petiolata*
Hedge Parsley *Torilis japonica*
Hedgehog *Erinaceus europaeus*
Hemp *Cannabis sativa*
Hemp Nettle *Galeopsis tetrahit*

Herb Hyssop *Hyssopus officinalis*
Herb Robert *Geranium robertianum*
Himalayan Balsam *Impatiens glandulifera*
Hoary Footman *Eilema caniola*
Holly Blue *Celastrina argiolus*
Holm Oak *Quercus ilex*
Honesty *Lunaria annua*
Hop *Humulus lupulus*
Hornet *Vespa crabro*
Horse Chestnut *Aesculus hippocastanum*
Horse Chestnut Leaf-miner *Cameraria ohridella*
Horseradish *Armoracia rusticana*
House Martin *Delichon urbicum*
House Mouse *Mus musculus*
House Sparrow *Passer domesticus*
Housefly *Musca domestica*
Hummingbird Hawkmoth *Macroglossum stellatarum*
Italian Ryegrass *Lolium multiflorum*
Jackdaw *Corvus monedula*
Japanese Knotweed *Fallopia japonica*
Jay *Garrulus glandarius*
Jersey Tiger *Euplagia quadripunctaria*
Kestrel *Falco tinnunculus*
Kidney Vetch *Anthyllis vulneraria*
Kingfisher *Alcedo atthis*
Lace Border *Scopula ornata*
Lady's Smock *Cardamine pratensis*
Larch *Larix decidua*
Large Black Slug *Arion ater*
Large White butterfly *Pieris brassicae*
Large-flowered Evening Primrose *Oenothera erythrosepala*
Larkspur *Consolida ajacis*
Lawn Camomile *Chamaemelum nobile*
Lesser Celandine *Ranunculus ficaria*
Leylandii *Callitropsis x leylandii*
Lily-of-the-valley *Convallaria majalis*
*Liriope mascari*
*Lithocolletis coryli*
Little Owl *Athene noctua*
Little Thorn *Cepphis advenaria*
Loddon Lily *Leucojum aestivum*
Lombardy Poplar *Populus nigra*
London Plane *Platanus x acerifolia*
Long-tailed Tit *Aegithalos caudatus*
Lords-and-ladies *Arum maculatum*
Lovage *Levisticum officinale*
Love-in-a-mist *Nigella damascena*
Lucerne *Medicago sativa*
Madagascar Periwinkle *Catharanthus roseus*
Madonna Lily *Lilium candidum*
Magpie *Pica pica*
Magpie Moth *Abraxas grossulariata*
Male Fern *Dryopteris filixmas*
Mallard *Anas platyrhynchos*
Manchester Treble-bar *Carsia sororiata*
Mandarin *Aix galericulata*
*Marasmius oreades*
Marbled Clover moth *Heliothis viriplaca*
Marjoram *Origanum majorana*
Marsh Frog *Pelophylax ridibundus*
Marsh Horsetail *Equisetum palustre*
Marsh Mallow *Althaea officinalis*

Marsh Marigold *Caltha palustris*
Marsh St John's-wort *Hypericum elodes*
Meadow Brown *Maniola jurtina*
Meadow Buttercup *Ranunculus acris*
Meadow Cranesbill *Geranium pratense*
Meadow Fescue *Festuca pratensis*
Meadow Grasshopper *Chorthippus parallelus*
Meadow Vetchling *Lathyrus pratensis*
Meadowsweet *Filipendula ulmaria*
*Metarhizium flavoviride*
Minnow *Phoxinus phoxinus*
Mistle Thrush *Turdus viscivorus*
Mole *Talpa europaeus*
Moorhen *Gallinula chloropus*
Mother Shipton *Callistege mi*
Motherwort *Leonurus cardiaca*
Mottled Umber *Erannis defoliaria*
Mouse-ear Hawkweed *Pilosella officinarum*
Muntjac *Muntiacus reevesi*
Mute Swan *Cygnus olor*
Narrow-bordered Bee Hawkmoth *Hemaris tityus*
Natterjack Toad *Epidalea calamita*
*Nepticula aurella*
Netted Slug *Deroceras reticulatum*
Nettle-leaved Bellflower *Campanula trachelium*
New Zealand Flatworm *Arthurdendyus triangulatus*
New Zealand Pigmyweed *Crassula helmsii*
Nightingale *Luscinia megarhynchos*
Night-scented Stock *Matthiola bicornis*
Noctule Bat *Nyctalus noctula*
Norwegian Wasp *Dolichovespula norvigica*
Nursery Web Spider *Pisaura mirablis*
Nuthatch *Sitta europaea*
Oak Beauty *Biston strataria*
Oak Eggar *Lasiocampa quercus*
*Oniscus asellus*
Opium Poppy *Papaver somniferum*
Orange Underwing *Archiearis parthenias*
Orange-tip *Anthocharis cardamines*
Orkney Vole *Microtus arvalis*
Oxeye Daisy *Leucanthemum vulgare*
Painted Lady *Vanessa cardui*
Palmate Newt *Lissotriton helveticus*
Parent Bug *Elasmucha grisea*
Parrot's Feather *Myriophyllum aquaticum*
Parsley *Petroselinum crispum*
Passion Flower
Pea Moth *Cydia nigricana*
Pea Mussel *Pisidium pseudosphaerium*
Pea Weevil *Bruchus pisorum*
Peacock *Pavo cristatus*
Peacock butterfly *Inachis io*
Pear Sucker *Psylla pyricola*
Pearly Underwing *Peridroma saucia*
Pedunculate Oak *Quercus robur*
Peppered Moth *Biston betularia*
Peppermint *Mentha x piperita*
Perennial Ryegrass *Lolium perenne*
*Perrisia ulmariae*
Periwinkle *Vinca major*
*Perrisia ulmariae*
Phantom Midge *Chaoborus crystillinus*
*Phasmarhabditis hermaphrodita*

Pheasant *Phasianus colchicus*
*Phoma lingam*
Pied Flycatcher *Ficedula hypoleuca*
Pied Wagtail *Motacilla alba*
Pill Woodlouse *Armadilium vulgare*
Pond Snail *Lymnaea stagnalis*
*Pontania proxima*
Pool Frog *Pelophylax lessonae*
Primrose *Primula vulgaris*
*Pteromalus puparum*
Purple Loosestrife *Lythrum salicaria*
Pygmy Shrew *Sorex minutus*
Rabbit *Oryctolagus cuniculus*
Raft Spider *Dolomedes fimbriatus*
Ramshorn *Planorbarius corneus*
Raven *Corvus corax*
Red Admiral *Vanessa atalanta*
Red Ant *Myrmica rubra*
Red Clover *Trifolium pratense*
Red Deer *Cervus elaphus*
Red Mason Bee *Osmia rufa*
Red Spider Mite
Red Wasp *Vespula rufa*
Redshank *Polygonum persicana*
Redwing *Turdus iliacus*
Reed Sweet-grass *Glyceria maxima*
*Reineckea cornea*
*Rhodites rosae*
Ringlet *Aphantopus hyperantus*
Robin *Erithacus rubecula*
Roe Deer *Capreolus capreolus*
Rook *Corvus frugilegus*
Rose Aphid *Macrosiphum rosae*
Rosemary *Rosmarinus officinalis*
Rosemary Beetle *Chrysolina americana*
Rosy Apple Aphid *Dysaphis plantaginea*
Rough-stalked Feather-moss *Brachythecium rutabulum*
Sage *Salvia officinalis*
Sand Lizard *Lacerta agilis*
*Sarcococca humilis*
*Scolytus destructor*
Scotch Burnet *Zygaena exulans*
Sea Beet *Beta vulgaris*
Self-heal *Prunella vulgaris*
Seven-spot Ladybird *Coccinella septempunctata*
Shaggy Inkcap *Coprinus comatus*
Sheep's Sorrel *Rumex acetosella*
Short-tailed Field Vole *Microtus agrestis*
Signal Crayfish *Pacifastacus leniusculus*
Silk Moth *Bombyx mori*
Silky Wall Feather-moss *Homalothecium sericeum*
Silverfish *Lepisma saccharina*
Silver Birch *Betta pendula*
Silver-Y moth *Autographa gamma*
Silvery Threadmoss *Bryum argenteum*
Six-spot Burnet *Zygaena filipendulae*
Slow-worm *Anguis fragilis*
Small Thistle moth *Tebenna micalis*
Small Tortoiseshell *Aglais urticae*
Small White *Pieris rapae*
Small Yellow Underwing *Panemeria tenebrata*
Small-flowered Evening Primrose *Oenothera parviflora*

Smooth Meadow-grass *Poa pratensis*
Smooth Newt *Lissotriton vulgaris*
Smooth Snake *Coronella austriaca*
Snowdrop *Galanthus nivalis*
Snowy Owl *Bubo scandiacus*
Soapwort *Saponaria officinalis*
Song Thrush *Turdus philomelos*
Soprano Pipistrelle *Pipistrelllus pygmaeus*
Southern Hawker *Aeshna cyanea*
Sparrowhawk *Accipiter nisus*
Spindle tree *Euonymus europaeus*
Spotted Flycatcher *Muscicapa striata*
Spring Usher moth *Agriopis leucophaearia*
Stag Beetle *Lucanus cervus*
Starling *Sturnus vulgaris*
Stinging Nettle *Urtica dioica*
Stoat *Mustela erminea*
Stock Dove *Columba oenas*
Strawberry Snail *Trichia striolata*
Strawberry Tree *Arbutus unedo*
Sunflower *Helianthus annuus*
Swallow *Hirundo rustica*
Sweet Briar *Rosa rubiginosa*
Sweet Violet *Viola odorata*
Swift *Apus apus*
Sycamore *Acer pseudoplatanus*
Tall Fescue *Festuca arundinacea*
Tansy *Tanacetum vulgare*
Tarragon *Artemisia dracunculus*
Tasteless Water-pepper
Tawny Mining Bee *Andrena fulva*
Tawny Owl *Strix aluco*
Teasel *Dipsacus fullonum*
Tench *Tinca tinca*
Three-spined Stickleback *Gasterosteus aculeatus*
Thyme *Thymus vulgaris*
Timothy *Phleum pratense*
Toadflax *Linaria vulgaris*
Tobacco Plant *Nicotania sylvestris*
Tomato Moth *Lacanobia oleracea*
Tree Wasp *Dolichovespula sylvestris*
Treecreeper *Certhia familiaris*
Turkey Oak *Quercus cerris*
Turtle Dove *Streptopelia turtur*
Two-spot Ladybird *Adalia bipunctata*
*Typhlodromus pyri*
Vapourer moth *Orgyia antiqua*
*Varroa destructor*
*Verticillium lecanii*
Vestal Cuckoo Bee *Bombus vestalis*
Vine Weevil *Otiorhynchus sulcatus*
Virginia Creeper *Parthenocissus quinquefolia*
Water Dock *Rumex hydrolapathum*
Water Fern *Azolla filiculoides*
Water Forget-me-not *Myosotis scorpiodes*
Water Horsetail *Equisetum fluviatile*
Water Mint *Mentha aquatica*
Water Pepper *Polygonum hydropiper*
Water Starwort *Callitriche stagnalis*
Water Violet *Hottonia palustris*
Water Vole *Arvicola terrestris*
Weasel *Mustela nivalis*
Weeping Willow *Salix babylonica*
White Admiral *Limenitis camilla*

White Bryony *Bryonia cretica*
White Clover *Trifolium repens*
White Waterlily *Nymphaea alba*
White Willow *Salix alba*
White-clawed Crayfish *Austropotamobius pallipes*
White-lipped Snail *Cepaea hortensis*
Whitethroat *Sylvia communis*
Wild Carrot *Daucus carota*
Wild Daffodil *Narcissus psuedonarcissus*
Wild Strawberry *Fragaria vesca*
Willow Moss *Fontinalis antipyretica*
Willow Warbler *Phylloscopus trochilus*
Winter Moth *Operophtera brumata*
Wood Mouse *Apodemus sylvaticus*
Wood Tiger moth *Parasemia plantaginis*
Woodavens *Geum urbanum*
Woodpigeon *Columba palumbus*
Wren *Troglodytes troglodytes*
Yarrow *Achillea millefolium*
Yellow Archangel *Lamiastrum galeobdolon*
Yellow Flag iris *Iris pseudacorus*
Yellow Meadow Ant *Lasius flavus*
Yellow-necked Mouse *Apodemus flavicollis*
Yellow Slug *Limacus flavus*
Yellow Waterlily *Nuphar lutea*
Zebra Spider *Salticus scenicus*
*Zoophthora radicans*

# Index

# Photo and illustration credits

A. Petelin/shutterstock 99b; A. Poselenov/shutterstock 247; A.von Dueren/shutterstock 78t; Adam Edwards/shutterstock 28, 262b; Agorafobia/shutterstock 75c; AISPIX/shutterstock 15, 16; Alan Bryant/shutterstock 119t; Alan Scheer/shutterstock 167b; Alan49/shutterstock 40t; Alexander Chelmodeev/shutterstock 74t; Alexander Komp/shutterstock 136; Alexandra Lande/shutterstock 11; Alexey Sokolov/shutterstock 272bl; Alis Leonte/shutterstock 154; alslutsky/shutterstock 277; Alucard2100/shutterstock 192b; Ana Marques/shutterstock 126tl; Andrea Haase/shutterstock 287t; Andreas Altenburger/shutterstock 273; Andrew Bailey/FLPA 138b, 209; Anest/shutterstock 82bl; Anette Linnea Rasmussen/shutterstock 234; Anmor Photography/shutterstock 79; Ann Badjura/shutterstock 265b; Anna Martynova/shutterstock 293b; Anne Kitzman/shutterstock 285; Anton Gvozdikov/shutterstock 298b; ArjaKo's/shutterstock 282lb; ArnoldW/shutterstock 159; Arpad Nagy-Bagoly / shutterstock 235t; Art_Maric/shutterstock 102t; Aviddoghug via Wikipedia Commons 130br; Awei/shutterstock 253b; Aynia Brennan/shutterstock 3, 236; azaphoto/shutterstock 301; B. Borrell Casals/FLPA 180b, 303; bbbb/shutterstock 228b, 256t; Bernd Juergens/shutterstock 29; bluecrayola/shutterstock 149; Bo Valentino/shutterstock 156; Bob Gibbons/FLPA 66b; Borislav Borisov/shutterstock 6, 8, 35t; Brian Maudsley/shutterstock 179r; catherinka/shutterstock 97; Cheryl Kunde/shutterstock 86b; Chrislofoto/shutterstock 212b, 224, 231t; 250; Christian Mueller/shutterstock 203b; Christian Musat/shutterstock 52bc; Christina Loehr/shutterstock 95; Christopher Elwell/shutterstock 160t; clearviewstock/shutterstock 183tr; Cosmin Manci/shutterstock 84l, 309t; CreativeNature.nl/shutterstock 191; D Tanner/shutterstock 268t; D Vande/shutterstock 214; D. Kucharski & K. Kucharska/shutterstock 145r; Dan Shutter/shutterstock 206; Daniel Petrescu/shutterstock 69; Daniel Rajszczak 56; Dave Massey/shutterstock 96; Dave McAleavy/shutterstock 289; David Benton/shutterstock 52br; Daul Dohnal/shutterstock 35b, 90, 237t; David Hosking/FLPA 83b, 150, 168t, 205; David Woolfenden/shutterstock 155bl; Derek Middleton/FLPA 3, 46, 55b, 62, 220b, 279b; Dieter Hopf/ Imagebroker/FLPA 55c; Dirk Ercken/shutterstock 221; DL Pohl/shutterstock 194l; Dmitriy Bryndin/shutterstock 298t; Dmitry Maslov/shutterstock 254; Doug Lemke 47t; Dr. Morley Read/shutterstock 87t; Duncan Usher/FN/Minden/FLPA 284b; Edward Westmacott/shutterstock 248b; Elena Elisseeva/shutterstock 109b; Elliotte Rusty Harold/shutterstock 140, 176; Emily Veinglory/shutterstock 86l; Emjay Smith/shutterstock 33, 63r, 171, 270lt; Era Pictures 56; Eric Isselée/shutterstock 148b; Erica Olsen/FLPA 297; errni/shutterstock 178t; Evgeni Stefanov/shutterstock 75c; Ewa Walicka/shutterstock 122; F. Mann/shutterstock 296b; Filip Fuxa/shutterstock 238t; Florian Andronache/shutterstock 123tr; fotoping/shutterstock 218c; FotoVeto/shutterstock 74bl, 100, 264; Francesco Scotto/shutterstock 54t; Gary K Smith/FLPA 195; Geanina Bechea/shutterstock 3, 139; Georgy Markov/shutterstock 37; Gerald A. DeBoer/shutterstock 263t; Gertjan Hooijer/shutterstock 61t, 123cr, 301t; Gill Martin/shutterstock 144b; Glen Gaffney/shutterstock 165; Gordana Sermek/shutterstock 107; Gucio_55/shutterstock 48b, 109r; Hadrian/shutterstock 291; Halina Yakushevich/shutterstock 24; Hallam Creations/shutterstock 163r; hansenn/shutterstock 132l; Hartmut Morgenthal/shutterstock 276b; Heiko Kiera/shutterstock 192l; Heinz Schrempp/FLPA 169rb; Henrik Larsson/shutterstock 26t, 26b, 48t, 85, 169ctl, 253c; Horia Bogdan/shutterstock 151; Hugh Clark/FLPA 91; Ian Grainger/shutterstock 177t; Igor

Plotnikov/shutterstock 92; Igor Semenov/shutterstock 204; Ilona Slavickova/shutterstock 126br; Ilya D. Gridnev/shutterstock 266tl; Inavan Hateren/shutterstock 218t; Ingo Arndt/Minden Pictures/FLPA 299t; Inna Felker/shutterstock 68t; J Gade/shutterstock 51, 271b; Jag_cz/shutterstock_ 262t; Jan Bussan/shutterstock 231tr; Jason Mintzer/shutterstock 101; JeniFoto/shutterstock 19; Jens Stolt/shutterstock 199; Jeremy Early/FLPA 252b; Jerome Whittingham/shutterstock 210b; Jesse Kunerth/shutterstock 256c; John Braid/shutterstock 133tr; John Hawkins/FLPA 105; John Lumb/shutterstock 207; Jon Brackpool-Photography/shutterstock 30t; Joseph Calev/shutterstock 173, 183b; Joy Stein/shutterstock 138l; Jubal Harshaw/shutterstock 99t; Julie Swale/FLPA 168b; kanusommer/shutterstock 93; Karel Gallas/shutterstock 75t, 126bl, 184t; Kenneth William Caleno/shutterstock 248t; Kerry Vanessa McQuaid/shutterstock 115; Kirsanov/shutterstock 180t; Klaus Kaulitzki/shutterstock 186t; kldy/shutterstock 201t; Kletr/shutterstock 160b, 268b; Konrad Wothe/Minden Pictures/FLPA 257b; Krzysztof Odziomek/shutterstock 217; kurt_G/shutterstock 203t, 203c, 303b; Kuttelvaserova/shutterstock 280; Lane V. Erickson/shutterstock 84b; LianeM/shutterstock 161b; lightpoet/shutterstock 166; Lijuan Guo/shutterstock 102b; Lin, Chun-Tso/shutterstock 73; Ljupco Smokovski/shutterstock 265t; Lobke Peers/shutterstock 202; Lucian Mares/shutterstock 274; Lukich/shutterstock 245; Lynne Carpenter/shutterstock 22; M Trebbin/shutterstock 228t; Madlen/shutterstock 40b ; Magdalena Bujak/shutterstock 189; Maigi/shutterstock 148tl; Malcolm Schuyl/FLPA 219c; Maljalen/shutterstock 258; Marcel Clemens/shutterstock 114l; Marcus Webb/FLPA 278cl; Marek R. Swadzba/shutterstock 186b; Maria Dryfhout/shutterstock 294; Marie C Fields/shutterstock 218b; Mariia Savoskula/shutterstock 113; Marilyn Barbone/shutterstock 281b; Mark Bridger/shutterstock 63b, 141, 190, 293t, 312; Mark William Richardson/shutterstock 14b; MarkMirror/shutterstock 30c, 30b, 52bl, 169cr, 237b; Martin Fowler/shutterstock 52cl, 61b, 67, 85b, 85t, 130tl, 131b, 158t, 162, 225t, 242, 267rb, 269, 278b, 292; Mary Terribery/shutterstock 134l; Maslov Dmitry/shutterstock 41c; Matt Hart/shutterstock 116; Matthijs Wetterauw/shutterstock 54bl; Mauro Rodrigues/shutterstock 299b; Menno Schaefer/shutterstock 38, 194r, 201b; Michael Durham/Minden Pictures/FLPA 220t; Michael Moeller/shutterstock 212t; Mikhail Dudarev/shutterstock 282t; Mike Lane/FLPA 223; Mikhail Hoboton Popov/shutterstock 47b; Mikhail Melnikov/shutterstock 64b; MilanB/shutterstock 197; Milena/shutterstock 43; Mircea Bezergheanu/shutterstock 7, 124tl; mitzy/shutterstock 53l, 53r, 213; mortalcris/shutterstock 295; N Almesjö/shutterstock 152; Neil Bowman/FLPA 219t; Nejron Photo/shutterstock 290; Nigel Cattlin/FLPA 120, 161t, 222, 229t, 235b, 276t; Olga Gavrilova/shutterstock 130bl; panda3800 56; papkin/shutterstock 187; pashabo/shutterstock 184tl; Paul Hobson/FLPA 306b; Paul Sawer/FLPA 4; Paula Fisher/shutterstock 12; Pavel Mikoska/shutterstock 157; Pavels Hotulevs/shutterstock 252t; Pawel Kielpinski/shutterstock 117; Peter Doomen/shutterstock 121; Peter Entwistle/FLPA 11; Peter Krejzl/shutterstock 270t, 308b; Peter Wey/shutterstock 125b; Peter Wollinga/shutterstock 31; Phoric/shutterstock 301b; Photo Researchers/FLPA 36; Photofun/shutterstock 129, 174b, 175; Pietus/shutterstock 118; Pincasso/shutterstock 137; plastique/shutterstock 71; Polina Truver/shutterstock 9; pwrmc/shutterstock 146; Ralf Gosch/shutterstock 240; Ramon Grosso Dolarea/shutterstock 27r; Rasmus Holmboe Dahl/shutterstock 284tl; Razvan Zinica/shutterstock 77;

Razvan Zinica/shutterstock 275; Reinhard Dirscherl/FLPA 303t; Richard Becker/FLPA 181, 257t; Richard Peterson/shutterstock 243b; Richard Thornton/shutterstock 283tr; Rikard Stadler/shutterstock 178b; Rob Francis/shutterstock 60b; Rob Kemp/shutterstock 255, 279t; Robert Biedermann/shutterstock 112bl; Robert Hardholt/shutterstock 270lb; Robin Keefe/shutterstock 27l; Roger Tidman/FLPA 82t, 263b; Roger Wilmshurst/FLPA 158b; Roland Syba/shutterstock 296t; Roman Ivaschenko/shutterstock 281t; Ron Rowan Photography/shutterstock 169cbl; Ron van Elst 56t; Ronnie Nijboer/Nijboer Collection via Wikipedia Commons 127tr; RTimages/shutterstock 80, 119r, 278tl; Rustam R. Fazlaev/shutterstock 219b; Ruta Saulyte-Laurinaviciene/shutterstock 17; Ruud Morijn Photographer/shutterstock 216; S V Philon/shutterstock 167t; S. Pytel/shutterstock 145b; Scorpp/shutterstock 25; Sergey Peterman/shutterstock 260; Shawn Hine/shutterstock 226; Shelli Jensen/shutterstock-20; shenk1/shutterstock 64tl; Shutterschock/shutterstock 225b; Silvia Reiche/Minden Pictures/FLPA 72; Sir Colin Spedding 45tr, 45c, 45br, 49, 50, 66t, 83tr, 87c, 87b, 88, 94, 98, 106, 108, 109t, 114b, 123b, 124bl/br, 127br, 131t, 132b, 133b, 134c, 142, 144t, 163t, 169rt, 174t, 179b, 182,185tr, 185c, 211, 215, 228bl, 246t, 249, 253t, 256b, 259r, 261, 267b, 283b, 286, 300, 305, 307b, 308t, 310b, 229b; skyfish/shutterstock 241; Sokolov Alexey/shutterstock 59, 112br; Sonya Etchison/shutterstock 42; Stefan Fierros/shutterstock 78b, 147c, 259b; Steve Mann/shutterstock 231br; Steve McWilliam/shutterstock 52tl, 55t, 306t; Sue Robinson/shutterstock-10, 13, 14t, 41t, 70, 81, 230, 238b; SunnyS/shutterstock 3; Supertrooper/shutterstock 18; Sven Butstraen/shutterstock 293c; T R E Wheeler BA (Hons)/shutterstock 103; Tamara Kulikova/shutterstock 164; Tania Zbrodko/shutterstock 246b; Thomas Payne/shutterstock 184bl; Todd Boland/shutterstock 135; Tony Wharton/FLPA 307t; Torsten Lorenz/shutterstock 147br; Tramper/shutterstock 155tr; TTphoto/shutterstock 267rt; turtleman/shutterstock 193; V. Borisov/shutterstock 39, 60bl; Vasily Vishnevskiy/shutterstock 125r, 155r, 185b, 188, 251, 272t, 287b; Velela/Wikipedia Commons 41b; vgm/shutterstock 244; visuall2/shutterstock 143; Vladimir Chernyanskiy/shutterstock 208; Volha Ahranovich/shutterstock 172; Wim Claes/shutterstock 44; WitR/shutterstock 271l; Xander Fotografie/shutterstock 60tl; Yanik Chauvin/shutterstock 76; Yegor Larin/shutterstock 128; Yellowj/shutterstock 111; Yuri Kravchenko/shutterstock 177b; Yuriy Kulyk/shutterstock 68l; yxm2008/shutterstock 243t; Zadiraka Evgenii/shutterstock 266b; zerohi/shutterstock 210l; zhuda/shutterstock 110; Zigzag Mountain Art/shutterstock 21
p.312 Robin on spade: Mark Bridger/shutterstock

Illustrations by Marc Dando
41, 54, 57, 58, 59, 65, 65, 68, 89, 98, 112, 122, 123, 135, 151, 152, 153, 217, 233, 233, 269, 300, 302, 304 and 311. All other illustrations by the author.

320